# LESSONS OF
# CRIMINOLOGY

## Gilbert Geis

Professor Emeritus
Criminology, Law, and Society

**University of California/Irvine**


## Mary Dodge

Assistant Professor
Graduate School of Public Affairs

**University of Colorado at Denver**

**anderson publishing co.**
2035 Reading Road
Cincinnati, OH 45202
800-582-7295

# Lessons of Criminology

Copyright © 2002
Anderson Publishing Co.
2035 Reading Rd.
Cincinnati, OH 45202

Phone 800.582.7295 or 513.421.4142
Web Site www.andersonpublishing.com

**Library of Congress Cataloging-in-Publication Data**

Lessons of criminology / edited by Gilbert Geis, Mary Dodge.
    p. cm.
  Includes bibliographical references.
  ISBN 1-58360-512-6 (pbk.)
  1. Criminology. I. Geis, Gilbert. II. Dodge, Mary, 1960-

HV6025 .L458 2001
364--dc21

                                        2001022089

Cover design by Tin Box Studio, Inc.

EDITOR Gail Eccleston
ACQUISITIONS EDITOR Michael C. Braswell

# Dedication

To Dolores and in memory of Robley Geis
And for Philip, Lucie, and Michael

# Acknowledgments

We owe thanks for those who helped us put together this volume, most notably the authors of each of the chapters who were so forthcoming about their experiences and the meaning that their careers had for them and suggestions that might be helpful to others.

At the University of California, Irvine, particular contributions to the book were made by Judy Omiya, Marilyn Wahlert, and Carol Wyatt. Thanks also are due Steve Reynard and Violet Oliver.

At Denver, colleagues Mark Pogrebin, Fred Rainquet, and Eric Poole provided valuable support and encouragement. Good friends—Valerie Cass, Tammy Shuminsky, Greg Sarkisian, and Julia Vidock—deserve mention for making life fun.

We are very grateful to Mickey Braswell for suggesting this project, and to Gail Eccleston for her skillful shepherding of the manuscript into print. It is a pleasure working with the people at Anderson Publishing.

# Table of Contents

# Introduction

Gilbert Geis

The chapters in this book have been written by teachers and scholars who have achieved a certain eminence in the field of criminology and criminal justice. Their names will be found heavily footnoted in textbooks and monographs. Articles and books that they have written will be discussed in classes. Several of them bittersweetly comment that they know too well that such fame is fleeting: their best aspiration, as one notes, is to have been able to put a pebble onto the rockpile of knowledge. But they have done well professionally, and that is why they were asked to reflect on their careers and to suggest pathways for others.

The chapter authors were requested to tell us about the acts, decisions, and the choices that led them to a position of intellectual leadership. Many, you will learn, give a good deal of credit to luck, others to fortuitous circumstances, and a number look back a bit ruefully on what they believe were career missteps. All of the authors tell you what they believe they have learned, what they have come to value, and, either implicitly or explicitly, they offer advice on how they think others might fashion a satisfying and successful research and teaching career in criminology and criminal justice—and, indeed, in any college and university teaching and research position.

There is, generally, a considerable humility demonstrated in the essays. Professors almost inevitably come to appreciate that any number of students that they face in class are, by reasonable standards, smarter than they are. Professors usually are aware that because they control the arena of discourse, and have been performing in it for longer than students, they can appear to possess more commanding intellects than those they face in their classes. Teaching too involves something of a performance and it is becoming more demanding with competition from television and the internet. Teaching, they also understand, usually has something of a narcissistic element: in how many other settings can you talk and have people more or less attend to every word you utter?

The writers, however, devote less attention to teaching than to research issues. They discuss matters such as collaborative work, balancing research and teaching, selecting subjects to address, and about publication tactics, such as how to deal with rejections. Several of the writers have edited major journals in the discipline and provide clues about how manuscripts ought to be prepared. One in particular stresses what he believes is a dire need for improved writing skills among criminologists and criminal justice scholars. It is also suggested that submissions should adhere to the format used by the journal to which they are sent.

We were pleased by the generous response to our invitation to contribute these chapters. The authors solicited were almost exclusively drawn from the roster of Fellows of the American Society of Criminology, a status conferred by their peers upon those who are deemed to have made notable contributions to the field. Only a few persons we asked felt obliged to beg off, generally citing deadlines and competing academic responsibilities that they felt precluded adequate attention to the preparation of a chapter.

We were even more than pleased by the nature of the responses. No reader can miss the note of personal pleasure and satisfaction that is found in most of the articles. The writers have few regrets about the way they have lived their professional lives. They tend to stress particularly the wonderful opportunities they have had to do research about things that caught their fancy, either because they thought the issues intriguing or, more often, because they believed that they might make a contribution that in however small a way would improve human existence.

They often exult (and that does not seem too strong a word) in having the privilege of living a life of the mind, though many observe how lonely research and especially writing can be: it's you by yourself facing a blank computer screen and trying to fill that screen with accurate, sophisticated, and sensible information. Most of the writers are a bit annoyed at what they see as the tendency of their field to have moved too far from the human material that in its earlier days was the core of its work and into secondary analyses of data that is far removed from the persons who supplied it.

Though the writers do not address the point directly, it is worth noting that one of attractions of an academic career has to be that it displays an inordinate amount of tolerance for personal idiosyncrasies. In addition, the privilege of tenure, though now under siege, allows faculty members without fear of termination to voice opinions both intramurally and to the wide world that may not be popular at the moment or ever, but which they believe need to be heard.

Academics can be snobs about professional credentials, but in the end they usually will, admiringly or grudgingly, acquiesce to claims of demonstrable achievement. You may dress sloppily, deplore your bosses in polite or more scurrilous terms, irritate most everybody with mass media commentary, or otherwise engage in actions bordering on the despicable, providing you stay within the boundaries of the criminal law and do not exploit others. Nobody may like you, but as Jane Smiley so well relates in her novel *Moo*, set on a midwestern campus, they will—however cheerlessly—put up with you. It is true, of course, that though they may be strikingly tolerant, university faculty and administrators fall far short of sainthood. The cliche is that faculty infighting often is so intense and grotesque because the issues that are to be decided by professors involve such inconsequential matters.

Note also might be made of the flexibility of academic work. It can be a double-edged benefit. A nonacademic spouse or companion often may have difficulty understanding why a scholar labors endlessly on a research project that appears to contribute nothing to the family financial coffers. "How much did you get paid for that?" is a common comment when a publication is paraded. When the writer sheepishly has to admit that no money was received and that reprints had to be purchased with family funds, those outside the academic world understandably may be mystified. Explanations for why the research was done that refer to future promotions, salary increases, and similar rewards are undercut by the fact that nobody quite knows whether this or that particular work is essential or superfluous.

The flexibility in university faculty work can often require the professorial spouse to carry a good deal more than her or his fair share of the couples' chores. "You have nothing else to do after class, why don't you. . . .? is a not uncommon opening conversational thrust in many families with one "working" partner and one academic. But this situation has another side. One partner may be occupied at work from eight to five each weekday, but the academic can always claim a relentness need to attend to business, to prepare a lecture or meet a writing deadline, particularly when an unappealing household or community chore has to be addressed.

By and large, the contributors entered the field in the first decades after the second World War. Many of them dwell on their formative experiences in graduate school and on the initial years of their first job. This is common: junior and senior faculty members, in relaxed moments, are wont to spin stories and relay anecdotes about the members of the department from which they received their doctorate. The pressure of graduate education and the personalities, pleasant and less so, of graduate school professors often seem to combine to leave a deep impression on students who almost invariably come into graduate school

with considerable anxiety. These heightened impressions tend to
become indelible. Typical, for instance, from an earlier period are the
reminisces of Edward Shils about Robert E. Park, a preeminent mentor
of University of Chicago writers on crime in the l920s, such as Frederic Thrasher, author of *The Gang* (1927). In time, Shils probably outshone
Park professionally, but he always retained strong memories of his
graduate advisor:

> When a student did a dissertation under Park, he lived in the
> student's subject, imposed himself on the student, went to the
> district where the student was doing his field work, adding his
> own observations to the student's. . . . If a graduate student
> worked with him on an interesting subject, he interested himself unrestrainedly in the student's work. He had no reservations about telling a student "I am interested in you." He once
> said that to me.

When they were graduate students the chapter authors usually
located (or were located by) faculty members who most notably offered
extraordinary guidance and displayed personal interest in them. They
remember these mentors with a good deal of gratitude, and often with
affection.

Most of the authors came into criminology with their formal training having been gained in other disciplines, particularly sociology.
They are uneasy that newcomers today tend to be too heavily trained
only in criminology and criminal justice, because they believe, perhaps
unreasonably and anachronistically, that understanding of adjacent
fields can enrich understanding of criminology. In this regard, several
of the writers endorse immersion in another not-notably-close subject
area in addition to criminology and criminal justice in order to provide
a more cosmopolitan insight into their major criminological concerns.

Those who raise the issue heavily support cross-cultural endeavors.
They point out that many of the generalizations in criminology and criminal justice are too parochial, and they stress the pleasure of learning
about foreign cultures. Indeed, the opportunity for travel and research
abroad is often mentioned as one of the fundamental delights of a
criminological career. Several writers, refreshingly, cannot resist telling
you where they have been and some adventures associated with these
excursions. Not least they testify to the stimulation of colleagues
around the globe who share their interest and enthusiasm for a common
field of intellectual endeavor.

Things, of course, have changed in dramatic and in subtle ways since
the chapter writers first began their careers. The proliferation of institutions of higher learning (and the jobs available) has been extraordinary. Salaries have increased: I began teaching at the University of
Oklahoma in 1952 with a salary of $3,000 and left there five years

later after having advanced to $3,500: it will not do to say that $3,000 was a lot of money in those days. It wasn't; it was a pittance.

The authors in this book convey a sense of steadily enhanced status and opportunity, not only in terms of their own achievements, but as an offshoot of the striking increase in the status of university and college faculties. Criminology and criminal justice split off from sociology, where they were regarded—along with marriage and the family—as waifs, tolerated because they kept enrollments high. Their later structural independence demonstrated clearly enough that the problems they addressed often were considerably more significant than the more esoteric menus offered by their parent discipline. Indeed, as sociology has tended to wane, criminology and criminal justice studies have flourished.

It might be noted that the unabridged Oxford University Dictionary indicates that the word "profess" was used before 1500 only in a religious sense, as a declaration of faith. The term "professor" entered into academia in medieval times largely because of the creation of five Regius Professors at Oxford and Cambridge Universities during the days of Henry VIII. They were originally called *praelectors*; then the term gave way to "professor." In his tour through the world of words, H.L. Mencken noted that the term "professor" through the nineteenth century in America and until relatively recent times "has been applied to an appalling range of virtuosos, mostly frauds." Among those routinely labeled professors were band leaders, high school teachers, and dancing instructors, as well as charlatans who sold patent medicines.

Currently, more respectable connotations of the term have become decidedly dominant and the possession of the title "professor" now generally carries the suggestion that the person who holds it deserves at least initial respect (in most circles, by most people, but certainly not everywhere by everybody). Such respect is one of the not inconsiderable number of rewards of the calling.

Whether this development—and more generally the upward momentum of academia—has peaked remains an open question. Certainly, few would argue that universities have taken on what for some of us is an ominous master role as businesses. Commercialism seems to be the order of the day. University presidents often are recruited from the business world and they press for cost-effective education, for profitable hands-off distance learning programs, and for the faculty to get research grants to contribute to the university's coffers. A great deal of the teaching, especially in public institutions, often devolves to part-timers, meanly paid and without medical benefits, persons who do not have continuing communication with students.

At the same time, though, publication outlets have increased almost exponentially, though the competition for space in the top journals inevitably has grown more intense. The press toward statistical sophistication may represent only a transient trend; more likely it will persist. John Kenneth Galbraith has noted that economics has become a subfield of applied mathematics; criminology and criminal justice may be moving down the same road, though other publication outlets probably will appear to provide a home for good qualitative work.

No commentary on the difference between post World War II criminology and today's field can fail to note the increasing involvement of women and the subject of women and crime in the field. Few would doubt that the movement has been invigorating. It is often said that if men could be made to behave as women do we would have come a long way toward a solution to the crime problem. But such a development seems quite unlikely, and, even if possible, it might (or might not) have unacceptable side effects. In the following pages, two women, both of whom were married to academics, recount their experience with nepotism rules that barred a husband and wife from holding tenure positions on the same faculty and with the juggling and thinking that went into their personal decisions about family priorities and academic demands.

All too often, newcomers to a working situation find themselves puzzled about what it is that is required of them, what choices they ought to make among several vocational options that confront them, and what is the difference between the formal rules that are promulgated and the real rules by which they are expected to do their job. These chapters address dilemmas that might confront a newly-hatched academic, they offer wisdom on what choices the writers believe are likely to be satisfying, and they press the reader mildly or more forcefully to confront head-on questions concerning what they want to do with their lives. Most of us probably resolve a majority of such issues intuitively or flow with the tide and only later look back and discern a pattern or ponder why one path was chosen and not another. These chapters offer a helping hand toward directly recognizing and resolving matters that will bear upon the way you live the remainder of your life. You may agree or disagree with some of the recommendations, but by having them stated outright they serve a prodding purpose about important matters that many of us often have no inclination or little time to ponder. In this regard, I would note the wisdom of novelist Louis Auchincloss, who was asked what he had learned after a prolonged period of sharing his concerns with a counselor. "I came to realize," Auchincloss said, "that I have but one life to live and if I don't live it in a way that pleases me nobody else really cares." We think it is an insight that highlights the importance of the following chapters.

# 1

# It's a Wonderful Life: Reflections on a Career in Progress*

Francis T. Cullen

Some two decades ago, my good friend, Terry Magel, observed that being a college professor was the "easiest job in the world." He did not share this sentiment in a cynical way—as though being a professor was a "scam" that we were somehow smart enough to be perpetrating on unknowing students and taxpayers who were footing the bill for our "easy gig." Instead, he was reminding me that we should appreciate our good fortune of having chanced upon an occupation that offered the *opportunity* for a "wonderful life." After all, we avoided the harsh realities of many jobs that expose workers to physically burdensome conditions and/or to coercive labor conditions. But more than this was involved in Terry's admonition to be appreciative of our employment fates—however much we might lament the follies of academic administrators who often unnecessarily complicate our lives.

First, we were being paid to do largely *what we wanted to do*. It sounds trite to say, but we felt privileged that the state—in this case Illinois—was financing our efforts to investigate whatever we wished to explore. We could imagine few occupations in which we would be given such flexibility and, in essence, be allowed to have so much fun.

Second, we were in an occupation in which we could—like James Stewart's memorable character, George Bailey, in *It's a Wonderful Life*—make a difference in people's lives. When faculty pass away, universities often hold a memorial service. These are sad occasions, of course, but they are filled with heartening testimonials as to how a faculty member touched, if not changed, one life after another. Professors have the chance to affect lives, in small ways and large, and to earn the respect, if not gratitude, of many students and colleagues. Given the

*I would like to thank Kristie Blevins, Leah Daigle, Travis Pratt, Sharon Levrant, Shannon Santana, and Luahna Winningham for their helpful comments.

number of people who cross paths with faculty members in the course of a career, the capacity to leave the world a better place—to achieve larger good beyond one's own narrow self-advancement—is ever-present. Not many other occupations offer this opportunity to achieve such meaning and to make such an enduring contribution.

It is this sense of appreciation of the special nature of our work that I would hope that those entering, or already making progress in, a career as a university-based criminologist have developed and will continue to embrace. Without it—if one's "calling" becomes "just another job"—I fear that one's career will not prove very rewarding and may, in the face of the many difficulties that are inevitably confronted, be enveloped by a deep cynicism that leads to a daily drudgery that is relieved only through early retirement. So my first lesson—and sincere hope—is that being a criminologist-professor will furnish this sense that we are granted the opportunity for a "wonderful life"—a life that allows us both to probe virtually any realm of ideas and to potentially shape the intellectual and, at times, personal development of those we encounter.

I am also mindful, however, of the challenges that our work poses. The editors have asked me to share my ideas on criminology and on being a criminologist. They have made the shaky assumption that by achieving a modest amount of success in the discipline (far more than I had ever imagined possible!), I have worthy advice to offer. I would be guilty of false modesty if I suggested that I was bereft of some *potentially* useful insights. Even so, I must caution that what is good for the goose is *not* always good for the gander. My intellectual development and career are, like those of others, a mixture of an idiosyncratic biography situated in a particular historical era. Whether what has "worked" for me in my career is generalizable to others who have a different biography and are situated in a different socio-historical context is open to question. At the very least, my suggestions should be viewed with appropriate caution—as theses to be tested empirically before being accepted as advice to be counted upon.

## All of the Above: Doing What Works

When I was an undergraduate, I hated—with some of this enmity tainting the professors who authored them—multiple-choice test questions that were followed by the answers "none of the above," "all of the above," and/or "only b and c" or "only a and d." It was hard enough, after all, to decipher which of the closely worded, if not poorly worded, answers was correct without having to figure out whether "none of the above" was really the answer the professor had in mind. Using such "trick" answers struck me as unfair and, in the strain of an exam, as mean-spirited. When I became a college professor, I applied this insight in formulating my pedagogical approach: I vowed in my teaching not to do any of the things that my professors did that really "pissed me off."

I have generally achieved highly positive teaching evaluations in my career, in large part, I believe, because I have followed this maxim of not repeating what I viewed to be the mistakes of my professors. In essence, this strategy has meant that I did not needlessly subject my students to noxious stimuli, such as a host of none-of-the above answers. I am not counseling pandering to students, of course, but rather a modest attempt to "take the role of the other"—to figure out how one's actions as a professor impact on students (and others) in ways that diminish or enhance one's effectiveness. I know that there are times to be demanding and unyielding, but I am struck by how often the difficulties that professors experience are inadvertently created and could have been avoided by anticipating how others would view their actions.

Daniel Goleman has used the term "emotional intelligence" to describe, among other aptitudes, this ability to figure out what inhibits successful human relations and, conversely, what "works" in human relations. I am not wed to his concept, but Goleman's larger point seems correct: Some people seem more aware of how to negotiate the murky waters of interpersonal relationships, including those in organizations, and among other things to advance their careers as a result. I am not certain that I have a high "emotional IQ," but I do think that my advice here can boost the IQ of those who are not reflexive about why they do what they do in their academic lives.

As just implied, I did not simply decide to avoid the mistakes of my professors but equally, if not more important, *to copy what they did that worked in their careers*. This conscious modeling seemed obvious to me: If these people had achieved a high degree of success in their careers, they must be doing something—indeed, most things—right. How might I peer into their lives and learn from them as to how to organize my academic life more successfully?

The insights gained were not usually profound, but taken together, they gave me a cumulative advantage over those who were trying to develop an academic career without such modeling. Let me share just one example. During the early stages of my career, Robert Merton—my former professor at Columbia University—was kind enough to answer my letters. I noticed, however, that most of his correspondences with me were accompanied by several reprints of articles he had written that pertained, at least in a loose way, to the topic we were discussing. I took two important lessons from those correspondences. First, Professor Merton answered his mail, something that many academics fail to do. Second, he took seriously the opportunity to share his work and thus his ideas. I am often amazed that many people from whom I request reprints never find the time to send them. Even more common, colleagues who write articles rarely send out copies of their work to people in the field who share common research interests. But I came to the conclusion that if Robert Merton—arguably the most famous sociologist of the twentieth century—would send out reprints, maybe—just maybe—it would be a good idea for me to follow his lead.

I have not been disappointed by my decision to model the behavior of Professor Merton (or "Bob" as he graciously asked me to call him in one letter—a fact that I quickly pointed out to my colleagues who were appropriately envious that "Bob and Frank" were now on a first-name basis!). By sending out reprints of my work, I have opened up scholarly relationships with colleagues at other universities, some of which have evolved into close friendships and collaborative partnerships on research projects. I am persuaded—although I do not have hard data to substantiate this suspicion—that my citation counts in studies of "most cited authors in criminology/criminal justice" have been boosted by my efforts to share my writings with scholars in the discipline. Further, a salient collateral benefit of this reprint practice is that other scholars now regularly send me their work. This enables me not only to have access to information that might have escaped my attention but also to see and use potentially important writings in their pre-publication stage—that is months before they will appear in journals. To put this point in sociological terms, the simple practice of sending out reprints has been a way of building "social capital" that has helped to advance my career in small and large ways.

In short, a key feature of emotional or practical intelligence within academia is the simple but critical realization that we should avoid doing what we have seen does not work and that we should model or copy what does work. I am convinced that some folks come by this realization naturally and early (that is, in the beginning stages of graduate school), and that it is a key ingredient to their career success. I am also optimistic, however, that the practice of effective modeling is not a branch of rocket science but something that can be learned *if only one pays attention*. Accordingly, my advice is this: *pay attention to the scholarly and occupational practices that allow professors to be successful in their teaching and research*. Do not copy what they do mindlessly, but do make an effort to understand how you might borrow from them those practices that will make your work in the field more rewarding to you and others.

## Liberal But Not Stupid: Developing a Perspective

It is often quipped that a liberal is someone who has not yet been mugged. Underlying this comment—usually offered smugly and in an insulting way—is the assumption that liberals are people who do not confront the realities of problems and thus can afford to be idealistic on issues. In the face of such sentiments, I often counter with the statement that I am "liberal but not stupid"—a remark that my Cincinnati colleague Larry Travis once greeted with the response: "Well, at least you are half right!"

Larry's rejoinder aside, my claiming to be "liberal but not stupid" was an effort to stake out a particular vantage point on criminology and, indirectly, on my career. I believe that being able to do so has been critical to my scholarly career both in publishing and in teaching. It has given my work a steady "voice," a voice that I hope has matured but that nonetheless has spoken rather consistently across my career. My sense is that finding one's own criminological voice is a difficult process, but a process that should be encouraged—not hurried, but encouraged— to evolve as one gains knowledge and experience.

To a large extent, I somewhat wandered into my "liberal but not stupid" perspective. I went to college and graduate school from the late 1960s to the mid-1970s. I was naturally liberally inclined, having grown up in an Irish neighborhood in Boston that was bereft of Protestants and Republicans. It is said that you know someone is from Boston if they think that the Kennedy's are misunderstood. I do. In any event, my liberal leanings were somewhat radicalized by the Vietnam War, Watergate, and similar events and by my graduate school experiences. In this latter regard, my valued Ph.D. mentor was Richard Cloward, who had moved beyond *Delinquency and Opportunity* to become a noted radical scholar, coauthoring works with Frances Fox Piven such as *Regulating the Poor*. And within criminology, a "critical" perspective had gained vitality; indeed, it seemed that virtually everyone in my academic cohort was an adherent.

I tried to be one, too, but in the end, I just did not have a radical temperament—for four reasons. First, I have an inherent mistrust of univariate causal theories, and radical theories seemed, despite their eloquence and attention to the complexities of history, to be excessively reductionistic—to attribute virtually everything to some sort of power relationship. The world appeared more complicated to me than that. Second, scholars on the far left often were critics of logical positivism. But I must confess that despite its limits, I find testing theories with falsifiable data preferable to the vagaries of deconstruction. Part of not being stupid, I think, is changing one's opinion in the face of mounting empirical evidence. Third, I had the uncomfortable feeling that critical criminologists, to use Elliott Currie's words, refused to acknowledge the "personal and social pathology" of criminals. It was comforting to unmask the injustices of how offenders were treated by "state agents of social control" and to claim that relief from crime would only come with the dawning of a new era of humanity and social justice in the United States. But I felt hypocritical in bearing this breastplate of humanity without having to confront the realities of the damage that offenders wreak.

John DiIulio—often dismissed by criminologists as some right-wing kook not to be taken seriously—struck me as coming closer to the truth than his critics ever imagined. DiIulio might be guilty of hyperbole, but he has been correct in worrying whether emptying prisons might not release numerous dangerous offenders into poor neighborhoods where they might well do considerable harm.

Fourth, critical criminologists had succeeded in helping to foster the view that "nothing works" to prevent crime—short, that is, of a socio-economic revolution that achieved broad social justice. There is truth in this claim, for I believe that there are good data showing that more supportive, equitable societies are blessed with lower crime rates. Even so, the "nothing works" doctrine had the dysfunctional consequence of leading scholars—as a matter of *occupational ideology*—to assert that virtually everything being done in the criminal justice system to reduce crime was a matter of "nonsense," if not of "repression." It seemed to me that most criminologists were secretly happy when an evaluation study showed that a juvenile program "widened the net" or that a policing intervention was scuttled because it only served to "displace crime."

I am not arguing that the organized skepticism of criminologists is a bad thing. Given the foolish and mean-spirited crime-control policies that are regularly put forth by policymakers, it is part of our professional responsibility to unmask these interventions for what they are. Still, I became, and remain, concerned with the tenacity of a "professional ideology," to use C. Wright Mills's phrase, that sponsors the view that all criminal justice interventions are destined to fail. This ideology, I believe, has had two untoward consequences. First, equipped with this pessimistic view, progressives could offer few realistic or persuasive answers as to how to confront the crime problem. In this situation, crime policy was, in effect, relinquished to conservatives—that is, to people who, brimming with unfounded confidence, were willing to provide a clear, "common-sense" strategy for making the nation safer from criminals: lock them up. Second, this ideology discouraged many in my generation of criminologists from engaging in the systematic attempt to find out what might work to reduce crime. In the end, we must ask whether our profession has the commitment to *construct knowledge* that can be used within the criminal justice system to reduce crime in ways that are more effective and more humane than those proposed by conservative commentators.

Some scholars recognized the poverty of the "nothing works" doctrine. Elliott Currie may be a radical at heart, but his *Confronting Crime* and more recent *Crime and Punishment in America* not only show the limits of "get tough" policies but also articulate a roster of programs that have been shown to *work to reduce crime*. Similarly, John Braithwaite's *Crime, Shame and Reintegration* was a prelude to his active involvement in the movement to improve the quality of intervention in offenders' lives by implementing "restorative justice" (see, e.g., his recent essay in volume 25 of Michael Tonry's *Crime and Justice* series). Most consequential for me personally, the Canadian scholars Paul Gendreau, Jim Bonta, and Don Andrews combined to amass a wealth of data showing that offender rehabilitation "worked" to diminish recidivism. I recall Jim Bonta praising my 1982 book with Karen Gilbert, *Reaffirming Rehabilitation*, but adding that this volume would have been really good if only I had incorporated some data into it. I took Jim's constructive criticism to heart; thereafter, I would endeavor to argue that the case for offender treatment hinged not merely on humane sentiments but also on hard empirical evidence—evidence showing that rehabilitation was clearly more effective than a punitive approach in cutting into recidivism. Most recently, the use of meta-analysis has been most powerful in revealing the benefits of treatment interventions and the limits of mean-spirited correctional programs (e.g., boot camps, "intensive" supervision probation).

Thus far, I have hinted at what a "liberal but not stupid" approach would entail. Perhaps I can summarize it as incorporating the following principles: (1) This approach is informed by a general belief that people's choices are bounded by social constraints, including constraints that are rooted in social inequalities—with many such inequalities tied to economic processes that may produce wealth but also have untoward, if not unfair, consequences. (2) Knowing that harsh living conditions are implicated in crime, it is irresponsible not to pursue social welfare policies that ameliorate these disadvantages. (3) Within the criminal justice system—a system that will affect millions of lives annually—it is irresponsible not to pursue policies that improve the plight of offenders, victims, and potential future victims. (4) For those with progressive sentiments, the key issue is not *non-intervention* but rather the *quality of the intervention* that takes place in the criminal justice system. (5) Beyond the values that inform policy choices, criminal justice interventions should not be based on prejudice, custom, or fashion but on "what works"—on what the data show are the most effective policies to pursue. (6) Liberal welfare approaches to crime control that are revealed to be ineffective should not be defended but relinquished. Again, in the end, we should be faithful to the principle that there are effective ways of achieving progressive goals within the criminal justice system.

This "liberal but not stupid" perspective is hardly beyond reproach, especially as expressed here in a truncated rather than a nuanced form. My point in relaying it is not to convince others of the wisdom of my "criminological voice"—although such a conversion to my way of seeing things certainly would be welcomed!—but rather to urge readers to think more clearly about what "voice" will inform their scholarly enterprises. It is easy to internalize the discipline's implicit occupational ideology—ideas about crime and its control that are unquestioned as "obviously true" and thus are not subjected to the slightest degree of scrutiny. Following the crowd in this way—something we all do to an extent—offers acceptance but it does so, I fear, at the price of stifling creativity and the opportunity to search more boldly for the truth.

What I consider my most important work, *Reaffirming Rehabilitation*, came about in the late 1970s and early 1980s because I was able to question existing views about offender treatment—especially Robert Martinson's "nothing works" views and the popular "justice model" for corrections. This book, which Larry Travis kindly described as my effort to "piss in the wind," would not have been possible if I had not ventured out from the criminological crowd to try to find my own voice. The lesson I offer, then, is not to "piss in the wind" just to be different, but rather to seek genuinely for what you believe criminology is "really all about." In doing so, you may relinquish some cherished beliefs, but you also may come to speak in a voice that is clearer and more knowledgeable, thus contributing to the commonweal of the discipline.

## Social Context, Social Context, Social Context

> 10.  Don't believe what Dr. Travis says.
>
>  9.  But (insert "mean" professor's name here) means well.
>
>  8.  Have you seen the new bathroom?
>
>  7.  Are you stupid?
>
>  6.  Ja Ja Ja Jaahden
>
>  5.  I pahked my caah in Hahvad Yaad.
>
>  4.  Go Bearcats!
>
>  3.  The world is multivariate.
>
>  2.  I'd like to say three things . . .
>
>  1.  Social context, social context, social context!

Upon receiving their doctorates, Brandon Applegate and Melissa Moon—two of my former students at Cincinnati—presented me with a plaque titled, "The Top Ten Things You're Likely to Hear from Dr. Cullen." These often-repeated remarks are listed above. I will not attempt to explain all of them here—each one has a story attached to it—but I will focus on two of the sayings included in this "top ten" roster.

First, I feel compelled to explain why I would wish to ask people if they had seen my bathroom. In the mid-1990s, an addition was built onto my house. As part of this structure, I incorporated a first-floor, red-and-black "Bearcat Bathroom" (my sociologist-wife, Paula Dubeck, was relieved that I relented in my plans to outfit our new master bathroom in a similar decor). Basketball fans will immediately recognize that "Bearcats" is the nickname of the University of Cincinnati sports teams and that red and black are the school's colors. Much to my spouse's dismay, my bathroom was featured—replete with a photo of me in my Bearcat shirt standing by our black toilet—in the faculty-staff newspaper. For several weeks, I enjoyed a special notoriety around campus, as one person after another looked at me, paused for a moment, and asked "if I was that bathroom guy." My lesson here is that 20 years of criminology brought me minimal attention on campus, but one bathroom made me a campus celebrity! The other lesson is that my Bearcat Bathroom reflects not only some deep pathology but also the deep affection I hold for my university. Universities can be frustrating places—a point to which I will return below—but life inside them is more pleasing if they are the object of at least some kind sentiments and not the object of complete alienation.

Second, take note that the Number 1 "Cullenism" is "social context, social context, social context." Next to the bathroom, I was most pleased by the appearance of this saying on the plaque. Why? Because it showed that a core theme of my courses—that ideas and the policies they engender are shaped by the prevailing social context—had not been lost on my students.

My understanding of this insight extended in an intellectual way back to graduate school, first at the University of Rhode Island where I read Alvin Gouldner's *The Coming Crisis of Western Sociology* and then to Columbia where Richard Cloward and Robert Merton—each in a distinctive way—impressed on me how "scientific ideas" were, at least in part, a social product. Later, this insight would be strikingly illuminated for me again by Stephen Jay Gould's *Mismeasure of Man*, a book that I still count among the best I have had the privilege of reading.

I stress that my understanding of the thesis that social context shapes people's thinking was *intellectual*, because in an implicitly arrogant way, I assumed that this phenomenon applied *to other people, not to me*. Reflexivity was not one of my strongest traits, but in the late 1970s it finally dawned on me that my thinking, too, was being shaped by the social context in which I had come of age (the 1960s) and in which I now was living as a citizen and as a professor. This insight was like a bolt of lightning that was both depressing and liberating—depressing because I had to admit that much of my thinking was based on unacknowledged socialization and liberating because it freed me to reconsider *why I thought the things I did*. Were my beliefs based on an honest search for the truth or on views that were inculcated in me as I lived out my college days in the late sixties and joined academia in the seventies when critical criminology was preeminent among my academic cohort?

My work on rehabilitation emerged in large part because I was able to consider the possibility that my previous rejection of offender treatment—a rejection that led me to teach my students that "nothing works" in correctional rehabilitation—was more rooted in how I was shaped by the social context that enveloped me than by a sober assessment of the pros and cons of abandoning rehabilitation in favor of punishment-oriented philosophies. When I stepped back and made such an assessment, I was shocked by the ease with which I had accepted the view that the "justice model"—the view that giving offenders an array of legal rights but no longer obligating the state to invest in and improve their lives—would represent a preferable alternative. I would now see that forfeiting the rehabilitative ideal—even with its problems—was a mistake. Progressives were, in Karen Gilbert's and my view, playing into the hands of repressive forces by admitting that punishment should be the *exclusive* goal of the correctional system. I take heart that John Braithwaite has recently commented that "for the record, I do think now that your position in *Reaffirming Rehabilitation* has been thoroughly vindicated against the doubts of doubters" (personal communication, November 13, 1999).

In reading my major works on corrections, corporate crime, and criminological theory, the role of social context in shaping ideas is a common theme. Thus, in *Reaffirming Rehabilitation*, the rejection of offender treatment is traced not to rising crime rates (as conservatives claimed) or to the coerciveness and failure of programs (as leftists claimed) but to a changing social context that caused those on the right to want to assert "law and order" and those on the left to curtail the power of the state. In *Corporate Crime Under Attack: The Ford Pinto Case and Beyond* (with Bill Maakestad and Gray Cavender), the movement to bring white-collar malfeasance within the reach of the *criminal law* is again linked to the social eruptions of the sixties that caused much of the public to mistrust big business and to challenge the government, under the threat of lost legitimacy, to do something about it. And in *Criminological Theory: Context and Consequences*, Bob Lilly, Dick Ball, and I attempt to demonstrate how social context influences which theoretical ideas about crime "make sense" and are accepted and, in turn, which crime-control policies come into place.

Returning to the theme of the previous section, finding one's criminological voice depends, at least to some extent, on achieving a more mature reflexivity as to why one believes what one does. Realities are socially constructed not only for others—especially those with whom we disagree—but for ourselves as well. We must begin to deconstruct our own lives to understand how we have come to embrace beliefs that may have scant empirical support. "Social context, social context, social context"—this theme reminds us that ideas, whether held by others or oneself, are social products. This realization does not mean that the ideas are incorrect, of course, but it does motivate us to scrutinize them more closely to see if their appeal rests on scientific truth or on comforting biases we have unwittingly accepted as comforting realities.

## Mentoring as Mating: Initiating a Career

I arrived at Columbia University in the Fall of 1974 with the intention of studying urban education, a by-product of my having attended an inner-city Boston high school at a time when racial equality had emerged as a salient social issue. I knew, however, that Richard Cloward—the noted "strain" theorist (who, sadly, passed away in 2001)—was on the faculty of Columbia's School of Social Work, which led me to explore whether he might be offering a course that semester. He was—"Deviance and the Social Structure"—and I decided to enroll. Consistent with the times, the course focused on the social control of "deviant" populations and had reading assignments that included Piven and Cloward's *Regulating the Poor*, David Rothman's *The Discovery of the Asylum*, and Thomas Szasz's *The Manufacture of Madness*. My course paper explored the emergence and application of "deviant labels" within schools and earned my first and only A+.

This grade emboldened me to ask Professor Cloward for a readings course on theories of deviance, a request he granted, to my delight. We started by my reading works from the Chicago School of sociology that, Cloward informed me, were at the heart of his concept of "illegitimate means." People, he explained, could not become any kind of deviant or criminal of their liking. How they adapted to the problems in their lives was "structured" by the learning environments and opportunities tied to their place in society—that is, by the illegitimate means available to them. What was innovative about his work—and Cloward's subsequent book with Lloyd Ohlin, *Delinquency and Opportunity*—was that it called attention not to the sources of the strains individuals experienced but to the necessity to develop a theory as to why particular types of responses were made to these strains. Gangs, for example, were not found everywhere in society but emerged in certain structural locations where collective subcultural delinquency was feasible. Most scholars missed this point in his work, reducing him to a "Mertonian strain theorist." He was, in fact, a student of Merton's, but his innovation was in extending Merton's work by linking it to the insight of the Chicago School that particular kinds of criminality—such as gang behavior (Thrasher), jack-rolling (Shaw and McKay), and professional thievery (Sutherland)—depended on access to the means to learn and perform the deviant activity in question.

I was enormously appreciative of the chance to work one-on-one with Professor Cloward, and I completed the assigned readings promptly and carefully. I manifested, I think, both an understanding of, and a commitment to, his ideas. Within a few weeks, I was shocked when, in the course of one of our meetings, he asked if I might like to do my dissertation with him. He explained that *Delinquency and Opportunity* had applied the "theory of illegitimate means" only to types of delinquent gangs. Subsequent research by James Short and others had failed to find the distinctive, ideal-types of gangs that Cloward and his co-author, Ohlin, had hypothesized (e.g., conflict versus criminal gangs). In response, scholars tended to "throw the baby out with the bathwater," assuming that their entire work, including the concept of illegitimate means, was limited to gang delinquency and thus was of questionable value. In fact, their theoretical ideas applied to the choice of *any course of deviant activity*. He explained that he and Ohlin had intended to write a more general statement of the theory of illegitimate means, but had not done so because life circumstances had led them in different directions—Ohlin to Washington, D.C. to government service and Cloward into the movement to empower poor people.

Would I, Professor Cloward asked, like to take up this project that Ohlin and he had abdondoned in the early 1960s and write this as my dissertation? I thought for at least two seconds before blurting out, "Yes." Perhaps I should have thought more carefully before making such an important career decision, but this was, for me at least, a case of "intellectual love at first sight." I was amazed at Professor Cloward's sharp mind and kind temperament. I would have the *privilege of being his graduate student*. As things turned out, I worked closely with him for the next several years. He constantly pushed me to find the "broader theoretical point" at hand, a skill that I unwittingly honed under his mentorship and that has been a major ingredient in whatever career success I have experienced. I crunched no numbers and collected no data; instead, I wrote a theoretical dissertation—a work explicating the theory of illegitimate means that ultimately was published in 1984 under the title *Rethinking Crime and Deviance Theory: The Emergence of a Structuring Tradition*.

Three potential lessons can be learned from this brief biographical tale. First, there is a lesson for graduate students seeking mentors. Richard Cloward was a good man, but he did not choose to work with me because he wished to "do good." I not only had done well in his course but also had shown that I appreciated the time he spent with me, was committed to his ideas (not blindly but deeply), and would work assiduously on the assignments he outlined. I believe that he saw that I was a worthy "investment"—someone who would, in the end, carry his ideas and his intellectual style into the field.

Graduate students might benefit by pausing for a moment to "take the role of the other." Imagine yourself as a faculty member. Who would you wish to mentor? What characteristics—motivation, skills, work habits—would you wish your student to manifest? Although bounded by other factors, rational choice theory is applicable here: faculty members like to mentor students who are highly motivated, reasonably skilled, reliable, and of "low maintenance." Some faculty may "play favorites," but if they do so, they pay the price of being stuck with students who are "more work than they are worth."

Second, not everything about mentoring, of course, is so coldly calculating. I was attracted to Professor Cloward not simply because he was a "star" but also because he was kind enough to share his time and to take an interest in me. I am not certain that we "connected" on an interpersonal level to the point of becoming "friends." But I do believe that during my time at Columbia, there was a special bond and that he saw me as a special student. In this sense, mentoring is much like "mating." Without some convergence of interpersonal style and sentiments— without the emergence of a special quality to the relationship—I fear that mentorship risks losing its capacity to have enduring effects on the student and, I might add, on the faculty member.

Third, I learned a *style of mentorship* from Professor Cloward: select a student early in his or her graduate career and then work with that student closely over the next several years. I will not pretend that this is the only way or even the best way for faculty to mentor students. But following the principle to "do what works," I imported this mentoring style into my own academic career. Much as in mating, I try to select students as mentees in the first year or two of their stay at Cincinnati who are compatible with me—who share my values and intellectual interests and who have personal styles I enjoy. Melissa Moon says that I like students who are "humble," an observation that I first denied but later was forced to admit. Actually, I would put it in slightly different terms: as I was with Professor Cloward, I am most comfortable with students who appreciate the chance to work with me and who are committed to the type of criminology in which I am engaged. Without such an orientation, I am not certain that I could have the kind of trusting relationship in which my most effective mentoring and a student's most effective learning takes place.

I cannot provide a rigorous empirical assessment of the effectiveness of my mentoring philosophy, but I can say that all of the students I have mentored—numbering more than 10 now—have embarked on successful academic careers in which they have been productive researchers and, I trust, good faculty members. Their success, of course, says more about them—their talents and hard work—than it does about me. Still, I am immodest enough to believe that my mentoring, which in almost all cases has involved collaborative research and publications, has helped "my students" to reach their potential. I also must confess that I find few aspects about being a professor more rewarding than watching my "academic offspring" mature and contribute to their students and to the discipline in general.

## The MacDonald's Franchise: Understanding Academic Life

Most new faculty members make the mistake of anticipating that upon starting a new position, they will be the recipient of a good deal of "support." In my experience, this is generally *not* how academic life operates. Rather than a welfare state, it is closer to a community run on the principles of social Darwinism—perhaps not in its crudest form but in a genteel form in which survival is mostly up to each individual with little help from others. In many ways, a new faculty member should try to follow the strategies, identified by Hans Toch in *Living in Prison*, that inmates use to survive: learn to carve out a "niche" that furnishes meaning and a way to survive as comfortably as possible.

Okay, likening academia to prison is excessive, especially for an essay carrying the title "It's a Wonderful Life." Perhaps a more apt comparison would be that securing a faculty position is similar to securing a MacDonald's franchise. There is some initial support: a desk, a filing cabinet, some supplies, a computer, and an office, and perhaps even someone to give some advice along the way. But in the end, it is up to each "franchise" to "turn a profit." Those franchises that prove successful tend to get more investment in them; those that do not tend to lose whatever backing they may have originally experienced.

Of course, different departments run differently (e.g., I have been fortunate to have had an inordinately supportive chair, Ed Latessa, while at Cincinnati). Even so, it is risky not to understand that we are mostly the architects of our own academic careers—that the niches we find ourselves in and the "profits" we make or do not make are largely of our own doing. Fair or unfair, I worry that too many beginning professors feel abandoned when the ill-defined support they anticipated does not arrive. They expect, moreover, that their scholarly work will be "appreciated," their service "rewarded," and their identities "validated." I have truly great colleagues, but few have read a fraction of my writings and I count myself fortunate if I receive a compliment or two for my "contributions" each academic year. Faculty members, it seems, are not part of the "caring professions," but rather are too busy trying to keep their own "franchise" in business.

Another mistake faculty make is in assuming that "justice" in a department—say, in the distribution of resources or in votes on policy issues—is rooted in clearly defined policies and process. To some extent, of course, it is, but my sense is that the dominant "rule" of academic life is not just deserts but rather *reciprocity*. At times, I joke with my students who become faculty members that in departmental politics they should vote their conscience—unless they don't care, and then they should vote with their friends! My message is that life in academic departments—as in other formal organizations—is intimately influenced by informal social relationships. People with high "emotional intelligence" seem to understand this reality and are good at building exchange-based relationships that give them political influence and perhaps access to collaborative research relationships. In this framework, "support" is not a "right" that is to be anticipated and received, but a resource that one should return through a genuine expression of appreciation, the performance of a favor, or the "scratching of a colleague's back."

Not everyone will be good at reciprocity; for some, it does not come naturally and is not part of their personal style. At a minimum, however, new faculty should be aware that the norm of reciprocity governs most academic exchanges. Violating it is likely to prompt displeasure from one's colleagues and exclusion from informal networks. Claims that one is unfairly treated and unsupported are likely only to send the message to colleagues that they should stay even farther away from you.

Let me hasten to say that I am not counseling the tolerance of injustices or of systematic mistreatment. When I was turned down (unjustly!) for promotion at Western Illinois University, I published a letter in the student newspaper criticizing the university president's decision. Terry Magel thought this was a good idea, and the student editors agreed, gleefully placing my scathing letter on the front page of the paper. Besides my buddy John Wozniak, a peacemaking criminologist for whom compassion is a core talent, few of my colleagues praised my defiance of the president. In fact, it was a stupid thing to do, and could have cost me my job had a faculty union not been there to protect me. But as concluded by the Delta boys in *Animal House*, sometimes in the face of adversity a truly stupid gesture is called for! More seriously, I do understand the need to stand up and challenge mistreatment. Still, I would caution you to pick your battles carefully and not to expect that engaging in conflict with others will make you popular.

## Publish, Publish, Publish: Building a Career

I chose a career as a professor because I wanted to "teach." I had some sense of research—a project I did as an undergraduate in an experimental psychology course was later published—but the pull to academia lay in the prospect of being a teacher. At Columbia, however, my older brother John—also a sociologist—warned me that we would not get jobs if we did not start publishing; after all, positions in sociology departments were in short supply in the 1970s. Now I have often followed in my brother's footsteps, attending the same high school and the same three universities and going into the same profession. Rumor has it that when I was being toilet trained, my mother told me to watch my older brother—which I did and apparently have continued to do so in the years since. The Freudians might have a field day with this account, although I suspect that Ron Akers could explain my behavior through differential social reinforcement. Regardless, on this occasion, I again followed John's lead and started to publish what I could.

My works were, to be kind to myself, of modest value, with all of them coming from course papers (two on "deviance in hockey"—a topic selected because I had played goalie at Bridgewater State College). Still, I had five publications when I entered the job market, which was enough to earn me the right to take Marvin Krohn's line at Western Illinois University (Marv had departed for the University of Iowa). I had never seen a cornfield in my life, but now I was surrounded by them. The people seemed nice in Macomb, Illinois. In my first week in town, a clerk kindly waited on me and then inquired as to what country I was from. I noted that the Pilgrims had landed in Massachusetts, not Macomb, and that it was not me who had the accent.

My career as a researcher did not get off to a fast start. At 25, I was young and inexperienced. Facing 12-hour teaching loads, having virtually no teaching experience, and feeling anxious every time I stepped in front of the classroom, I found I had no time for research as I tried valiantly to stay one lecture ahead of the students. I loved my job—being a "professor" was special—but my unfinished dissertation loomed constantly in the background, making it difficult to enjoy any "leisure time." In the end, it took me three long years to complete my dissertation. In the interim, I experienced only limited publishing success, suffering a string of rejections. I also dutifully applied to 30 or so jobs each year, hoping to escape rural America and return to a city with a professional baseball team. And each year, I received 30 or so standardized rejection letters from universities letting me know that their failure to hire me was not due to my personal or professional inadequacies but to the surplus of qualified candidates. I was especially galled when one university noted that I was not in their top 12 candidates but offered to keep my application active in their second group of candidates just in case everyone ahead of me declined their position. This was my "standardized" response:

Dear Employer:

Thank you for your letter informing me that I have been placed in the top twenty-five candidates, though not in the elite twelve. While I very much appreciate your invitation to keep my candidacy under consideration, I must at this time decline your offer.

Due to the unusual number of qualified job offers I have received this year, I have been forced to turn down many competent and prestigious departments. It appears that some departments have particular specializations that match my needs more directly. However, should my situation change in the future, I will be in touch.

Again, I appreciate your interest in me. I wish you luck in your search for a promising young academic to fill the position in your department.

> Sincerely,
> Francis T. Cullen, Jr.
> Assistant Professor
> PYA (Promising Young Academic)

Eventually, of course, I did come to experience a good amount of success in publishing my works (and after six good years in the cornfields was able to move to the city of Cincinnati). I have come to realize that not everyone has a knack for research. I was blessed with some natural ability and, as noted, with mentoring from Richard Cloward that nurtured my ability to "see the big picture" and to generate researchable ideas. But I also feel it necessary to state here that in no way was my entry into the research/publishing enterprise easy. It was a rugged journey that started slowly and left my ego damaged on more than a few occasions. How, then, did I turn around my career and start to publish, first with a degree of regularity and then at a fairly high rate? I must admit that I did so not with any grand plan, but rather I stumbled along, experimenting and creating the design as I proceeded. Retrospectively, however, I can identify six pieces of advice that newer scholars—and perhaps some maturing scholars—may find of some utility.

First, at the earliest feasible time, it is essential *to organize your academic life around your research*. An insurmountable barrier to publishing is when a scholar devotes *no time to the enterprise*. My main problem in finishing my dissertation, for example, was that I was so overwhelmed by my faculty responsibilities that I simply devoted no time to it. Even today, papers and books go unwritten unless I *make time for research*. I say "make time for research," because *there is never a good time for research to be undertaken*. Teaching and service activities—never mind the other exigencies in one's life—are sufficiently greedy to exhaust all available time. They also have the trait of being immediate—

there is a lecture to prepare or a meeting to attend—while research seemingly can be put off to another day. In actuality, this is a false assumption. Especially for junior faculty, the tenure and promotion clock is ticking inexorably toward the time when momentous decisions about your fate within a university will be reached. Ultimately, it takes a conscious decision to allocate time to research—one way or another. For example, I tend to engage in "binge research and writing," working feverishly on a paper until it is done, putting everything else on hold (and then working feverishly to catch up on the things I have set aside). Regardless of the style that works for you, it is essential to allocate blocks of time to your scholarship. Keep a log each week on how many hours are devoted to your research. If the log says "zero," you will know why your publication record is lagging behind.

Second, *develop a plan for your research agenda*. For new faculty members, this means knowing which articles are to be written from your dissertation. I recommend following a practice I employ to this day: making up a folder for each "article in progress" that carries a label with a title attached. For me, this practice allows the article to assume a more concrete form—something I can envision ending up in print some day. Devising a title is important because it captures, if only provisionally, what the thrust of the article will entail. The folder is important because it is a handy place into which materials relevant to the article can be placed—such stuff as quotes or publications one runs across or ideas about the project that one jots down onto scraps of paper or develops into a systematic outline.

Writing from one's dissertation is but the first step, however. At the same time, a new faculty member should be in the process of collecting data for his or her next set of articles. This cycle—writing and finishing articles from one data set while collecting the next data set (or finding a relevant secondary data set)—should continue throughout one's career. More generally, the lesson is that research agendas do not simply take care of themselves; they require careful attention and a clear idea of what scholarly products they can yield.

Third, *expect and learn from criticism and rejection*. When I was in grade school, I recall that one Sister of Notre Dame gave me the grade of "D" on my report card in the behavioral category of "takes criticism well." To this day in academia, I continue to believe that what I write is correct, and that those reviewing the articles I submit to journals raise mainly specious critical comments. If not taken too far, this orientation to externalize blame is not a bad thing. The review process can be harsh and can attack one's ego. You have to expect to be bruised and you should have enough confidence to withstand the pain. Although not applicable to truly flawed works that warrant revision, I would advise a three-day policy after receiving a rejection: one day to weep; one day to find a new journal; and one day to send the manuscript out again.

The review process, however, can also be an invaluable learning experience. As noted, I suffered one rejection after another early in my career. Although not forfeiting the belief that these works had some value (most eventually ended up in print in lesser journals), I also tried to discern if I was engaging in scholarly practices that condemned my articles to rejection. I learned, for example, that I had to clearly demonstrate the importance of what I was researching and that I had to use much better data (surveys of college students and of Macomb residents would not do for first-tier journals). The challenge, of course, is not to repeat the same mistakes in future works.

Fourth, when appropriate and within limits, *seize opportunities and be persistent*. I had written a 410-page dissertation that had been rejected for publication as a book by 39 publishers. I had one chance left: Rowman and Allenheld, who had given the publication decision to their editorial consultant, Edward Sagarin. As chance would have it, Professor Sagarin was spending the summer at Ohio State University and invited me to come and talk with him about the manuscript. So, I hopped in my VW Rabbit and drove from Macomb to Columbus, Ohio. In our conference, Professor Sagarin said that during our earlier correspondence, he had become cautious about the project because he had the impression I would "do anything to get it published;" after meeting and liking me, he felt this was not the case. Of course, he was wrong. Why else would I have made a day-long drive through Midwestern cornfields for a one-hour meeting if not to "get it published?" Perhaps, though, Professor Sagarin sensed that my interest in the book extended beyond securing a line on my vitae to a belief in the ideas it was putting forward. In any event, because I traveled to Columbus, *Rethinking Crime and Deviance Theory* was published. In 1986, it was one of two books selected for "Honorable Mention" for the Distinguished Scholarship Award given by the Criminology Division of the American Sociological Association.

I will not elaborate much further on this tale because the lessons, I trust, are clear. My experience with my dissertation was idiosyncratic, but the broader point is that achieving career successes at times requires one to "hang in and not give up" and to recognize when a chance to move ahead has presented itself.

Fifth, *find good co-authors*. At last count, in my published writings (in print and forthcoming), I had collaborated with 121 different coauthors, including relatives (who are academics), friends from graduate school, departmental colleagues, graduate students, scholars at other universities, and people I have never met or talked with. Again, my proclivity for working with others may not be appropriate for all scholars. Some people prefer to work alone or with one or two others. Further, joint projects are rewarding only if you are able to select co-authors who are talented and, equally important, who you like and can get along with.

These caveats stated, I have learned that scholarly collaboration has three important benefits: (1) Co-authors have allowed my work to be of higher *quality*, sharing ideas and shoring up my weaknesses (e.g., on tricky statistical issues). (2) Co-authors have enabled me to be more productive, both because there are more hands to share the workload and because interdependence with others creates pressures to finish projects and bring them to print. (3) By working with others, I have developed some of my closest friendships and most rewarding collegial relationships in the field (e.g., Bob Agnew, Mike Benson, and Paul Gendreau).

Finally, in an idea borrowed from my colleague Paul Mazerolle, I would raise the possibility of developing a "working group" of scholars who come together to focus on—and publish articles about—a particular topic. Some time ago, Bob Agnew, Tim Brezina, John Wright, and I decided to have dinner each year at the American Society of Criminology Conference to discuss research plans on strain and social support theories. Until recently, our most noteworthy accomplishment was to meet annually to *talk about* what projects we might undertake. But eventually, our evolving friendships—and perhaps the embarassment of doing more eating and conversing than writing—prompted us to undertake works that resulted in the publication of articles in *Criminology* and in *Justice Quarterly*. We now have another pretty exciting paper near completion. I anticipate that in the years ahead, we will end up producing a series of articles that, given our collective criminological wisdom, may potentially make a meaningful contribution to the discipline (and to our careers).

Sixth, productive researchers not only are good scholars but also *are effective managers of projects and people*. In graduate school, students are often not taught that there is a wide gap between having a good idea for a research project and having that idea appear in print. But publishing is a production process—analogous to starting with a conceptual design for an automobile and then having to develop the operational mechanisms needed to transform the concept into a car rolling off the assembly line. In a sense, this is why we say we are working on a research *project*. Such projects can take months, if not years, to plan and complete, and often involve managing multiple stages of the project as well as graduate students and other collaborators. Space prohibits a more detailed discussion of this topic, but let me add this much more: successful projects—those that yield publications—usually are carefully planned, involve making practical decisions as to what the project can actually achieve, and attend to the intellectual styles and personal oddities of the people involved.

Let me close this section by reiterating that publishing is not everyone's cup of tea. Some scholars cannot do it well, and some want to devote their careers more fully to teaching and service. I respect those who devote themselves earnestly to using their scholarly talents in this latter way. As noted, I entered the field to be a teacher, not a researcher, and I did not have any clue that I would end up being pretty good at publishing.

Still, for newer scholars entering the field, there is the hard reality that published works are the "currency" by which one is often measured. Those who publish tend to secure better jobs, have the ability to move to new jobs, are more able to obtain tenure and promotion and the job security this entails, gain more status in the discipline and within their universities, and have opportunities presented to them (e.g., I was asked to write this essay not because of my teaching evaluations but because of my research record). Thus, with the provision that this is what one wishes to do, I would urge you to *publish, publish, publish*!

## Conclusion: A Career in Progress

In 2001, I turned 50 years of age, which meant that I have been a professor for a quarter of a century. I could dwell on my lost youth and on a career that has perhaps seen its best days. But another reason why being a college professor offers a wonderful life is that I can look ahead and see that my career might well have another quarter of a century to go. As one colleague noted to me when asked if he might retire: "I've thought about it, but we have the kind of job people retire to."

This essay has endeavored to present a balanced view of being an academic criminologist. I see my work as being less of a "job" and more of a "calling," with the special rewards and obligations that this entails. At the same time, academia is an occupation and doing the work can be a struggle. It certainly has, at times, been for me, as I have experienced my share of failures, missteps, and disappointments. I have had the good fortune of working in good departments, of making good friends, and of having good co-authors. I have been most fortunate, however, somehow to have had the perceptiveness—the emotional intelligence—to "figure out," whether by modeling what works or by trial and error, the "business" or "career" side of being a professor: how to get research done, how to organize projects, how to develop and nurture collaborative relationships with co-authors, how to manage the research process, and so on. Hopefully, this essay will prove successful in sharing what I have learned with you so that you can negotiate the hurdles of academic life more easily than I did.

Again, I offer these observations from a career that is, I trust, but half over. Academic life can be what someone once called a "greedy profession," consuming your time and much of your psychological energy; after all, is the work day ever really over when we are prone to carry home from the office an unfinished research paper, a novel but unsettled idea, a set of papers, or a departmental worry? As in other work, the daily grind and yearly grind can cause one to seek relief and renewal (thank goodness for sabbaticals). Still, even after all these years, I remain excited about the projects I am working on or those that lie just ahead. With Bonnie Fisher as lead author and Mike Turner as a coauthor, for example, I am engaged in research on the measurement of sexual assault that is yielding publication that I trust will meaningfully extend the work of Mary Koss and others. With John Wright, I have a research agenda exploring the impact of social support on criminal involvement, a venture that I hope will result shortly in a book-length work systematically articulating a theory of social support and crime. With Paul Gendreau, I am planning to continue investigating the features of effective treatment interventions, a process that may yet yield a volume on "what works in corrections." With Brandon Applegate, a revision of *Reaffirming Rehabilitation* also seems worth pursuing—perhaps as a follow-up to our recently completed national public opinion survey on rehabilitation attitudes and the nature of support for faith-based programs (a project coauthored with Jennifer Pealer and Shannon Santanna, among others). With Travis Pratt leading the way—and Leah Daigle and Kristie Blevins making substantial contributions—I am part of a team subjecting a number of criminological theories to meta-analysis, with the goal of assessing their relative empirical merits. Travis and I have a similar project on social learning theory with Chris Sellers and Tom Winfree that should soon find its way into print. I would be remiss if I did not note that Tom Vander Ven, who has involved me in a line of inquiry exploring the impact—or lack of impact—of mothers' employment on delinquency and mention Liqun Cao, who keeps me involved in topics as varied as domestic views toward firearms and cross-national views on crime and control. Jim Unnever and Mark Colvin—scholars from distant universities—have generously joined me via the Internet in projects extending and testing contemporary ideas about crime. And with Jody Sundt and colleagues, I have an interest in investigating more deeply the occupational experiences of correctional workers, from prison chaplains to correctional officers. Many other learned coauthors with whom I have collaborative ventures in progress or in the planning stages should be highlighted, but space is limited and I anticipate that I have already made my point: I have more than enough exciting work under way and valued colleagues at my side to enrich my academic life well into the foreseeable future.

I am optimistic that these and related projects will come to fruition. If so, I trust that they will not only inspire my career and make my life a bit more "wonderful" but also be worthy of your attention and contribute to your criminological knowledge and imagination. In turn, I hope that you will honor the norm of reciprocity and share your research with me. Who knows? Maybe we might even end up being coauthors.

# 2

# Reflections of a Reluctant but Committed Criminologist

Charles R. Tittle

I didn't intend to become a criminologist. Rather, happenstance led me to investigate certain sociological problems that resulted in my being labeled a criminologist (Tittle, 1991). After a while the reactions of others had the effects that symbolic interactionist theory would predict—I began to think of myself as a criminologist, although one with a larger allegiance. In fact, one of the first conclusions I drew as a criminologist is that criminology ought not be thought of as a discipline. Disciplines have unifying perspectives; criminology does not. Criminology is an umbrella term encompassing diverse studies of crime and crime-relevant phenomena undertaken from many disciplinary points of view. It makes sense to speak of an economic perspective, a political perspective, a historical perspective, or a sociological perspective. It makes no sense to speak of a criminological, a criminal justice, or a criminal perspective (at least not in an academic context). In my mind, the best criminology is done by those with a firm grounding in some discipline, or by those with an appreciation of several different disciplines, the insights of which are then brought to bear on criminological issues. My discipline is sociology, which directs me toward the study of social norms and their violation—a focus that encompasses deviant behavior as well as crime-relevant phenomena (Tittle, 2002).

## Beginning Influences

Ironically, I did not start out wanting to be a sociologist either. My first passion was history. However, history students at Ouachita Baptist College, where I earned my bachelor's degree, were required to take some supportive work in sociology. That first sociology course opened my eyes and convinced me that history could benefit from some alliance with sociology; later I realized that sociology could also benefit from a better understanding of history. In any case, I found both history and sociology fascinating and, after being awarded Woodrow Wilson and Danforth Fellowships for graduate study, decided that I would merge the two. My teachers touted the University of Texas and, not having any other information, I followed their advice. It was a lucky choice, which highlighted a second lesson about academe—and criminology. It is that our system for identifying and attracting new scholars is exceptionally haphazard and weak. Without an efficient plan for recruitment that produces a steady stream of talented scholars, neither criminology nor its constituent disciplines can ever hope to advance very far.

Most promising undergraduates do not realize that they might become scholars, that the life of the mind is exceptionally rewarding, or that they can receive financial help in pursuing advanced training; in addition, they do not know the best places for training to pursue a life of scholarship. Undergraduates generally are utterly dependent on mentors for guidance. Unfortunately, most talented students do not have trusted mentors who recognize their potential, convince them of their talent, inform them of the possibilities for graduate subsidies, and advise them of the best options for graduate work. This is particularly true in large universities with huge classes, where students can seldom show their creativity and where teachers rarely come to know their students' names, much less their capabilities, fears, ambitions, and aspirations. That is one reason that a disproportionate number of graduate students started in small colleges, which ironically often do not adequately prepare students academically for graduate work. Intellectual advancement will be slow unless we recruit more effectively and begin preparing the scholars of the future earlier.

Having studied at a small college near my home town of Hope, Arkansas, I was blessed with mentors who encouraged me to become a scholar, and even though their advice to study at the University of Texas was not well informed, that choice turned out to be fortuitous. The downside of being at a small college was that I actually learned little sociology (though I did not know it at the time), arrived for graduate study with a strong preconceived notion about human behavior, and did not realize the impracticality of trying to combine sociology and history in pursuit of the Ph.D. My assumption that human behavior could be explained by moral values was a product of my religious background but it also fit nicely with the dominant theoretical motif of the time—Parsonian functionalism. That mode of thought, however, was anathema to one of my graduate school mentors, Jack Gibbs, who interpreted human behavior and social phenomena by reference to structural influences, especially "control." Although Jack did not know it, the first several years of my professional career were spent in a shadow fight with him about this fundamental question. His influence finally led me to treat it and all other questions as matters of systematic evidence. That was the third, and one of the most important, lessons of my career.

The necessity for empirical evidence collected and organized by scientific principles will be elaborated later; for now I will return to the story of how I came to do criminological work. Having arrived at graduate school in 1961 planning to study the sociology of organization and social psychology in order to pursue a teaching career in some liberal arts college, I soon fell under the influence of two mentors—the aforementioned Jack P. Gibbs and Richard J. Hill. They inspired me to change career objectives, foci of interest, and ultimately my entire way of thinking. Those changes, however, were slow and they were produced in subtle and different ways.

## An Early Research Opportunity

Dick Hill was a father figure rather than an intellectual leader. Even though I did a master's thesis with Reece McGee concerning the social organization of small colleges, it was Dick who arranged a fellowship for me to conduct research at a mental health facility in the Dallas-Fort Worth area during the summer following my second year in graduate school. In the planning phase we visited several hospitals and clinics, including the Federal Narcotics Hospital in Fort Worth. The narcotics hospital seemed the most interesting, mainly because it was a lot more like a prison than a hospital. In addition, the medical officer in charge was highly receptive to sociological research, having read and appreciated Goffman's work on total institutions (and mistakenly believing that other sociologists were as talented as Goffman). So, I went back to Austin to bone up on the appropriate literature in order to design a meaningful piece of research. That was my first in-depth exposure to the professional literature bearing on criminology.

Although the focus of that summer research was to be on mental health or medical sociology, the literature that drew my attention concerned inmate organization, mainly because the study of prison inmates seemed to raise fundamental questions about social order. The predominant perspective in sociology at that time contended that social order rests on shared values/goals and internalized commitments to norms stemming from such values. But the order that prevails in prisons seems to contradict that notion. At first glance it would appear that prison inmates actually oppose the goals and values of their keepers and the derivative norms of the prison system. Yet, behavior is as orderly and predictable in prison as it is on the outside. Either Parsons and his followers were wrong or something not obvious was going on. I thought it would be important to find out. Moreover, because the inmate population included men with court sentences as well as "volunteers" seeking treatment for drug addiction, the institution appeared to pose many contrasts that, studied carefully, might enrich the prison literature.

The narcotic hospital research convinced me that the inmates and the officials were, in fact, committed to a common goal—maintaining orderly relations—and that reciprocal concessions played a key part in the maintenance of institutional order; however, it was also obvious that control and coercion loomed large. Moreover, I found that inmates shared a common set of values among themselves that helped shape a dual social order in the institution, a formal and an informal system. Thus, in my mind the Parsonian perspective was vindicated; however, I concluded it was incomplete because it did not incorporate enough about coercion to paint an accurate picture of social organization and it did not put enough emphasis on competing normative systems. Later on, of course, the sociological pendulum swung to the opposite extreme with the predominant perspectives coming to focus almost totally on coercion while ignoring the part played by shared values and goals.

That experience at the narcotics hospital, thus, was the beginning of the fourth important lesson of my career: things are more complicated than our theories acknowledge. An accurate theory has to accommodate a variety of causal forces but it has to do more than simply identify them and say they are all important. Over time I became convinced that one of the keys to this more accurate approach, which later became known as "integrated theory," was the use of contingency statements (Tittle, 1989b, 1994, 1995). Shared goals explain social order better under some conditions than others and coercion has more effect in some circumstances than in others. It is incumbent upon scholars to specify those contingent conditions, but they are impeded in the effort by the adversarial nature of much of our work. Far too much scholarship is designed to prove that one causal force is all that matters, is "more important" than another, or should be taken seriously because it has previously been ignored. We will make more progress when we try to understand how explanatory variables fit together.

This first significant research experience not only turned my thinking toward criminological issues (how and why people obey rules in a given context and how and why some people, drug addicts in this case, adopt lifestyles that are generally socially unacceptable), but it also led to publications that helped identify me as a criminologist. I thought the papers that grew out of the Fort Worth research (Tittle & Tittle, 1964, 1965) addressed fundamental sociological concerns; however, disciplinary audiences tend to interpret scholarly work in narrow, context-specific terms. Even though my work concerns social psychology (Schulman & Tittle, 1968; Tittle & Hill, 1967a; Tittle & Villemez, 1976), organizations (Hall & Tittle, 1966), sociology of religion (Tittle & Welch, 1983; Welch et al., 1991), urban sociology (Tittle, 1989a, 1989c; Tittle & Stafford, 1992), survey methodology (Tittle & Hill, 1967b), stratification (Tittle, 1994; Tittle & Rotolo, 2000), and theory (Jackson et al., 1986; Paternoster & Tittle, 1990; Tittle, 1985a, 1989b, 1994, 1995, 1997, 2000; Tittle et al, 1986), most people who know my work define me as a criminologist. That is probably because the research context for most of my scholarship bears on deviant or criminal behavior and people remember the context rather than the larger implications. Hence, ideas and research focused on prisons will be regarded as criminology even though the theoretical issues transcend the research context. Similarly, ideas and research focused on population phenomena will be regarded as demography even though the theoretical issues concern social organization and social change. And so it is with every research context. That is why sociology (and increasingly criminology) is so fragmented into specialty areas.

Every research context seems to spawn its own "area," and in the process the larger, transcendent general questions are ignored or given short shrift. The undesirability of such fragmentation constitutes my fifth major insight (Tittle, 1985a, 1989b, 1995; Tittle & Paternoster, 2000). We cannot make much progress until we define our questions in general terms and pull together the research from numerous specific contexts to draw its implications for general principles of human behavior. Without a generalizing focus we will end up with a thousand different bodies of knowledge, much of it overlapping. Furthermore, each "area" will find itself doing the equivalent of "reinventing the wheel." Resources and good scholars are scarce. If ideas and conclusions cannot be directed toward basic questions, progress will indeed be slow.

My development and identity as a criminologist was later aided by additional work concerning inmate organization (Tittle, 1972a, 1972b, 1972c, 1974, 1969b) but in the meantime I burned up a lot of intellectual energy struggling with the issues that Gibbs continued to pose. Late in my graduate school career he was turning his attention more fully away from human ecology and symbiotic relationships to "control" and its significance in social life. In addition, he continued to harp on the importance of theory to explain things and on the absolutely essential requirement for solid evidence about sociological questions. Learning those precepts was an important advancement, but it was not until somewhat later that I came to really appreciate them. More immediately, Gibbs put a bug in my ear about the potential effects of criminal sanctions, pointing out that we actually had very little evidence concerning deterrence despite the tendency of most criminologists and sociologists (including me) to contend that sanctions did not matter much because, after all, moral conscience and value commitments determine behavior.

## The Academic World

By and by I earned the Ph.D., forsaking criminological issues altogether to write a social psychological/methodological dissertation,
supervised by Dick Hill. My first job was at Indiana University in Bloomington. Initially, I devoted my efforts to the social psychological and organizational interests with which I began, but I was soon drawn back
toward the control questions that Gibbs had first raised and to the
anomalies I had discovered in the narcotics hospital research. A Federal
grant permitted a follow-up study of inmates at the narcotic hospital in
Lexington, Kentucky, where both males and females were housed in the
same institution. This resulted in a book (Tittle, 1972c) and several articles (Tittle, 1972a; 1972b; 1969b). In addition, I set my mind to figur-
ing out a way to compile evidence about the deterrence question, not
realizing that Gibbs was thinking along the same lines. My first deterrence paper (Tittle, 1969a) was accepted for publication before Gibbs',
but did not actually appear in print until after his (Gibbs, 1968). In any
case, both those papers served notice that deterrence may be more likely than most social scientists thought. I know I was astonished at the
results and consequently became quite interested in doing additional
work on deterrence and the effect of sanctions (Tittle, 1973, 1975,
1977a, 1977b, 1978a, 1978b, 1979, 1980a, 1980b, 1980c, 1985b; Tittle
& Logan, 1973; Tittle & Rowe, 1973, 1974, 1978; Ward & Tittle, 1993).

After five years at Indiana, where I had the privilege of associating
with excellent criminological scholars such as Austin Turk, Alfred Lin-
desmith, Michael Schwartz, and Karl Schuessler and where the halls were
haunted with memories of Edwin Sutherland, Albert Cohen, William
Chambliss, and Donald Cressey, I decided to move to a brand new,
completely undistinguished university in Boca Raton, Florida. Most
serious scholars who knew me thought that it would be a career ending move. I did not see it that way. The decision to abandon major university contexts was motivated by the tug of previous commitments. I
continued to harbor the moral obligation toward undergraduate education with which I began graduate school. It appeared to me at that time
that Indiana was simply exploiting undergraduates for the benefit of the
graduate program. As at most large universities, undergraduates were
taught in mass lecture sections or mostly by teaching assistants, and
nobody seemed to care much about their welfare. In particular I knew
that I was ineffective as an undergraduate educator under those conditions, and I believed the problem was structural, not personal.

## The Challenge of a Minor League School

The appeal of a school featuring small classes filled with juniors and seniors (Florida Atlantic University had no freshmen until many years later) was irresistible. The appeal was particularly strong because I completely rejected the popular notion that there is a conflict between research and effective undergraduate teaching. Indeed, in my mind the best teachers are active scholars. I was convinced that I could develop as a scholar while serving on the faculty of a school devoted almost exclusively to undergraduate education.

I was lucky enough to get a grant to conduct a three-state survey addressing the deterrence question. The data led to a book and several articles on deterrence (Richards & Tittle, 1981, 1982; Tittle, 1977b, 1980c) but were used for numerous articles about subjects besides deterrence—socioeconomic status and crime (Tittle & Villemez, 1977), age and crime (Rowe & Tittle, 1977; Tittle & Ward, 1993), religiosity and crime (Tittle & Welch, 1983), differential association and crime (Tittle et al., 1986; Jackson et al., 1986), geographic mobility and crime (Tittle & Paternoster, 1988), and urbanism and crime (Tittle, 1989a, 1989c; Tittle & Stafford, 1992). And I was able to call upon other kinds of data to address issues about sanctions and deviant behavior (Tittle & Rowe, 1973; 1974, 1978). By then my reputation as a criminologist was hardened although I continued to think of my work as fundamentally sociological and fundamentally general. Also while at Florida Atlantic, I "inherited" a grant project funded by the State Attorney General's Office to ascertain the extent and distribution of racial discrimination in the Florida juvenile justice system. The funds had been awarded to two colleagues who hired Debra Curran, then a graduate student and later my wife, to collect the data. However, before the project was begun they took other jobs. I was asked to complete the project. This was fortuitous because it turned my thinking toward issues about how the justice system works (Tittle, 1994; Britt & Tittle, 1975; Tittle & Curran, 1988).

## Return to a Research Context

Eventually, after 18 years, I accepted a position at Washington State University, returning to a research context. My disenchantment with Florida Atlantic University had grown steadily because it turned away from liberal education to focus heavily on professional training for numerous specific careers such as nursing, health administration, social work, criminal justice, urban and regional planning, and others. I believe that universities have two sacred missions. One is to expand and hone knowledge—the research mission—and the second is to educate students in the liberal tradition—freeing their minds from the constraints of ignorance. Colleges and universities cannot discharge those duties if they try to teach too many students in mass lectures, as Indiana did; nor can they accomplish those goals if they are mainly training grounds for occupational pursuits, as Florida Atlantic and numerous other schools have become. Furthermore, institutions that make no time or place for scholarship while emphasizing only "teaching" will also fall short of the mark. Because few schools achieve a good balance between liberal education and scholarship, it began to seem to me that a mismatch in favor of scholarship was the lesser of several evils, at least as long as the mismatch was not too extreme. It was not too out of balance at Washington State University and I expect it will not be at North Carolina State University, where I will be located when this paper appears in print.

## Accumulating Observations about Criminology

It was at Washington State that several of the lessons of my academic career fully crystallized. Four in particular came into sharp focus. They are: (1) our body of verified scientific knowledge is exceptionally weak, (2) science is the best model for criminological work, (3) bias is pervasive in social science, including criminology, and is an archenemy of knowledge, (4) recommendations or guidelines from criminologists for social policy should be delayed until there is a strong scientific base of relevant knowledge. Each of these lessons is intertwined with the others and to fully comprehend their import one must share certain definitions and orientations about the meaning of science. Those meanings will be specified later, but for now I will elaborate on the path that led to my strong feelings about these four issues.

Early in my career I became acutely aware of our dearth of knowledge and the need for systematic compilation of reliable evidence concerning human behavior. My first job interview as a soon-to-be Ph.D. was at the Baylor University Medical School. During the tour I was taken to a lab where medical doctors were conducting experiments with astronauts. The plan was to isolate several people in a simulated spacecraft for several weeks during which time their bodily functions and activity were to be observed and monitored. As I was being introduced around, one of the experimenters said something like the following: "We need you; we do not know what will happen with our experimental subjects after being in isolation for a long time. We are afraid they may become aggressive and violent and we want to be able to pull them out of the isolation chamber before they do harm to each other. But because we are medical doctors we don't know what the clues are that would enable us to know when violence is imminent. We need a sociologist to tell us that."

Unfortunately, even though I had some personal beliefs about this issue and was tempted to invoke them under the guise of scientific knowledge, I knew that criminologists did not then, nor now, know enough about violent behavior to provide reliable advice. In this case and many others, lack of knowledge is particularly telling because being wrong would have had very costly and dangerous consequences. Moreover, I knew it would be irresponsible and dishonest to pretend that I had the appropriate knowledge those experimenters sought. I decided right then that sociologists and criminologists must build a reliable, verified body of knowledge that is compiled in systematic ways to enable us to answer relevant questions about human behavior.

Further, delving into the literature about deterrence led to the realization that there was little actual evidence concerning the effects of sanctions and that the quality of much of the evidence that existed was poor. Using reasonable scientific criteria, any objective observer would have concluded that the effect of sanctions was simply unknown. Nevertheless, the literature was filled with strong statements suggesting that the issue was settled. Moreover, many criminologists had been advocating social policy supposedly based on this body of evidence. It seemed to me that those advocates either had exceptionally weak standards for evidence or they were acting on ideology. In any case, it was a revelation to discover that knowledge about one of the most important issues in criminology rested on a reed. I began to wonder if the same might be true of other issues as well.

I turned my attention to socioeconomic status and crime. The class-crime relationship was at the time thought by most to be well established—"everybody knew" that there was a strong negative relationship between the two. Even now, at least one major figure contends that questioning whether the data support a negative class-crime relationship is the equivalent of declaring the earth to be flat. Again, however, the picture turned out to be a lot muddier than anybody thought (Tittle, 1983; Tittle & Meier, 1990, 1991; Tittle & Villemez, 1977; Tittle et al., 1978). Even though some criminologists still believe the evidence favors the classic interpretation, few now think the data are compelling (for citations to the literature about this controversy see Tittle & Paternoster, 2000:339; recent installments to the body of evidence include Dunaway et al., 2000; Wright et al., 1999). Yet, in this case, like that of deterrence, numerous people were and are willing to make strong statements one way or another. Moreover, many advocates seem uninterested in the actual evidence, being convinced that their particular view is right—even to the point of questioning the motives or competence of those who raise questions about the evidence.

This experience with the SES/crime controversy fueled my growing skepticism about criminological knowledge. That skepticism led to additional reviews of evidence about age and crime (Tittle, 1988; Tittle & Grasmick, 1997; Tittle & Rowe, 1977; Tittle and Ward, 1993), religiosity and deviant behavior (Tittle & Welch, 1983), urban residence and crime (Tittle, 1989a, 1989c, Tittle & Stafford, 1992), IQ and crime (Ward & Tittle, 1993, 1994), geographic mobility and crime/deviance (Tittle & Paternoster, 1988), discrimination in the juvenile justice system (Tittle & Curran, 1988), and labeling (Tittle, 1975, 1980b). In each instance I found an insufficient basis for firm conclusions. In some instances the collective research proved to be consistent with widespread beliefs and in other instances it did not. In all cases, however, I came away amazed at how little we knew about these important relationships and about how weak the available data really are. Even less is known about the actual causes of human behavior, especially crime and deviance. More astonishing, however, is the fact that the absence of knowledge does not seem to bother a lot of people—they are quite confident in asserting conclusions and some even press to be consulted about social policy, claiming to have scientific knowledge needed by policymakers.

My increasing frustration with the volume and quality of data came to be matched by a concern that we have poor explanations for those empirical regularities that most people think have been reasonably established. Our most reliable knowledge concerns simple relationships between demographic factors and crime/deviance, but even for those relationships we have poor understanding of the causal mechanisms involved. For example, it is not intellectually satisfying simply to know that crime is predictably linked to age, assuming that it turns out to be so linked (Tittle, 1988). We really ought to know why that is and why the relationship might be somewhat different for different individuals and categories of persons. Moreover, even if we could establish that age affects crime, we would need to know the causal mechanisms. Expanded knowledge is particularly important if one is to try to do something about crime. It is not practical, for example, to think about eliminating age categories to control crime although it might be practical to think about eliminating some of the linkages that permit age to cause crime. But we have to know what those linkages are and how they work. Without adequate answers to the questions of "why" and "how," we simply cannot claim to know much and we cannot make meaningful policy recommendations.

## A Guiding Paradigm

### *The Scientific Process*

These concerns about evidence and explanation produced much thought about how to do criminology. There are, of course, many paradigms, all with their own persuasive followers. After contemplating the various approaches, however, I came to the conclusion that criminologists must adopt the scientific paradigm if they are to be successful. This means specifically that (1) we should eschew intuition and personal experience as sources of data, relying instead upon empirical evidence (that which can conceivably be measured and replicated), (2) we should seek to find the causes of the phenomena of interest, and (3) we should strive to organize our knowledge into general theories that permit answers to questions of "why" and "how." This does not imply that intuition and personal experience are not valuable—they are, but only as sources of inspiration, insight, and clues to explanation. It also does not mean that purely descriptive work is unimportant; in fact, description is essential—but only to establish regularities that are then to be accounted for within explanatory systems that specify causal connections. In addition, the model of science I came to embrace does not imply that limited, ad hoc explanations are of no import; they are crucial—but only as building blocks for more general explanatory schemes, which I call theories.

As I conceive it, scientific knowledge is built through sequential feedback, beginning with descriptions of empirical regularities, proceeding to explanation that satisfies the intellectual curiosity of other scholars who are trained to be skeptical. Explanations are then put to empirical test by deriving specific hypotheses about interconnections and causes among variables suggested by the proposed explanation and checking the hypotheses with data relevant to that purpose. When the test results are supportive, the community of scholars gains some confidence in the proposed explanation. More often than not, however, a test will yield some support and some challenge. That stimulates revision of the explanation, taking into account the pattern of evidence. Eventually, refined explanations are united within more general explanatory schemes called theories. Those theories in turn are tested, refined, and made more accurate. Such theory then permits explanation, prediction, and sometimes control of criminal/deviant or other human behavior. The whole process, however, is long and tedious, with knowledge growing in a cumulative process. One study means nothing; collections of large numbers and varieties of progressively more refined studies are required.

For science to operate and to produce the desired outcomes, it must be supported by a community of scholars dedicated to the scientific enterprise. This community of scholars must structure itself to reward those who follow its dictates and ignore those who do not, and it must socialize new members in the values and methods of science. Those values include dedication to: (1) knowledge gained through the scientific method, (2) objectivity, (3) the search for truth, (4) open discussion and sharing of information, and (5) skepticism and mutual criticism. Science, therefore, is not value free. It is absolutely committed to a value system—the values of science. Moreover, science is a jealous master, insisting that other values (ideology and personal commitments) be rejected or overcome, at least while attempting to do science. However, because scientists recognize that individuals do have other values and goals that cannot be easily suppressed, the community of scientists organizes itself to counter those competing impulses. It does that by insisting on review by demanding critics, rewarding those who work against their own personal interests and values, and granting prestige to those who most fully exhibit the ideals of science while stigmatizing those who betray the cause.

If practiced according to ideal dictates, science can lead to knowledge that is more reliable, satisfying, and useful than any other paradigm by which people seek to understand human behavior and social organization. This is generally acknowledged by scholars and laypersons alike. However, practicing science is difficult, especially for those who study social phenomena. Science is obstructed because the objects of research may react to being studied, thereby introducing bias, and because developing good empirical measures of many of the concepts thought to be crucial to social behavior is difficult, sometimes perhaps even impossible. Many causal effects may have very long time lags, making it impractical to document their influence, and the possibility of reciprocal causation involving large numbers of variables is very real, posing methodological challenges of the highest order. In addition, extensive research, replication, and refinement necessary for valid scientific conclusions are inhibited by costs. Finally, there is the ever-present danger of uncontrolled personal bias by researchers and by those who interpret research. Therefore, the best that we criminologists can do is to practice science to the fullest extent possible, recognizing that our work often falls short and being cautious in our claims.

## Difficulties in Following the Paradigm

Collectively, however, we criminologists do not practice science to the fullest extent possible, and humility and caution do not come easy for us. A goodly proportion consciously reject the scientific model altogether, some believing it inappropriate and others believing it impossible to employ. And among those who ostensibly embrace the scientific approach many fail to follow its mandates. While there are numerous ways we deviate from science, perhaps the most obvious and destructive are lack of patience, a penchant for ad hoc research, and a pervasive weakness for ideology and bias.

Impatience. The scientific process is necessarily slow and cumulative. Establishing regularities, developing and testing explanations, and merging explanations through theories, which are then tested and refined, takes a very long time and involves hundreds of pieces of research to address adequately even one issue. Most criminologists cannot wait for that process to unfold. Their impatience leads them to leap to conclusions from limited evidence and their arrogance leads them to tell others what to do based on that same limited evidence. One study does not make a science; in fact, dozens of studies do not necessarily make a science. Yet many of us are already sure we know the answers to any question about crime. Unfortunately, however, the answers various scholars offer differ and the evidence is too weak to adjudicate among the diverse points of view. The truth that many do not want to face is that we simply do not have the empirical or theoretical basis for claiming adequate knowledge about criminal or deviant behavior.

Ignoring our weaknesses is nowhere more obvious than in the willingness of so many criminologists to offer advice to policymakers and to make statements for mass media consumption. Some are not only willing to try to make policy and influence public discourse, they insist upon it. During the six years I served on the Executive Board of the American Society of Criminology, we repeatedly dealt with movements to get the association to become politically active, to publicize research, or to endorse policy-oriented research. And these efforts continue. Quite a few believe, for instance, that the association should issue press releases, written for laypeople, with summaries of the articles published in our journal. This is presumably to provide citizens with information to use in influencing public policy about crime or to fashion their own actions, or perhaps to convince the public that we are doing something interesting and important. Offering professional research for public consumption, however, ignores the fact that no piece of research means anything except in context with all that has gone before, and no piece of research can be taken seriously until it has been subjected to repeated replication and the scrutiny of critical scientists.

Serving the ingredients of early-stage science to the public and policymakers is not just contrary to an informed scientific approach; it is counterproductive. Anything we say has a good probability of being wrong, or at least of being only partially correct. At best, when we are wrong we undermine future claims to be heard in those instances where our knowledge may be more advanced and accurate. Perhaps the best example of this is the distrust citizens now have of public reports about medical research. So many statements such as "X is good for you" have been followed later by other reports denying X's benefits that few people take publicly disseminated medical advice anymore. At worst, our policy proclamations may produce costly and dangerous outcomes (Tittle, 1985b). If punishment deters crime (which we do not know), then successfully advocating policies against punishment may cost numerous citizens their money or lives. If punishment does not deter (which, again we do not know), then successfully advocating policies to accomplish more certain or severe punishments may cost numerous accused persons their freedom or lives. Since we have inadequate knowledge about the effects of sanctions under various conditions, deciding punishment policy must be a matter of values and preferences—issues best left to public debate, free of scientific pretense.

Misplaced foci. The urge to do good and to perform useful public service is strong among criminologists. I share that commitment (Tittle, 1974, 1978b, 1979, 1985b). However, the way to accomplish that purpose is to do the basic science that will lead to reliable knowledge. We cannot cut corners; we must be patient. In the meantime, we must restrain ourselves from leaping to the public pulpit and we must minimize distractions that divert us from building a science of human behavior that will allow explanation, prediction, and perhaps control of behavior. One of those distractions is ad hoc research.

Many criminologists orient their work around a particular issue or type of crime and treat that issue or crime as if it were different from other issues and from other behavior. We have bodies of literature about drug use—even separate literatures about specific forms of drug use—robbery, white-collar crime, street crime, female crime, male crime, youth crime, adult or aged crime, and so on. As noted before, such fragmentation leads to duplication and discourages cross fertilization. For maximum advancement we must focus more on general, unifying themes. Two of my books (Tittle, 1995; Tittle & Paternoster, 2000) have tried to set an example of how to do that.

This tendency for ad hoc work is particularly prominent in policy research. Scholars inclined toward ad hoc, policy-oriented research think that they can learn how to deal with specific issues about crime in specific contexts by focusing on those particular sites. Indeed, many policy-oriented scholars as well as most laypersons are highly critical of general, theoretically oriented research that does not seem to have an obvious practical application. They do not see how, for example, an experiment about the way people manipulate probabilities, using judgments about the chances of seeing a green or a yellow taxi, could possibly have anything to do with crime and its management. They think one has to study actual criminals doing criminal acts in order to learn useful things about criminal behavior. In fact, however, learning the general principles of probability manipulation is crucial to understanding the conditions under which sanction threats are likely to deter criminal behavior as well as how other decisionmaking bears on crime. And unless the experiences and thought processes of those who commit criminal acts (or make laws and manage the justice process) are very different from those who do not (a highly unlikely possibility because almost everybody at one time or another commits criminal acts) establishing those principles of probability manipulation involves many kinds of studies, using many different kinds of subjects in numerous types of situations, only some of which will include actual criminals making criminal decisions.

Some ad hoc research is useful for science and for public policy. Any good data provide building blocks that an integratively oriented scholar might ultimately use to develop explanations or theories. And serendipity sometimes provides insights for a problem distant from the immediate context. Moreover, public issues occasionally hinge on evaluation research. For instance, exposing discrimination in the justice system, determining whether various programs "work" or not, and showing the unintended by-products of government policies and programs are valuable activities. Nevertheless, such ad hoc efforts should be secondary to building general knowledge about human behavior that will permit future scholars to answer questions by drawing on a corpus of empirically verified theories. The quickest way to establish a knowledge base with powerful potential applicability is to conduct theoretically driven research designed to build or test theory, not to address an immediate practical issue. To the extent that practicality is foremost, one is likely to overlook crucial theoretical points and thereby actually delay the accumulation of knowledge necessary for practical solutions.

A natural science illustration is pertinent (*Newsweek*, 1966), even if one has an aversion to the practical problem being addressed. During the Vietnam war the Defense Department was looking for ways to combat enemy forces hiding in the jungle. An engineer happened to see a scientific report about bedbugs. It seems they can smell human blood at long distances, and when they do, they become very excited, jumping up and down, and emitting screeching noises undetectable by the human ear. This engineer then got the idea to encase bedbugs in plastic pellets, along with tiny transmitters, to be dropped or shot into dense foliage. If people were in the jungle, the encased bedbugs would make noises, which would be transmitted to the allies, warning them of potential danger. Thus was derived a practical solution.

But that derivation did not come from research undertaken directly to address the military problem. It was an application of *basic* knowledge compiled by someone whose interests were far removed from military issues—by entomologists driven by purely scientific interests. It is difficult to imagine an entomologist saying: "I think I will study bedbugs because what I discover may enable a weapons engineer to solve a military problem." It is equally unlikely that the defense department would be able to foresee the advantage of bedbug research. In fact, a Federal grant of any kind, especially from the Defense Department, to study bedbugs on the pretense of solving a military problem would probably be met with derision.

In reality, the purposes of science are separate from practical concerns. Nobody can foresee the uses to which knowledge may be put, and if scientists design their research mainly for practical application, they will do poor science and in the process neglect esoteric things that may ultimately prove useful for addressing pragmatic concerns. The entomologist was doing what scientists do, which in this case was plugging gaps in knowledge about insects, without regard for its practical import or its ideological ramifications. When criminologists collectively make a similar commitment, they can build a base of knowledge that is both scientifically satisfying and useful for policy. The road to that goal is a high one, incrementally built on well-structured, empirically verified theory.

A second distraction inhibiting science is personal bias, especially ideology. It is pervasive in criminology, sometimes well concealed but often open and active. One form is embedded in the research process. Research biases include tendencies to focus on results supporting the author's point of view while deemphasizing contrary evidence, to distort the positions of those who report contrary evidence, and to draw conclusions not justified by the data. Such biases are the easiest to combat, however. Critical review by scientific audiences, diminution of prestige for those who fail to control their biases and enhancement of prestige for those who do, and replication can all help reduce biasing influences. Along with structural safeguards, training in the tenets of science are essential. Socialization for scientific work helps scholars take pride in recognizing the import of data contrary to their personal inclinations and in implementing measures to counteract biases. Contrary to the view of some, it is not enough to recognize and declare one's own biases; scholars must try to do something about them.

Destructive ideology and personal biases no doubt also intrude into the publication process, although no data demonstrate it. We all have experienced, or know about, the difficulty of getting into print competent and important but controversial work (that which provokes strong feelings among reviewers or which reports results contrary to their positions or beliefs). It is not hard to see, especially for a former editor, that some reviewers nitpick papers whose problem, approach, or conclusions they do not like while letting more agreeable work escape with cursory comments. Departures from conventionality face an especially rough gauntlet. These ideological intrusions are exacerbated when editors rely on advice from those known to be spokespersons for specific positions or lines of research, many of whom have firmly held positions concerning the issues under consideration. Nevertheless, there are some protections in the arena of publication to prevent ideology and personal biases from making science impossible. Primary among them is the plethora of potential publication outlets. Competent work can almost always be published somewhere, even if not in a prestigious outlet, partly because some editors are more broadminded and professionally conscientious than others, partly because there is not enough good work to fill the pages of all journals, and partly because controversial work is sometimes commercially attractive enough to be published in book form.

The most onerous effects of biases in the social sciences are manifest in concerted efforts to prevent the conduct of, or the distribution of the results of, research that one or another group finds distasteful. Recent history is filled with instances where politically organized groups of ideologues on both the left and the right have tried to prevent research, either because they fear the results or because they think the answers to the questions are already known (Hunt, 1999). And it is well understood that many issues simply cannot be studied unless the scholar is willing to sacrifice his/her reputation and suffer persecution (Farberow, 1963). In criminology specifically there are numerous ideas concerning potential causal elements that could contribute to our knowledge were they pursued to their logical end. Yet some of them have hardly been articulated and many others have waxed or waned in response to political currents—not the imperatives of science.

The most obvious illustration concerns the idea that personal defects, such as neurological deficits, hormone deficiencies, personality patterns, or genetic predispositions, cause or contribute to criminal behavior. It is theoretically useful and easy to imagine that some people have such defects and that under some conditions those defects interact or converge with other variables or conditions to increase the chances of criminal outcomes. Spelling out those possibilities theoretically and then testing carefully drawn hypotheses through the scientific process would permit the actual import of individual defects to be established. They may turn out to be of no consequence or they may be shown to have important causal influence. We simply do not now know, and we are likely to be slow in finding out the part played in criminal behavior by personal defects because it is politically costly to pursue such work (for some, of course, it may be politically advantageous). The case of IQ and crime is but one instance where many who entertained this question did so in the face of derision (see Devlin et al., 1997; Jacoby & Glauberman, 1995). On the other hand, some have made outrageous claims about IQ and crime without attending to the theory or research necessary to justify such claims (Herrnstein & Murray, 1994).

Neither extreme encourages good scholarship. Progress is most likely when scholars pursue all theoretical questions freely (though ethically) in search of the truth, not when they shirk ideas for fear of offending others or losing prestige, become inhibited out of concern for jeopardizing financial or publication possibilities, or choose to remain ignorant because they fear how results of research might be used. We must be committed to knowledge, and as scholars we have a moral obligation to oppose inhibitions on truth seeking, to resist claims from incomplete knowledge, and to counter inappropriate applications of actual knowledge.

## A Lesson Only Partially Learned

A final lesson I have learned, although I have often been ineffective in acting on it, is that civility in our work and in our relations with other scholars, students, and laypersons is essential. My mentor in this regard has been James F. Short, Jr. (Jim), friend and departmental colleague at Washington State University for 12 years. Jim's career has featured outstanding scholarly contributions, important critical work, high-level editorial activities, and leadership in our professional associations. Through it all he has maintained a reputation as the nicest and most trustworthy person in our business. Jim has shown that people can do their work well while remaining sensitive to the feelings and needs of others and he has demonstrated by practice that one can maintain the distinction between intellectual issues and the personal characteristics of individuals concerned with those issues. Authors of work criticized by Jim invariably go away feeling uplifted, enlightened, and energized, not denigrated or diminished.

No matter how much we might disagree among ourselves and regardless of differences in style or capability, we must treat each other with respect if we are to share a productive work environment. It is not necessary to attribute bad motives or incompetence in order to evaluate scholarly work, and it is not consistent with scientific principles to try to undermine research or lines of thought by associating them with assumed or actual political agendas, sources of funding, or the particular publication outlets. Furthermore, name calling, ad hominem criticism, and shrill calls for emotional response add nothing of value to scholarly interchange. Good scientific work is good, no matter who does it or why, and poor scientific work is poor, no matter its source. Furthermore, scholarly work outside ones favorite paradigm may challenge conclusions, force greater diligence, and open new lines of thought and research. For those reasons it must be acknowledged and its practitioners granted respect.

## Summary

I have tried to identify the major principles for an effective criminology, as I have come to understand them in my own career. Briefly summarized they are: (1) criminology is not a discipline but a topical area dependent on a variety of disciplines and that criminological knowledge is best pursued and dispensed within the context of liberal arts education, (2) our methods of identifying and recruiting new scholars must be improved, (3) evidence concerning most important issues having to do with crime and crime-relevant phenomena is weak; success requires that we commit ourselves to a long-range mission of improving that situation, (4) things are more complicated than our extant theories show, calling for improved theories specifying contingent and interactive effects, (5) the most effective criminology demands that we be aware of and committed to the goal of developing general explanatory schemes refined through test and feedback, (6) science is the best model to follow in developing criminological knowledge, (7) weak science, which is likely to continue to characterize criminology for some time, is hardly a basis for policy, and (8) the barriers to, and distractions from, good scientific criminology, especially the widespread practice of ad hoc work and the intrusion of personal biases and larger ideologies, must be countered, and (9) civility within the scholarly community is necessary for maximum collective effort.

There are many other, more limited lessons, especially about doing research and teaching, that could be shared. They are too numerous to detail here and can only be transmitted effectively through long-term teacher-student or colleague-colleague interactions. Moreover, those lessons are dynamic, growing and shifting with experience and new situations. The nine lessons of criminology noted in the previous paragraph, however, are fundamental. They rest on solid principles with enduring significance. I wish I had learned them a lot earlier in my academic life.

# References

Britt, D.W. & C.R. Tittle (1975). "Crime Rates and Police Behavior: A Test of Contradictory Hypotheses." *Social Forces*, 54:441-451.

Devlin, B., S.E. Fienberg, D.P. Resnick & K. Roeder (eds.) (1997). *Intelligence, Genes, and Success: Scientists Respond to* The Bell Curve. New York, NY: Springer-Verlag.

Dunaway, R.G., F.T. Cullen, V.S. Burton, Jr. & T.D. Evans (2000). "The Myth of Social Class and Crime Revisited: An Examination of Class and Adult Criminality." *Criminology*, 38:589-632.

Farberow, N.L. (ed.) (1963). *Taboo Topics*. New York, NY: Atherton.

Gibbs, J.P. (1968). "Crime, Punishment, and Deterrence." *Southwestern Social Science Quarterly*, 48:515-530.

Herrnstein, R.J. & C. Murray (1994). *The Bell Curve: Intelligence and Class Structure in American Life*. New York, NY: Free Press Paperbacks.

Hall, R.H. & C.R. Tittle (1966). "A Note on Bureaucracy and Its 'Correlates.'" *American Journal of Sociology*, 72:267-272.

Hunt, M. (1999). *The New Know-Nothings: The Political Foes of the Scientific Study of Human Nature*. New Brunswick, NJ: Transaction.

Jackson, E.F., C.R. Tittle & M.J. Burke (1986). "Offense-Specific Models of Differential Association." *Social Problems*, 33:335-356.

Jacoby, R. & N. Glauberman (eds.) (1995). *The Bell Curve Debate: History, Documents, Opinions*. New York, NY: Random House.

*Newsweek* (1966). "Technology Versus the Viet Cong." 68, Dec. 19:108-112.

Paternoster, R. & C.R. Tittle (1990). "Parental Work Control and Delinquency: A Theoretical and Empirical Critique." In *Advances in Criminological Theory*, Vol. 2, edited by W.S. Laufer & F. Adler, pp. 39-70. Newark, NJ: Transaction Publishers.

Richards, P. & C.R. Tittle (1982). "Socioeconomic Status and Perceptions of Personal Arrest Probabilities." *Criminology*, 20:329-346.

Richards, P. & C.R. Tittle (1981). "Gender and Perceived Chances of Arrest." *Social Forces*, 59:1182-1199.

Rowe, A.R. & C.R. Tittle (1977). "Life Cycle Changes and Criminal Propensity." *Sociological Quarterly*, 18:223-236.

Schulman, G.I. & C.R. Tittle (1968). "Assimilation-Contrast Effects and Item Selection in Thurstone Scaling." *Social Forces*, 46:484-491.

Tittle, C.R. (2002). "Deviance." Encyclopedia of Crime and Justice. New York, NY: Macmillan. Reference 2:519-528.

Tittle, C.R. (2000). "Theoretical Developments in Criminology." *Justice 2000*. Washington, DC: National Institute of Justice (in press).

Tittle, C.R. (1997). "Thoughts Stimulated by Braithwaite's Analysis of Control Balance Theory." *Theoretical Criminology*, 1:99-107.

Tittle, C.R. (1995). *Control Balance: Toward a General Theory of Deviance*. Boulder, CO: Westview Press.

Tittle, C.R. (1994). "The Theoretical Bases for Inequality in Formal Social Control." In *Inequality and Social Control*, edited by M. Myers & G. Bridges, pp. 21-52. Boulder, CO: Westview Press.

Tittle, C.R. (1991). "On Being Labeled a Criminologist." *The Criminologist*, June-July.

Tittle, C.R. (1989a). "Influences on Urbanism: A Test of Predictions from Three Perspectives." *Social Problems*, 36:170-188.

Tittle, C.R. (1989b). "Prospects for Synthetic Theory: Consideration of Macro-Level Criminological Activity," In *Theoretical Integration in the Study of Crime and Delinquency*, edited by S. Messner, M. Krohn & A.E. Liska, pp. 161-178. Albany, NY: SUNY Press, 1989.

Tittle, C.R. (1989c). "Urbanness and Unconventional Behavior: A Partial Test of Claude Fischer's Subcultural Theory." *Criminology*, 27:273-306.

Tittle, C.R. (1988). "Two Empirical Regularities (Maybe) in Search of an Explanation: Commentary on the Age/Crime Debate." *Criminology*, 26:75-85.

Tittle, C.R. (1985a). "The Assumption that General Theories are Not Possible." *In Theoretical Methods in Criminology*, edited by R.F. Meier, pp. 93-121. Beverly Hills, CA: Sage.

Tittle, C.R. (1985b). "Can Social Science Answer Questions About Deterrence for Policy Use?" In *Social Science and Social Policy*, edited by R.L. Shotland & M.M. Mark, pp. 265-294. Beverly Hills, CA: Sage.

Tittle, C.R. (1983). "Social Class and Criminal Behavior: A Critique of the Theoretical Foundation." *Social Forces*, 61:334-358.

Tittle, C.R. (1980a). "Evaluating the Deterrent Effects of Criminal Sanctions." In *Handbook of Criminal Justice Evaluation*, edited by M.W. Klein & K. Teilmann, pp. 381-402. Beverly Hills, CA: Sage.

Tittle, C.R. (1980b). "Labelling and Crime: An Empirical Evaluation." In *Societal Reaction and Deviant Behavior: The Evaluation of a Theory*, 2nd Ed, edited by W. Gove, pp. 157-179. Beverly Hills, CA: Sage.

Tittle, C.R. (1980c). *Sanctions and Social Deviance: The Question of Deterrence*. New York, NY: Praeger.

Tittle, C.R. (1979). "Statement on Capital Punishment." *Southern Sociologist*, 11:16-17,ff.

Tittle, C.R. (1978a). "Comment on 'Deterrence: Theory vs. Practice.'" *Criminology*, l6:31-35.

Tittle, C.R. (1978b). "Restitution and Deterrence: An Evaluation of Compatibility." In *Offender Restitution in Theory and Action*, edited by B. Galaway & J. Hudson, pp. 33-58. Lexington, MA: Heath.

Tittle, C.R. (1977a). "Introduction to Part I: Social Control and Deviance." *Social Forces*, 56:315-319.

Tittle, C.R. (1977b). "Sanction Fear and the Maintenance of Social Order." *Social Forces*, 55:579-596.

Tittle, C.R. (1975). "Deterrents or Labeling?" *Social Forces*, 53:399-410.

Tittle, C.R. (1974). "Prisons and Rehabilitation: The Inevitability of Disfavor." *Social Problems*, 21:385-395.

Tittle, C.R. (1973). "Punishment and Deterrence of Deviance," In *The Economics of Crime and Punishment*, edited by S. Rottenberg, pp. 85-102. Washington, DC: The American Enterprise Institute.

Tittle, C.R. (1972a). "Institutional Living and Rehabilitation." *Journal of Health and Social Behavior*, 13:263-275.

Tittle, C.R. (1972b). "Institutional Living and Self-Esteem." *Social Problems*, 20:65-77.

Tittle, C.R. (1972c). *Society of Subordinates: Inmate Organization in a Narcotic Hospital*. Bloomington, IN: Indiana University Press.

Tittle, C.R. (1969a). "Crime Rates and Legal Sanctions." *Social Problems,* 16:409-423.

Tittle, C.R. (1969b). "Inmate Organization: Sex Differentiation and the Influence of Criminal Subcultures." *American Sociological Review*, 34:492-505.

Tittle, C.R. & D.A. Curran (1988). "Contingencies for Dispositional Disparities in Juvenile Justice." *Social Forces*, 67:23-58.

Tittle, C.R. & H.G. Grasmick (1997). "Criminal Behavior and Age: A Test of Three Provocative Hypotheses." *Journal of Criminal Law and Criminology*, 88:309-342.

C.R. Tittle & R.J. Hill (1967a). "Attitude Measurement and Prediction of Behavior: An Evaluation of Conditions and Measurement Techniques." *Sociometry*, 30:199-213.

C.R. Tittle & R.J. Hill (1967b). "A Note on the Accuracy of Self-Reported data and Prediction of Political Activity." *Public Opinion Quarterly*, 31:103-106.

Tittle, C.R. & C.H. Logan (1973). "Sanctions and Deviance: Evidence and Remaining Questions." *Law and Society Review*, 7:371-392.

Tittle, C.R. & R.F. Meier (1991). "Specifying the SES/Delinquency Relationship by Social Characteristics of Contexts." *Journal of Research in Crime and Delinquency*, 28:430-455.

Tittle, C.R. & R.F. Meier (1990). "Specifying the SES/Delinquency Relationship." *Criminology*, 28:271-299.

Tittle, C.R. & R. Paternoster (2000). *Social Deviance and Crime: An Organizational and Theoretical Approach*. Los Angeles, CA: Roxbury.

Tittle, C.R. & R. Paternoster (1988). "Geographic Mobility and Criminal Behavior." *Journal of Research in Crime and Delinquency*, 25:301-343.

Tittle, C.R. & T. Rotolo (2000). "IQ and Stratification: A Test of Herrnstein and Murray's Social Change Hypothesis." *Social Forces*, 79 (in press).

Tittle, C.R. & A.R. Rowe (1978). "Arrest and Crime: More on the Deterrence Problem." In *The New and the Old Criminology*, edited by E. Flynn & J. Conrad, pp. 85-95. New York, NY: Praeger.

Tittle, C.R. & A.R. Rowe (1974). "Certainty of Arrest and Crime Rates: A Further Test of the Deterrence Hypothesis." *Social Forces*, 52:455-462.

Tittle, C.R. & A.R. Rowe (1973). "Moral Appeal, Sanction Threat, and Deviance: An Experimental Test." *Social Problems*, 20:488-498.

Tittle, C.R. & M.C. Stafford (1992). "Urban Theory, Urbanism, and Suburban Residence." *Social Forces*, 70:725-744.

Tittle, C.R. & D.P. Tittle (1965). "Structural Handicaps to Therapeutic Participation: A Case Study," *Social Problems*, 13:65-82.

Tittle, C.R. & D.P. Tittle (1964). "Social Organization of Prisoners: An Empirical Test." *Social Forces*, 43 (December, 1964):216-221.

Tittle, C.R. & W.J. Villemez (1977). "Social Class and Criminality." *Social Forces*, 56:474-502.

Tittle, C.R. & W.J. Villemez (1976). "Category/Continuum Thought Styles and Survey Research." *Sociological Focus*, 9:1-10.

Tittle, C.R. & D.A. Ward (1993). "The Interaction of Age with the Causes and Correlates of Crime." *Journal of Quantitative Criminology*, 9:3-53.

Tittle, C.R. & M.R. Welch (1983). "Religiosity and Deviance: Toward a Contingency Theory of Constraining Effects." *Social Forces*, 61:653-682.

Tittle, C.R., E.F. Jackson & M.J. Burke (1986). "Modeling Sutherland's Theory of Differential Association: Toward an Empirical Clarification." *Social Forces*, 65:405-432.

Tittle, C.R., W.J. Villemez & D.A. Smith (1978). "The Myth of Social Class and Criminality: An Empirical Assessment of the Empirical Evidence." *American Sociological Review*, 43:643-56.

Ward, D.A. & C.R. Tittle (1994). "IQ and Delinquency: A Test of Two Competing Explanations." *Journal of Quantitative Criminology*, 10:189-212.

Ward, D.A. & C.R. Tittle (1993). "Deterrence or Secondary Deviation?: The Effect of Informal Sanctions." *Deviant Behavior*, 14:43-64.

Welch, M.R., T. Petee & C.R. Tittle (1991). "Religion and Deviance Among Adult Catholics: A Test of the 'Moral Communities' Hypothesis." *Journal for the Scientific Study of Religion*, 30:159-172.

Wright, B., R. Entner, A. Caspi, T.E. Moffitt, R.A. Miech & P.A. Silva (1999). "Reconsidering the Relationship Between SES and Delinquency: Causation But Not Correlation." *Criminology*, 37:175-194.

# 3

# Surrounded by Crime: Lessons from One Academic Career

Malcolm W. Klein

I came from an academic family. My father was a widely revered professor, and I thought being a PROFESSOR was a great honor, far beyond anything I could achieve. Now here I am, decades later, a PROFESSOR, asked to pass lessons on to future generations, including some individuals who in turn will become PROFESSORS, whether they know it or not. So how does one determine when such a career starts? How do we learn who we will be?

## Lesson #1: Accidents and Probabilities May Determine Our Paths

Surely one of the more common experiences among many professionals is that they got to their careers—or their several careers—as much by accident as by forethought. As I neared completion of my undergraduate days, I applied to the Master of Arts program in psychology in several graduate schools with good reputations, as recommended to me by my favorite department chairman. One of them—Boston University—accepted me with a very generous graduate assistantship, so that's where I went; I followed the money.

Two days after I arrived, I found myself taken under the wing of Professor Nathan Maccoby, distinguished social psychologist, survey researcher, and handball player.[1] He was to be, he announced, my mentor. He started by taking me to lunch in Cambridge, which required a subway ride under the Charles River in Boston. As we waited for the train he launched into a mentor's lecture on the nature of graduate study and the life I could expect to lead for the next few years. Somewhere in this routine, he dropped the phrase: "You know, a master's degree is a quitter's degree." That's how I found out I was a Ph.D. candidate. Certainly, I could not own up to being a quitter's candidate, so the die was cast. Quite accidentally, I became a doctoral student in social psychology.

One can learn about one's style as well as one's trajectory. Following a seminar run by Professor Warren Bennis, another early mentor,[2] my closest friend and fellow student and I stayed on to discuss weighty matters of graduate and postdoctoral careers. After a while, Bennis looked at us and asked, "Would you rather be loved or respected?" My friend blurted out "loved" just as I firmly opted for "respected." I had never realized this about myself until the question was posed. OK; now I knew something more about myself—I was after respect, not love. Like my father the professor before me, I'm sure my colleagues would agree that many look to me more with respect than love![3]

I ended up, upon completion of the Ph.D., in a survey research job in Los Angeles. I had assumed from the many jokes that I would hate Los Angeles, having been born and bred in New York. But quite to the contrary, I found it a delightful location—the weather, the ski-to-surf topology, the ethnic heterogeneity, and the social openness of the place was a great contrast to the closed society of my Boston years. After two years, however, the next career accident took place.

Prepared to move north to Berkeley for a public health research position, I was approached by local colleagues to consider the position as director of a project to reduce street gang crime in Los Angeles. When I noted that I had absolutely no background in youth, or criminology, or urban problems, I was told not to worry. I was bright and competent and I could learn all I needed to in six weeks.[4] There followed a week of seduction—meetings, interviews with cops and gang workers, intensive exposure to the street gang literature, and finally attendance on the last night at a weekly meeting of one of the street gangs involved. For a social psychologist who had taken courses in group dynamics, leadership, and social perception, this was a fascinating experience. The meeting was the culmination of discussions of leadership over the past year and the competing factions were anything but subtle about pressing their points. There was excitement here—even clear hints of physical danger (I sat close to the single exit from the room)—and a real-life dramatization of the very principles of group process I had studied from the textbooks.

Later that night in my living room, the chief "seducer," who was resigning as project director, used every argument he could muster to persuade me to stay in L.A. and take over the project. Finally, he said loudly enough for my wife to hear it and groan in the bedroom, "Frankly, you'd just be chicken not to take this on." My wife told me later that as soon as she heard that, she knew she would have to start unpacking: we were not going north to Berkeley and, quite accidentally, I became a criminologist.

My final case in point came six years or so later. Still located in the research institute that had housed the gang project, I was approached by the chair of the psychology department and later by the chair of the sociology department. I had done some part-time teaching for both. Would I be interested in an appointment as associate professor, each one asked. My inclination was to say yes—a tenured position set on the plate before me was tempting indeed. But I was unwilling to give up my valued research position. Would they consider a joint appointment, split between the institute and the department? The psychology chair said yes, that would be fine, but of course my loyalty must be to the department first; "joint" did not mean "equal." The sociology chair said yes, that would be fine: 50 percent at the institute, 50 percent teaching (one course a semester). That was one good way to build the department, he said. And so, quite accidentally, I became a sociologist.[5] In fact, against all logic, I was unanimously elected as chairperson of the sociology department three and a half years later, and remained in the position for 13 years. What a tolerant group they were!

In sum, my trajectory as a social psychologist was determined by chance and equally altered by chance to that of sociologist and criminologist and street gang specialist. There was no way to predict all this. Paths open up; our choice is to decide whether or not to follow them.

## Lesson #2: You Don't Have to Be a Criminologist to Be a Criminologist

This lesson is perhaps obvious from the foregoing. I never set out to be a criminologist and never formally trained for it. Yet this was true of many criminologists, for until the last two decades the field was less a coherent discipline than a tenuous molding of disparate fields—sociology, psychology, economics, biology, political science, criminal justice, law, public administration, and more. The disadvantage of this array of disciplines is sometimes the absence of a central thrust, of unifying theory, of compatible methodologies. The advantage is the flip side of these—balancing perspectives, alternative approaches, and distaste for doctrinaire or ideological supremacies. We are, indeed, a cosmopolitan discipline.

My own writings have in some ways exemplified this situation. I draw principally from social psychological, organizational, and sociological perspectives. My methods at various times have included experimentation, survey research, field observation, personal interviews, demographic analyses, and archival research into police, probation, court, and social agency files. They have been both qualitative and quantitative, with appreciation for both.

The greatest struggle of this field over my decades within it, however, has been in the sheer growth of knowledge concerning crime, its perpetration, and its contexts. There is now a legitimate discipline called criminology, and students must familiarize themselves with this body of knowledge, regardless of the disciplinary background from which they approach it. It is an area where ignorance is now easily revealed, as is evident from reference to media coverage of crime and to politicians' assertions about it. Conventional wisdoms no longer suffice.

## Lesson #3: Your Choice of Favorite Topic May Not Be the Choice of Your Audiences

Over my years in criminology, I have studied, written about, and taught about a series of topics: delinquency, police and court responses to delinquents, self-report methods of crime measurement, diversion of juveniles from court to community, community policing, drug sales, the juvenile justice system, cross-national comparisons of these issues, and street gangs. When I took a hiatus from gang research in 1970, I was told by an old hand in the field that I would never escape gangs, that I would be known more for that work than any other I might undertake. And, indeed, he was correct. I even said in the prologue of my 1971 book on gangs, "I've had it with gangs!" Ever since, colleagues have thrown that phrase in my face, especially when I took up gang research again in 1980.

The issue is similar to that of "newsworthiness" in journalism. Dull doesn't sell; normal doesn't sell; complexity doesn't sell. What sells is drama, exotica, excitement. Of my various research topics, only that of street gangs has those elements in the public eye—even in the eye of many criminologists. Street gangs, usually incorrectly, are thought to involve high levels of violence and drug sales. Attached to them are words like predators, rat packs, terrorists, and conspiracy. Gangs are the "them" versus the "us." Gangs reap headlines, reporters' inquiries, and over-enrolled college classes.

My personal preference, the source of my greatest rewards and satisfaction, has been my cross-national work on the nature of juvenile justice systems and self-report methodology. These have been intellectually challenging and mind-expanding. There's nothing like looking at other people's systems to understand your own better. In this regard, two study trips to China have been the most valuable by far, as the Chinese group-oriented culture yields a justice system far different from that produced by our individual-oriented culture.

But if I offer a choice between lectures on cross-national crime or street gangs, or an article on China or south-central Los Angeles, or self-reported delinquency in Europe or crime patterns of street gangs, the choice is always made for me: gangs, please. This sort of external demand is of little consequence if one's areas of study do not capture public officials' attention. In the absence of public glare, one can maintain the comforts of the ivy tower. But if the topic is publicly relevant—organized crime, spousal battering, public corruption, police abuses, child abuse, street gangs—then even the ivy tower becomes transparent. So, in the eyes of most, I've been a gang researcher; the rest, the bulk of my work, has been obscured. I resent it, but I understand it.

## Lesson #4: Eventually, You May Have to Go Public, or You May Want to Go Public

When I started out in gang research in the early 1960s, "street gangs" was an esoteric topic. Only a few notable books had been produced, such as Frederic Thrasher's pioneering *The Gang*, Lewis Yablonsky's imaginative but overstated *The Violent Gang*, and James F. Short and Fred Strodtbeck's *Group Process and Gang Delinquency*, a brilliant and comprehensive empirical study of the topic. At the time, street gangs were thought to exist in only a few large urban areas—New York, Philadelphia, Boston, Chicago, San Francisco, Los Angeles, and El Paso were best known. Later research revealed more than 50 cities to be gang-involved, but nobody knew that at the time.

To the general public, gangs at worst meant *West Side Story*, a romanticized image of fun-loving if alienated pranksters involved in only occasional violence against each other: not an issue to engage the rest of us. Gang researchers, of whom there were only a few, could concentrate on theoretical development and basic data gathering without much concern for putting their knowledge to work in the public domain or for engaging in explanations of gang affairs in the media.

Further, through the 1960s and 1970s gang activity did not seem to warrant much attention. Gang violence was relatively low, gangs weren't known to be prevalent nationally, the idea of gangs controlling illegal drug markets had not yet been elaborated, and gangs seemed to be an inner-city urban problem like many others that largely could be ignored by public officials and an unconcerned suburban America. What wasn't understood was that street gangs were slowly proliferating across the country and were becoming more dangerous.

We know better now. The number of gang-involved cities doubled through the 1960s, and that number doubled again through the 1970s, and then the number leapt forward at an accelerating pace in the next two decades. We went from 50 gang cities to several **thousand** cities and towns. We went from large urban centers to smaller cities to suburban communities, and even to rural areas. Along with this proliferation came expanded media coverage and the diffusion of gang "culture" through TV, movies, magazines, news reports, and public lectures by the police and other agencies. We got to the point where almost any teenager in the nation could mimic the dress, the walk, the language, and the signs of gang membership.

At the same time, weaponry advanced both in terms of technology and availability. The "zipguns," tire irons, chains, and fists of the 1960s were slowly replaced by truly lethal firearms—mostly handguns, but occasionally automatic rifles as well. Gang fights that used to yield bruises and stitches now more often resulted in gaping wounds and death. Los Angeles County, the most active gang location in the nation, went from fewer than a 100 gang-related deaths per year in the 1970s to more than 800 in the mid-1990s—fully 45 percent of all county homicides of all types.

One result of all this was increased funding for gang research and a minor explosion of gang researchers. Suddenly I had new colleagues and a rapidly expanding body of knowledge about street gangs. This new knowledge meant that, if called upon, academics could become involved in public policy to an extent heretofore not feasible. We could be "experts" because we were developing **generic** knowledge about our topic.

This new knowledge base took on particular significance because of another major development in the gang world, the growth—even the domination—of suppressive approaches in gang policy and practice. With the election of Ronald Reagan in 1980 and the conservative sweep that overtook the nation, the "war on crime" began to move from a simple political slogan to an ideology implemented in reality. The proliferation of street gangs and greater attention to street violence led to new anti-gang tactics that eschewed prevention and rehabilitation in favor of active suppression. Police departments developed special gang units devoted to gang intelligence and crackdowns. Prosecutors and correctional agencies also formed special gang units, aimed at more convictions and increased incarceration of gang members. Federal agencies, such as the FBI, the Drug Enforcement Agency (DEA), and the Bureau of Alcohol, Tobacco, and Firearms (ATF), launched new initiatives against street gangs. Many states passed special gang legislation, defining "criminal street gangs" and providing stiffer sentences for convicted members, while local jurisdictions targeted gangs for civil abatement and injunction measures to prohibit activities thought to be typical of gangs (many of these activities being otherwise perfectly legal).

Were these new and enhanced forms of suppression based on the expanded knowledge base about gangs, it would have been fine. But instead, most of them ignored knowledge in favor of ideology. Indeed, many of them were directly opposite to what was being learned about gangs and how they respond to efforts at control. Street gangs, we have learned, develop an "oppositional culture"; the more attention paid to them, the more society intervenes in their world, the stronger become the bonds between gang members. Group cohesiveness grows in the face of control. Young people join gangs first and foremost out of needs for identity, belonging, status, and protection. The effect of most intervention, from special social intervention to outright suppression, is to increase that identity and status and to glorify the gang to potential recruits. We have the data to demonstrate this, but law enforcement, the courts, and political leaders do not attend to such data in formulating their practices and pronouncements.

For gang researchers, especially long-termers like me, this presented, during the 1980s and 1990s, a serious dilemma. Should we remain in our ivy towers, collecting our data and expanding them to include reactions to this new and misguided national wave of suppression? I decided, partly out of social conscience and partly out of fear that a bad gang situation was inadvertently being worsened by the attempts to better it, that I would use our data base—40 years of accumulated knowledge from many researchers—to sound a warning.

Where previously I had ducked reporters covering gang stories, I now engaged in dialogues with them. Where previously I had turned down television and radio interviews, I now accepted them from local stations and national network news shows. Where previously I had published for my professional colleagues only, I now launched into a more lay-friendly book called *The American Street Gang*, spelling out the problems for colleagues, students, and the general public alike. The outcomes of these efforts have been several:

1. Some public agencies have listened and altered their practices at least to some extent.

2. Most public agencies have not.

3. A number of people in law enforcement have decided I am the "enemy"; an ivy tower egghead with no relevant "street time." Well, egghead maybe, but one with thousands of hours of "street time" in direct connection to gang members, cops, and social practitioners.

4. I am now hounded by print and broadcast media people who seem fascinated by the idea that legal crackdowns may have boomerang effects.

5. I have become a much sought after "gang expert" in court cases, where defense attorneys almost in desperation turn to the research to counter the overreach of the law in the hands of the prosecutors and their police expert witnesses.

At best, I have become a knowledge-based whistle-blower; at worst I am a public nuisance. My pride is that I say nothing to agencies, or to the press, or to politicians, or to judge and jury, that is not based on the accumulated research of many scholars.

## Lesson #5: Stick Around Long Enough, and Your Field Will Change

When I started out, criminology was a relatively new and small field of interest. In part because of this, but also in reflection of a changed world, it has grown from a polyglot collection of disparate disciplinary backgrounds into a coherent, sophisticated area of study with its own departments and schools across the country. Some of the changes most directly related to my own teaching and research include the following:

### 1. The Juvenile Justice System

In the 1960s, the American juvenile justice system—especially juvenile courts and probation—still attempted to reflect the spirit of prevention and rehabilitation that had been its wellspring decades earlier. Most juvenile offenders were assumed to be malleable and amenable to treatment, primarily the subjects for family and community rehabilitation rather than punishment and incarceration. Indeed, the 1960s saw further amplification of this spirit in legislation that decriminalized "status offenses," non-criminal and strictly juvenile behavior such as incorrigibility, running away, alcohol possession, curfew violation, and habitual truancy. Status offenders were defined as the best targets for strictly preventive efforts such as individual and family counseling, remedial education, and job training.

At the same time, status offenders and other non-serious violators were separated in detention and incarceration from adult prisoners and even from serious juvenile offenders. The purpose was to avoid labeling minor offenders as criminal for fear of enveloping them in a criminal subculture. At the same time, there was an expansion of juvenile "experts" in police, probation, and parole departments and an infusion of financial resources and training for social service agencies in the community, allowing the diversion of juvenile offenders from the court system into the social service and welfare system. Finally, all this was accomplished by major judicial rulings that provided juveniles with greatly expanded civil rights, so that the "due process" long available to adults increasingly became available to juveniles as well.

This was the liberal context in which I began my work as a criminologist. In the years following these developments, major national studies of diversion and community treatment undertaken by me and my colleagues seemed to confirm and consolidate a widening body of research that was most discouraging. In essence, the data revealed that most prevention, diversion, and treatment programs for juvenile offenders were having very little positive effect; in some instances the data suggested that many programs inadvertently **increased** offending levels among the program recipients.

These findings, along with greater recognition of the "revolving door" nature of the juvenile justice system, the increasing sophistication and maturation of young people, and signs that serious, violent delinquency was on the upswing, combined to suggest that juvenile offenders were not, after all, very amenable to the social service treatments at our disposal. In addition, these problems surfaced publicly at the same time as the entire nation's swing to the right politically. Conservative ideologies as expressed in the Reagan, Bush, and even Clinton administrations formed fertile ground in a "war on crime" that quickly expanded into the juvenile system. Labeling theory and other liberal philosophies were replaced by deterrence theory and a "just desserts" philosophy that, at the juvenile level, led to the handling of juvenile offenders more and more like their adult counterparts.

Juvenile courts are losing much of their discretion, and many of their would-be clients are remanded to adult courts and prisons. Police juvenile officers devote less time to concerns with minor offenders and concentrate on those for whom court convictions are most likely. As in adult systems, juvenile officers become part of the "prosecution team." At the same time, probation and parole officers have transformed themselves from social workers and service providers to peace officers, with sidearms and warrant-less searches aimed at returning to incarceration clients who fail to observe provisions of their probation or parole status. And of greatest relevance to my research, street gangs with their increased prevalence and violence have become the quintessential examples of the need for massive crackdowns. Gangs, many of which do and most of which do not meet the stereotype provided by police and prosecutors, have been redefined, demonized, and subjected to unthinking and ideologically driven suppression.

Gang research, needless to say, reflects some of this change; there is less field observation and ethnography and more data gathering in police and court files. Interviews with police officers replace "street time"; media and police depictions of gang structure, violence, and drug distribution are more often accepted at face value by researchers who fail to dig below the level of aggregate data analysis to seek incident-level data. The more the response of the justice system to juveniles' changes, it seems to me, the more criminologists ought to be skeptical about the public images that result.

## *2. Methodological Sophistication*

However methodologically sophisticated you may be on entering the field of criminology, be prepared to update yourself periodically. At least three areas are of principal concern: statistical procedures, computer expertise, and information technology. When I started out, the most sophisticated statistical procedures were within my grasp after just two semester courses. Computers were massive, room-size complexes available only to large companies. Information technology was unknown (unless you count printing presses and rotary telephones).

Today's advanced statistical packages such as various forms of multiple regressions, or LISREL in its several progressions are the coin of the realm in much research. While I can still do chi-squares and t-tests by hand, the mere mention of such "skills" brings raucous laughter from my students sitting at their laptop computers. Yet as advanced as the procedures are, and as rapid are the computer outputs, and as sophisticated are the procedures for dissemination over the Internet, these are merely the rudimentary foundations of what is yet to come. Today's student cannot assume that the apex of his or her methodological training will suffice 10 years from now. The rate of change is not additive, it is geometric; to fall behind is to fall behind further at the same time. And to retreat into strictly qualitative methods is less an alternative than an admission of personal limitations.[6]

There is one domain of methodology, however, which has not exhibited the same rapid progress and that is the area of research design. In many ways, the **logics** of research design have been well established over many decades. This is true of ethnography, of archival research, of survey procedures, of epidemiology, and of experimental and quasi-experimental designs. Yes, there are variations, but they are variations on familiar themes that have calculable relationships to the production of shared knowledge. That "production of shared knowledge" is what I take our enterprise to be about.

The problem with the greater stability in the logics of research methods is that they are often taken for granted, first by teachers and then understandably by students. In many instances, I have been shocked by graduate students spewing out analyses of covariance and logistic regressions from their laptops with little or no idea how they relate to the particular data-gathering methods that generated the numbers. The role of the ethnographer, the validity of the self-report and police crime data, and the purpose of various control or comparison groups are lost. It is the **logic of the research** that informs the utility of the statistical and computer sophistication, not the latter. And I haven't even begun to spell out the role of criminological **theory**!

### 3. Crime Measurement

Here is an area that has changed dramatically and I've been pleased to play a small role. Until around 1960, most estimates of crime prevalence and individual criminal involvement were based on official data, and usually on police reports. We have learned since then that these data produce vast undercounts of actual crime and delinquency rates and at the same time provide very inaccurate estimates of race, ethnicity, class, and gender differences. To offer one example, most theories of street gang development prior to 1970 assumed the validity of major differentials between minority and white delinquency rates. As these theories were then used to explain delinquency generally, they greatly overstated the role of race and ethnicity.

Nowadays, in addition to better police reporting—better, not uniformly good—there are two more valid forms of crime data collection that have seriously affected our understanding of criminal patterns. One is the use of victim surveys that can capture much of the crime not reported to the police or recorded by them. The other is the use of self-report surveys, in which individuals report their own involvement in delinquent and criminal activities. I have been involved in this latter development by instigating the emergence of the International Self-Report Delinquency (ISRD) scale which has been used in more than a dozen countries to date. Indeed, because victim and self-report surveys overcome many problems in comparing data from different police systems, both are rapidly advancing the state of the art in international crime measurement.

For those who understandably question whether victim and self-report surveys can yield valid and reliable data, there are two answers. First, they are generally far more valid than police reports. Second, their reliability has been tested in numerous situations and with numerous populations. Their reliability, while anything but perfect, is frequently shown to be comparable to the majority of measurements used in psychology and sociology to assess human attributes, attitudes, and behaviors. Advances in both types of surveys continue to improve the situation. The result has been a criminology far superior to that of just a few decades ago.

## 4. Street Gangs

I mentioned earlier that the knowledge base on gangs has changed. Although a few gang scholars might challenge my thoughts here, I think we can safely list several areas in which our gang knowledge has become far more secure. Because this is the arena of research for which I have become most widely known, I'll take the liberty to be a bit more expansive about these changes.

(a) Gang-related crime is highly versatile. Gang members, on average, engage in a wide variety of offenses rather than being specialists in violence, or drug sales, or graffiti, or theft, or anything else. We coined the term "cafeteria-style" delinquency for this; during a recent lecture in Sweden, it was suggested I call it smorgasbord delinquency. Whatever the term, versatility is the pattern, not the narrow range of offending usually portrayed in the media.

(b) Another form of versatility is in the nature of gang members themselves. Contrary to stereotype and assumption, there is almost as much individual diversity among gang members as among, say, the readers of this essay. Some are boisterous and some are quiet; some are very involved in criminal activities and some only mildly so; some are bright and some are dull; some are articulate and easy to talk with, while others are hard to approach; some are emotionally disturbed but most are not, and so on. And, by the way, some are female, although the majority is male, and they come in many, many ethnicities and national origins. In sum, gang members do not lend themselves easily to generalizations (which does not, of course, dissuade people from employing such generalizations).

(c) Another form of diversity has to do with the group structure of gangs. The usual stereotype is of highly organized groups, large and violent with clear leadership roles and rules about loyalty and turf protection, and identities symbolized in special tattoos, hand signs, clothing styles, and shared gang argot. There are **some** street gangs that more or less fit this stereotype, but they are the exceptions. They are a caricature of one of five types of gang structure that have emerged from our national research and encompass the vast majority of street gangs both here and abroad.

The stereotype just described fits under the heading of "traditional" gangs, large, long-standing and self-regenerating groups with strong territorial affiliation, and fairly clear subgroups based on age, residence, and often gender. Yet their cohesiveness is only moderate and the leadership often distributed across quite a few members.

"Neo-traditional" gangs are similar but lack self-regeneration and therefore are of shorter duration. "Collective" gangs may also be large but are far more amorphous and unstable, lasting only a few years and lacking subgroup structure.

By far the most common street gangs are what we call "compressed" gangs. Smaller than these first three types, they are without clear subgroups, have a narrower age range (often being predominantly composed of teenagers) and may or may not lay claim to special territories. It is these compressed gangs that are most responsible for the enormous proliferation of gangs across the country over the last 20 years.

While each of these fours gang types exhibit versatile or cafeteria-style offending, the fifth type does not. These are the "specialty" gangs that tend to concentrate on just one form or one pattern of crime. Whatever their origination, they have evolved into better-organized, smaller, more cohesive, more secretive groups with a clear leadership structure. These characteristics are fundamentally necessary to support their criminal enterprise, whether this is home burglaries, theft, extortion, graffiti spread (as in "tagger" crews), or drug sales. Such groups—especially drug gangs—receive a great deal of attention from the justice system and the media, but they are no more typical of the street gang scene than are the traditional gangs described above. Most public officials, police, media, and social service providers are only vaguely aware, if at all, of these structural differences. If they were, they would learn to respond differently to the several types. But stereotyping is easier.

(d) Early street gang ethnographers often suggested on the basis of their personal observations that street gangs were **qualitatively** different from the myriad of other youth groups that constituted the bulk of informal adolescent collections. Gangs were something above and beyond other youth groups, even those that occasionally indulged in antisocial activities. Recent analyses of survey research studies of gangs have come to the same conclusion. Gangs tend to recruit from a somewhat different pool of youngsters, and more importantly, transform the values and behaviors of those who commit themselves to gang membership. This is particularly the case with respect to delinquent and violent behaviors and the rationalizations needed to maintain them.

The significance of these strong qualitative differences is at least twofold. For criminology, it means we must develop a special **gang** knowledge that recognizes that group process in gangs is different from, not just more of, those in other groups. For practitioners, be they police, judges, gang workers, or social workers, it means they must develop intervention procedures specific to the nature of various gang structures; they cannot simply rely on knowledge of youth groups in general.

(e) I end this list, somewhat arbitrarily, with the most discouraging of all the forms of knowledge we have accumulated about gangs. Incidentally, it is the one firm piece of gang knowledge that makes students, media, and practitioners most unhappy with me when I discuss it. They don't like the message, namely that almost everything we have done over the last half century to correct the gang problem has failed (or, at best, failed to demonstrate any success).

Part of the problem is that most gang intervention efforts are unaccompanied by serious attempts to evaluate their effectiveness. It is the conceit of the practitioner that what he or she does to intervene in gang affairs must be a good thing (else why do it?). Social workers, ministers, teachers, police, and prosecutors all tell us of the success of their efforts. Few, if any, bother to have independent assessments that could prove otherwise.

Part of my career in gang research has been devoted to assessing program success, either of my own efforts or those of others. In the few cases of **adequate** program assessment, the programs have come up wanting. This is usually because they are poorly implemented and occasionally because research has revealed them to have no impact or, worst of all, the effect of increasing the gang problem.

And it doesn't really matter whether the programs are aimed at gang prevention or gang intervention or gang suppression; there is precious little evidence to show that we can really control gang processes. The irony is that the most carefully evaluated programs are the ones yielding the most discouraging evidence. Sloppy research allows greater claims to success than does careful research. To be associated, as I have been, with a tradition of inquiry that is less than praiseworthy is not a source of pride. It is left for people like me to blow the whistle, and hope that someone will hear it.

The good news is that, as this essay is written, some public officials are beginning to listen, to get beyond the rhetoric of the program directors and to require program evaluations. This has not really happened since the 1960s in gang programming, but the door has again been opened a bit by federal agencies funding gang programs. If the effort is sustained, then this is a change of great promise, including the promise of our not continuing to make the errors in gang control that we have been re-inventing for the past half century.

The lesson here is not only that your field **has** changed, but that inevitably it **will** change; to embrace the field one must commit one's self to attend to change and use it to advance the field even further.

## Lesson #6: Retirement Does Not Mean Death

I overheard it prior to the most recent annual convention of the American Society of Criminology. A special panel presentation by several very prominent criminologists was to be devoted to discussions triggered by my own research career in community treatment of delinquents, in gang research, and in cross-national research on crime. It was a panel that had been organized in my honor, and I was honored indeed. But the snippet of conversation I overheard was about how sweet it was that this posthumous honor had been arranged and oh, by the way, how long ago had I died?

Well, some time prior to this death, I retired. But for me, retirement was merely from the classroom—after some 43 years of teaching. I have still continued research with former students and many colleagues, and I have continued my writing. Retirement for me, it turns out, means a greater life without compulsions and deadlines, but certainly not without tasks of interest. I will complete this essay with a brief description of my newest endeavor, especially pleasing because it combines several of the academic interests I have addressed in the preceding pages.

Two sabbatical leaves in Europe, one in the 1980s, and one in the 1990s, exposed me to a new and varied set of colleagues. With them, I explored the areas of cross-national crime measurement and of street gangs in Europe. The first area has culminated in the development of the International Self-Report Delinquency (ISRD) program, which has seen applications in more than a dozen countries and the publication of two books and numerous articles, mostly by colleagues overseas. I also explored what appeared to be the emergence of a street gang problem in Europe, and this is the area that engages me now.

Through personal observations and a review of a very sparse literature on gangs in Europe, it seemed clear that a problem was developing almost without notice. In the early 1990s, I was able to identify a number of cities facing the development of street gangs—Stockholm, Berlin, Frankfurt, Stuttgart, London, Manchester, Zurich, Brussels, and Kazan among other Russian cities. I brought together a small group of North American and European scholars to discuss the value of investigating further if there was an emerging gang problem in Europe and if so, what might we learn about it and how might our extensive American experience be pertinent. The response was positive and enthusiastic, with the result that in the past few years the Eurogang Program has developed.

To date, four international workshops have been conducted, with researchers and policymakers coming together in Germany, then Norway, then Belgium, and finally in Holland. Attended by up to 50 scholars from dozens of countries, these workshops have produced, to date:

- The first published book on gangs in Europe

- A proposal to the European Union to form an international network of gang researchers

- An Internet network of more than 100 interested researchers

- The identification, as of this writing, of several dozen European cities in more than a dozen countries now facing some level of street gang problem — in most cases, not yet a serious problem

The book, which emerged from the first of the workshops, is titled *The Eurogang Paradox*, so named because of an early identified problem. Many European officials and some scholars initially denied the existence of street gangs, in part because they compared their groups to the common stereotype of American gangs. Thus, believing our gangs were large, highly organized, led by a few psychopathic characters, very cohesive with strong codes of loyalty, and almost invariably violent, they felt that their antisocial youth groups could not be considered street gangs.

The paradox, of course, is that most American gangs do not fit this stereotype. Indeed, if they did we'd all be in serious trouble. But American gangs are really a widespread proliferation of groups that usually are not very organized, only moderately cohesive, with constantly changing leadership and membership. While they engage in a wide range of delinquent or criminal behavior—"cafeteria style"—most of this is non-violent. Further, the most common victim of gang violence when it does occur is another gang member. The rest of us are in more danger when we step into our cars or go for a swim.

It has taken several years, but I believe most of our European colleagues now understand that many of their cities do contain some street gangs, that many of these are similar to ours, and that therefore there is already a major body of knowledge that they can apply to their own situations. My hope, and that of the other American gang researchers who have contributed to the Eurogang Program, is that any continuation or expansion of gang problems in Europe can be met with more planned, organized research and program development than we have seen in the United States.

I continue to work to this end. And if truth were told, continuing my involvement yields personal dividends. One of these is maintaining my professional life even after my unnoticed death. Another is the foreign travel involved and the opportunity to see ourselves as others see us. The comparative perspective is one I urge on each and every reader of this essay. It's good to be an American criminologist, but even better to find the context that gives such a profession its fuller meaning.

## Recommended Readings

Empey, Lamar T. & Mark C. Stafford (1991). *American Delinquency, Its Meaning and Constructions*, Third Edition. Belmont, CA: Wadsworth Publishing Co.

Humes, Edward (1996). *No Matter How Loud I Shout: A Year in the Life of Juvenile Court*. New York, NY: Simon and Schuster.

Covey, Herbert C., Scott Menard & Robert J. Franzese (1997). *Juvenile Gangs*, Second Edition. Springfield, IL: Charles C Thomas.

Decker, Scott H. & Barrick Van Winkle (1996). *Life in the Gang: Family, Friends, and Violence*. New York, NY: Cambridge University Press.

## Selected Personal Bibliography

Carter, R.M. & M.W. Klein (1975). *Back on the Street: The Diversion of Juvenile Offenders*. Englewood Cliffs, NJ: Prentice-Hall.

Carter, R.M. & M.W. Klein (1971). *Street Gangs and Street Workers*. Englewood Cliffs, NJ: Prentice-Hall.

Junger-Tas, J., G.-J. Terlouw & M.W. Klein (1994). *Delinquent Behavior Among Young People in the Western World*. Amsterdam: Kugler Publications.

Junger-Tas, J., G.-J. Terlouw & M.W. Klein (1989). *Cross-National Research in Self-Reported Crime and Delinquency*. Dordrecht: Kluwer Academic Press.

Junger-Tas, J., G.-J. Terlouw & M.W. Klein (1984). *Western Systems of Juvenile Justice*. Thousand Oaks, CA: Sage Publications.

Klein, M.W., H.-J. Kerner, C.L. Maxson & E.G.M (2000). *The Eurogang Paradox: Street Gangs and Youth Groups in the U.S. and Europe*. Weitekamp, Dordrecht: Kluwer Academic Press.

Klein, M.W. & K.S. Teilmann (1980). *Handbook of Criminal Justice Evaluation*. Thousand Oaks, CA: Sage Publications.

Klein, M.W. & K.S. Teilmann (1976). *The Juvenile Justice System*. Thousand Oaks, CA: Sage Publications.

Kobrin, S. & M.W. Klein (1983). *Community Treatment of Juvenile Offenders: The DSO Experiments*. Thousand Oaks, CA: Sage Publications.

Miller, J., C.L. Maxson & M.W. Klein (2000). *The Modern Gang Reader*, Second Edition. Los Angeles, CA: Roxbury.

Maxson, C.L. & M.W. Klein (1997). *Responding to Troubled Youth*. New York, NY: Oxford University Press.

Maxson, C.L. & M.W. Klein (1995). *The American Street Gang: Its Nature, Prevalence, and Control*. New York, NY: Oxford University Press.

## Endnotes

[1] Maccoby later was named "University Professor" at Stanford Unviersity.

[2] He was later to be President of the University of Cincinnati, and then "University Professor" of the University of Southern California.

[3] Bennis' question was based on recent social psychological research on group leadership, which suggested that those in leadership positions generally found that achieving *both* respect and liking was unlikely.

[4] They were wrong. It's been almost 40 years, and I still need to learn more!

[5] My background for this consisted of one undergraduate course in sociology in my sophomore year. I had never read Weber, or Durkheim, or Parsons (but had read Merton).

[6] This comment could cost me half my readership, but it does force an important issue into the discussion.

# 4

# The Good Boy in a High-Delinquency Area—40 Years Later

Frank R. Scarpitti

It was a blistering cold January afternoon in Cleveland, Ohio, as the local college junior, attempting to earn a dollar an hour, explained to the elderly woman looking out at him through a slightly opened door that he was doing a market survey and would like to ask her some questions. Without waiting for her reply, he asked, "What product is associated with Elsie the cow?" "Are you crazy?" the woman asked incredulously, as she slammed the door and retreated into the warm house. I was that student, and that was my first attempt at research.

Now, more than 40 years since that afternoon in Cleveland, the answer to the elderly woman's question is still not clear, and I continue to ask questions of people in the name of research. While this inauspicious beginning hardly would have predicted a career of social science research and teaching, it did uncork a curiosity about why people act as they do that later was instrumental in my choosing to study sociology in graduate school. Although a standard dictionary defines research as "diligent and systematic inquiry or investigation into a subject in order to discover facts or principles," that definition always seemed too formal to describe my motivations. Actually, to me research is very much like detective work, and the researcher very much like the detective, looking for clues, investigating relationships, posing questions, seeking answers based on fact. My own fascination with mystery, detective novels, puzzles, the unexplained, why things happen as they do, made me a natural for a research career. I never really wanted to be a police detective, but I have wanted to do what detectives do.

And so, when I graduated from Fenn College, now Cleveland State University, and stopped asking incredulous respondents about Elsie the cow and whether they thought of J.C. Penney's when they wanted to buy "good" clothing, I went on to graduate school at The Ohio State University. Even though *Time* magazine had sarcastically described sociology as the scientific study of the obvious, I knew that sociologists were interested in the human condition, and that was my interest as well. It wasn't that the natural sciences were uninterested in people problems, of course. After all, it was natural scientists who had discovered many of the advancements that have eased human suffering and prolonged life, and as a high school student I had thought of a medical career. But, I had a problem with the natural sciences: I kept seeing my eyelashes whenever I looked into a microscope. So, I determined early in my college life that I had better look for a career elsewhere. I found it in sociology, where I could do what detectives do and believe that I was helping the human condition as well.

In retrospect, my choice of sociology is quite understandable. My parents were working-class, first-generation Italian-Americans who raised a family of five children during the Depression and World War II. Paying the rent, feeding and clothing the family, and coping with my father's endless medical bills was a constant struggle that had a profound impact on me, as did the family's adoration of Franklin Delano Roosevelt, and faith in the Democratic Party. Through first-hand experience I learned the value of government programs for the poor and the working class, as well as of the great unmet social needs that existed in the country. Although I was too young to place any of this into a political context, I was drawn even as a teenager to ideas and movements that I believed were meant to help the working person achieve greater equality and security.

My family moved from a small steel-belt community in western Pennsylvania to Cleveland when I was 12 years old, settling in an apartment in the Glenville section of the city. At the time, this once largely Jewish section of the city was undergoing a transition that in a few years would see it change almost completely in terms of race, class, employment, safety, and neighborhood integration. What I would later learn was that a classic ecological pattern of invasion and succession accompanied by the usual social disorganization was taking place. Whites were fleeing to the suburbs, African-Americans were moving in from areas closer to the central city, unemployment was high, crime and delinquency rates were rising rapidly, and a street culture unknown to the neighborhood in the past was now evident everywhere. For a family from a small town with very limited cultural diversity, this was a unique and sometimes challenging experience. Although reasonably tolerant liberals, my parents sometimes had a difficult time adapting to the changes they saw going on around them. On the other hand, for me, it was an opportunity to learn about social and cultural differences, and to experience real-life situations that would otherwise be known only in the abstract. I was not precocious enough as a teenager to realize what was happening to me, especially as I acted out my own forms of rebellion, but spending my teen years in the sometimes chaotic environment of our urban neighborhood had a great deal to do with my eventual interest in the study of sociology.

The 1950s was the era of *The Shook-up Generation* and *The Blackboard Jungle*, a time when we saw a rather dramatic escalation in the rates of juvenile delinquency. What was happening in the Glenville section of Cleveland was no exception to what was happening nationally. As the number of kids getting into trouble with the police grew, the pressure increased on all of the teenagers in the neighborhood to be one of the crowd, to choose sides, to fight, in other words, to be delinquent. Although some of my friends and acquaintances did get into trouble with the law, I resisted, for reasons I couldn't articulate then, and took refuge in my academic work and numerous part-time jobs that kept me busy and off the street. I got through high school unscathed and without a police record. For all the reasons cited by William Foote Whyte and Albert Cohen, I became a "college boy" determined to achieve upward mobility and middle-class respectability. It was not the end of my association with delinquents, however.

Fenn College was an urban commuter school based on the principle of cooperative education. After the first year, students spent every other quarter in the workforce, applying ideas learned in class to real situations in industrial or other jobs consistent with one's major or career interests. While college administrators and some faculty seemed to believe in the integrative value of alternating between study and work, most of my friends and I saw it as the only way we could earn our way through college. After working as an occupational therapy aide in a local mental hospital and as a drill press operator in a small factory, my third co-op job, in the summer between my sophomore and junior years, was as a unit supervisor in the Cuyahoga County Juvenile Detention Center. For nearly three months, I spent 44 hours each week living with approximately 30 15- and 16-year-olds who were awaiting court appearances or transfers to the state industrial school. Although my primary task was security (my coworkers and I may have been called supervisors, but we were first and foremost guards), the proximity of my age to that of the detainees and the fact that I knew some of them or their families from the neighborhood allowed me to talk with them about what they had done, why they had done it, and what they believed would happen to them. It also gave me the opportunity to practice some of the sophomore sociology and psychology I had learned in my classes. What was their motivation; did they learn their delinquency from friends (I remembered differential association); were they really striking out at society; and so on? By and large, most of them seemed to be confused, inarticulate, and unaware of their motivation. By the end of summer I didn't understand them much better than I had at the beginning, but I had heard a number of interesting stories, learned a number of techniques for committing crime that I hadn't known before, and knew that I wanted to understand more about crime and delinquency. Apparently my curiosity about the lives and behavior of my charges was interpreted as earnestness by the Superintendent of the Center because he offered me a full-time job as a night supervisor. I jumped at the offer, and for the next 24 months, I worked the midnight to 8:00 a.m. shift while attending college and working as a market surveyor during the daytime. As a result of my full-time employment, the College waived further cooperative education experiences and I was able to graduate in four years.

For a short period of time I also worked for the YMCA as a Youth Worker assigned to a small outpost in a downtown housing project. In addition to the usual duties (I learned to play ping pong pretty well), I was expected to work especially closely with a group of young men from the projects who had started to act like a gang (they had neither a name nor formal structure, however). I spent a number of nights and weekends in their company, and soon discovered that I had neither the commitment nor courage for this line of work. Social service was not for me. This experience did, however, add to my already intense interest in learning more about social behavior. It seemed that the last 10 years of my life had been pointing me in the direction of sociology and its subfield of criminology. I decided to go to graduate school, at least to earn a master's degree.

I chose Ohio State for my graduate work for two equally important reasons, one professional and one personal. As an undergraduate I had taken a course in criminology and had read the text, *The Crime Problem* by Walter C. Reckless, with great fascination. This book addressed many of the issues I wondered about pertaining to my own experiences growing up, my neighborhood, friends who had gotten into trouble, rackets and scams I had seen on the street, and so much more I wanted to know about crime. At the time, I thought I hadn't read a more interesting book in my entire college career. Coincidentally, Reckless taught at Ohio State, and one of my undergraduate professors thought I could surely become one of his students if I went there for graduate education. On the personal side, it was also convenient that Columbus was not too far from Yellow Springs, Ohio, home of Antioch College. I had been dating a girl from Antioch and hoped the relationship would develop further and faster if I were closer (it did; we've been married for 41 years). In September, 1958, I started graduate school.

## Learning To Do Research

Several years prior to my entering Ohio State, Walter Reckless had proposed Containment Theory, a theoretical model for understanding the factors responsible for making some youths vulnerable to delinquency and others resistant to nonnormative behavior. He proposed two types of factors that control behavior, an inner control system and an outer control system which are able or unable to work alone or together to handle the forces conducive to delinquency. The outer control system refers to the individual's social world, the value system predominant in his or her culture, the external social structure designed to guide one's behavior in a socially approved manner. Inner controls, on the other hand, consist mainly of self components that provide an internal buffer against deviation. These two control systems should form a solid, united front against the adversities and pressures of the environment. In industrial societies external containment resides primarily in the family and other groups in which the individual participates. When the outer controls are adequate, they will contain the individual and prevent deviation. When they are inadequate and structural supports cannot contain the actor, the inner control system must hold the person in line. The ability to do this is dependent upon the presence of either a good or poor self-concept.

According to Reckless, the direction of socialization and the resulting good or bad concept of self are the chief factors responsible for the child's insulation against deviancy or involvement in unlawful behavior. This is especially true in areas characterized by great social disorganization. Here the outer controls on the youth's behavior are weak, if they have not broken down completely, and the direction of one's actions will be dependent upon his or her self image. But, since the self-image is a composite of the youth's interactive experiences, chances of developing a law-abiding self-image are fewer in a bad environment than they would be in an adequate social environment. In spite of this, most lower-class boys socialized by lower-class parents in lower-class neighborhoods are able to develop a self-concept that is strong enough to protect them from norm-violating behavior.

The two containing systems (or lack of them) were not seen by Reckless as causes of juvenile delinquency. The "causes" or contributing factors may be delinquent companions, status frustration, differential opportunity, exposure to a delinquent subculture, or a deviant value system (to account for the most popular etiological reasons of the period). The containing systems serve as the individual's insulation or protection against those forces that might influence the boy or girl toward delinquency. When the containing systems are weak, the person is vulnerable and might succumb. When they are strong, the child is likely to be law-abiding despite environmental pressures.

This attempt to integrate personal and structural factors into a theoretical explanation of delinquency was consistent with Walter Reckless' background and experience. Trained in the 1920s at the University of Chicago, his teachers were Park, Burgess, and Mead. While steeped in the tradition of social disorganization and the effects of family and community integration, he was also committed to understanding the role of individual differences in explaining human behavior. In fact, he was one of the first sociologists to write a social psychology textbook, an early attempt to demonstrate the reciprocal relationship between social and individual considerations. By the 1950s he was a well-known criminologist who had written numerous books and articles about various aspects of crime and corrections, but he had not constructed an enduring theory of crime or delinquency. Containment Theory was not only a natural outgrowth of his early training and past professional work, but it also represented his burning desire to explain juvenile delinquency and leave a lasting mark in theoretical criminology.

Reckless was not an armchair theorist, however. Throughout his career he had collected data on various aspects of crime and corrections and he continued this commitment to empiricism to test his new theory. He hypothesized that boys living in high-delinquency areas were exposed to similar environmental circumstances, but not all became delinquent. Most, in fact, did not. If the elements of outer containment available in high-delinquency neighborhoods were not particularly powerful forces for controlling nonnormative behavior, then the difference between delinquents and nondelinquents living in these areas must be the individual factor of self-concept. Assessing the strength of the self-concept among "good" and "bad" boys in a high-delinquency area would be a powerful test of the idea.

In the mid-1950s, Columbus, Ohio, sixth-grade school teachers in high-delinquency areas of the city were asked to nominate boys in their classes whom they would characterize as "good," not headed for trouble with the law, or "bad," likely to get into legal trouble in the future. Although a crude measure, the teachers' perceptions of the 12-year-olds provided two groups of 125 youngsters each who manifested behavioral differences at a relatively early age of life. The boy and his mother were interviewed in their home, responding to questions designed to determine how the boy saw himself and how his significant other saw him. Some questions were taken from standard sources, while others were developed by Reckless and his assistants. All, of course, appeared to have face validity, essentially asking the boy what he thought of himself and how those feelings related to his getting into trouble or not. Overwhelmingly, based on the instruments used, the so-called "good" boys saw themselves as good, conforming, and able to stay out of trouble with the law. The so-called "bad" boys, on the other hand, were less certain of their futures, often believing that their parents and others saw them as bad kids headed for trouble. Articles reporting these findings were published in various outlets, including the *American Sociological Review*.

When I entered the Sociology Department at Ohio State, I found Walter Reckless to be a charming, charismatic, paternalistic figure who was ably assisted by a young assistant professor, Simon Dinitz. Reckless didn't have much time for a new graduate student, but Dinitz did, and for that I shall be forever grateful. While I admired and respected Reckless, Dinitz became my role model. He was a brilliant teacher, a warm and caring friend, and a first-rate sociological scholar who was genuinely concerned about the welfare of graduate students. Later I would learn that Reckless shared this concern, but at the time, Dinitz was the one to whom I could go for assistance and encouragement. Much of what I have done over the years as a graduate teacher is the result of what I learned from him.

Toward the end of my first year, I was ready to begin a master's thesis. The tradition, however, was that criminology students worked on some part of what we called the self-concept research for master theses and doctoral dissertations. My assignment was to follow up the "good" boys who had been contacted originally four years earlier. I knew about the study, of course, and found it fascinating because I applied its finding to myself. I had been a good boy in a high-delinquency area; I had delinquent friends but didn't do what they did; I had always thought of myself as a good boy and knew my parents believed this also. Could this be why I hadn't become delinquent? This research was about me, so I jumped at the chance of doing a follow-up study of the good boy in a high-delinquency area. Although Reckless supervised the research, as he did all of the projects, Dinitz was my official advisor who guided me through the day-to-day problems of field work, data analysis, and thesis writing.

The good boys were located in the community and they and their mothers were interviewed in the home by a research companion and me. Questions were similar to the ones asked four years earlier. The findings of the research indicated that after passing through the most delinquency-vulnerable years, the 101 boys whom we located continued to view themselves as good, unlikely to get involved in delinquency or crime. Their mothers viewed them the same way. Ninety-seven of the 101 had no police contact during the four-year period, and the four who had contact were relatively minor offenders. With the help of Sy Dinitz, the findings of this research were published in the *American Sociological Review*, in an article titled, "A Follow-Up Study of the Good Boy in a High Delinquency Area." For years after, colleagues whom I met would remember me as "the good boy in a high delinquency area." And, indeed, I was.

This research was followed the next year by a follow-up of the "bad" boys four years later. Results confirmed what was shown four years earlier, that they viewed themselves much less positively than the "good" boys, and their mothers were inclined to agree with them. By age 16, nearly 40 percent had a police record, often for serious delinquencies. I had shown that good and bad boys saw themselves differently, conceived of different behavioral possibilities for themselves, and were influenced differently by elements of their environment. These findings were interesting but not revolutionary. They only led to more questions, some of which were asked a few years later in my doctoral dissertation, where I attempted to integrate the role of self-concept in personal decisionmaking with status frustration and differential opportunity theories. Even then, I didn't have the definitive answers I was naively seeking about delinquency causation and I realized, perhaps for the first time, the true nature of the enterprise I had chosen for a career.

As I have attempted to explain to several generations of students, doing research is like building a pyramid of pebbles. Each piece of research, each project, is like a pebble being cast on a pile, one supporting another, the pyramid getting narrower and taking shape as the pebbles accumulate and build. On some occasions research pyramids get finished, questions are ultimately answered, but only because the top is held up by the countless pebbles that have been placed below. Occasionally, some researcher is able to place a stone on the pile, and very rarely a boulder is contributed. But, there aren't very many Newtons or Lockes or Einsteins, those who have placed stones and boulders on the pyramid of science. Most pyramids are made up of the pebbles, the contributions of countless scientists who place limited research findings in the scientific literature to be used by others to conceptualize a problem, to modify their own experiments, to replicate, in other words, to build that metaphorical pyramid. We all benefit from the research of those who come before us and make contributions to science.

By now I was a true believer in Containment Theory and shared Reckless' disappointment when it was criticized in a number of subsequent articles published by professional colleagues, and realized that our "metaphorical pebbles" were not quite as large as I had believed. The research was criticized on several grounds, including the naive assumptions about self-concept upon which it rested, the difficulty of measuring one's self-image, the questions used to determine self-image, the manner in which the boys were chosen, and others equally painful to relate. Nevertheless, my original enthusiasm for the idea that delinquency results from a combination of social and personal factors remains with me, and has structured a great deal of the teaching and research I have done since then.

The research I did as a graduate student, under the watchful eyes of Reckless and Dinitz, taught me a number of valuable lessons. Perhaps the most important is the value of field work. I learned a great deal from talking with the boys and their mothers, sitting in their homes on hot summer afternoons and evenings, listening to stories only tangentially related to the objectives of the research, and realizing that I had a responsibility to do more than merely exploit them for the information I wanted. Because I could do little more than be a compassionate listener, I did that, sometimes offering advice or encouragement. I learned as much about them and their lives in this way as I did from the structured questionnaires we used, and I know that I became a better research sociologist because of it. It is a pattern I have attempted to follow in all of the projects I have been involved with over the past four decades.

I learned another lesson at this time as a result of having one of my early manuscripts rejected by a journal. Shortly after receiving my doctorate, I submitted a manuscript to a very prestigious journal for publication consideration. At the time, I thought the paper was pretty good, because it was based on interesting data and offered thoughtful conclusions. After the obligatory four months wait, I eagerly opened the letter that would bring me the expected good news. Unfortunately, the news wasn't good; in fact, it was devastating. Not only was the paper rejected, but the reviewers and the editor himself wrote comments that were highly critical of what I had done and even the manner in which it was presented. Without doubt, I was convinced that I was incapable of ever getting anything published, that my career was over before it had really begun. I sank into a "rejection depression," a condition that is common among academics and is so feared by some that it paralyzes them as productive scholars. In my case, it lasted about 24 hours. The next day I decided to rework the data and rewrite the paper, determined to salvage my career by learning from my mistakes and working harder than I had in the past. This time the paper was accepted with only minor revisions. I have had my share of rejections since then, and I continue to feel despair when they arrive, but that early experience has proved to be of continuing value, recalled whenever I need to remind myself that perseverance usually pays off and that punctured egos usually heal. It is a lesson that I also pass on to graduate students who are permitted to grieve when they receive a rejection, but only for a maximum of two days.

## Doing Evaluation Research

Up until the early 1960s, mental patients diagnosed with a psychotic illness were confined to large state hospitals under lock and key as virtual prisoners. Even though the powerful tranquilizer drugs introduced several years earlier had shown that the most adverse symptoms of mental disease could be controlled and made the behavior of the seriously ill less obtrusive, conventional wisdom assumed that this meant change only for the ways in which hospitals were operated. Therapeutic communities within hospitals were being experimented with, as were "open door" hospitals, where patients could move about the institution with fewer restrictions. If these innovations were possible, some thought, why not treat the patient at home in his or her natural community rather than in the artificial setting of the institution? Community treatment of sorts had been tried in some European locations with

encouraging results. It had never been tried in the United States, however, for patients hospitalized with serious psychoses. Benjamin Pasamanick, Director of Research at the Ohio State University Psychiatric Institute, though it was worth trying and designed a study to test the efficacy
of home treatment for schizophrenics. The National Institute of Mental
Health (NIMH) agreed with him and funded the research in 1960.

The design called for adult patients to be referred to the research program when they had been diagnosed by a state hospital admissions psychiatrist as schizophrenic in need of immediate hospitalization, and not
dangerous to themselves or others. Once a second psychiatrist on the
staff of the research team confirmed the diagnosis, the patient was randomly assigned to one of three treatment groups: home on medication,
home on placebo, or admitted to the state hospital for conventional treatment. The families of those selected for home care had to agree with the
home treatment program before the patient was allowed to return to the
community. Treatment was delivered to the home care patients in the
form of frequent visits by public health nurses who delivered the medication, and a research staff psychiatrist, social worker, and psychologist, all of whom were available on a scheduled basis as well as when
crises arose. In order to guarantee that all community-based patients
were treated uniformly by the treatment staff, only one person, the project director who had no direct contact with patients, knew which were
being given real medication and which were receiving placebos.

The research was to be conducted in Columbus, and it received the
approval of state mental health officials when the grant was written and
submitted to NIMH. Once the study was funded and ready to start, however, state officials backed out, citing the dangers of having confirmed
mental patients treated in the community. For some months nothing
could be done, until the Commissioner of Mental Health for the State
of Kentucky heard of the situation and invited Pasamanick to conduct
the study in Louisville. The offer was accepted, even though no one from
the Institute was available to move to Kentucky and manage the project.

At the time I had a fellowship that allowed me to devote my full-time
to writing a doctoral dissertation. It, of course, was on the subject of
delinquency, which is where I saw myself working as a teacher/schol-
ar once I received the Ph.D. degree. When Sy Dinitz, who had a joint
research appointment at the Psychiatric Institute, approached me about
the possibility of moving to Louisville to set up and manage the nation's
first home care study, I was not particularly interested. After all, it was
not in criminology, I didn't know very much about mental illness, and
evaluation research didn't particularly appeal to me. Out of respect for
Sy, however, I agreed to talk with Pasamanick. And, the opportunity was
unique: implement a complex research design, hire a staff, administer
a small experimental clinic, and, most importantly, contribute to what
might become a revolution in mental health care. Although it was not

crime research, it was consistent with my desire to do research that has a meaningful social impact. I accepted the job, packed our Rambler American, and headed south.

After four months, a building had been rented, furniture purchased, staff hired and trained, logistics worked out, and patients referred. Over the next couple of years this important study proceeded as planned with only minor problems. Several hundred patients were recruited, the public health nurses demonstrated a remarkable ability to serve as an effective liaison between the clinic staff and the patients and their families, and more than 70 percent of those maintained in the community with drugs were able to function successfully for at least two years. As expected, those taking placebos did not do nearly as well, exhibiting much more disruptive behavior and higher rates of hospital admissions. The hospital control group functioned least well, however, with many of these patients institutionalized for long periods of time and others doomed to a pattern of repeated admissions and releases. Here, then, for the first time there was powerful evidence that those with serious mental disorders did not have to be confined to a hospital to effect recovery. Under supervised medical treatment and with important family and social support, those who were once relegated to mental hospitals were now able to resume useful roles in the community.

Directing this project taught me a great deal about research and how to do it in a community setting. Although social science graduate students are taught that the community is their obvious laboratory, it is far from the controlled environment in which natural and physical scientists are accustomed to working. Subjects disappear, politicians become angry, cooperating agencies lose interest, and newspapers threaten exposure. These are all issues that must be dealt with in the real world in order to carry out successful community-based research. Stressful issues such as these also make the work exciting and the work-day unpredictable. Believing that one's research may also have significant public policy implications and actually make a difference in the lives of thousands of people is a stimulant that becomes intoxicating. By the time I was ready to leave Louisville, I was committed to what I defined as "meaningful" research, that which I believed would have a positive and demonstrable social impact. Although I recognized its intellectual importance, I knew that conducting research to test abstract theories was not what I would be doing much of in the future.

Evaluating the efficacy of home care for the mentally ill turned out to be an excellent way to launch a career. A number of articles were published in a variety of journals, and a book, *Schizophrenics in the Community*, coauthored with Pasamanick and Dinitz, won the American Psychiatric Association's Hofheimer Prize for Research. Those of us involved in this work believed we were in the forefront of an important movement, especially when community mental health and deinstitutionalɔn became the dominant concepts in mental health care. We never ɩgined that the movement would be usurped and corrupted by bud-ɛt-cutting politicians and ultimately contribute to problems that some consider worse than the original one.

Although this first job experience as a professional sociologist was rewarding and pleasurable, I knew I wanted to combine research with teaching. I had several ideas about self-concept development and delinquency I wanted to research, and believed that the best way to do that was to get a job at a research university where I could combine original research with being a professor. That almost happened when I accepted a position as an assistant professor at Rutgers University. The opportunity to teach was available, and even to teach criminology, but doing my original research was not what the department had in mind. Instead, I was hired to assume co-responsibility for an evaluation of a program for delinquent boys operating in Newark, New Jersey. Patterned after the Highfields Guided Group Interaction model, Essexfields was a non-residential facility accommodating 20 boys at a time in a program of work and intensive group interaction. My collaborator on this Ford Foundation-funded project was to be Richard Stephenson, then the chair of the Sociology and Economics Department at Douglass College, the women's division of Rutgers, located across town from the men's division where I would work. Apparently, the Rutgers faculty found me acceptable because I had been trained in criminology, had research experience, and had worked with other collaborators. In addition, as the chair of the Rutgers department said, "we believe in giving a young man from the Midwest a chance."

Having spent my entire higher education career in Ohio, I hadn't given much thought to regional differences in prestige among schools until I was preparing to assume my new position at Rutgers. The chair's earlier comment during my interview now resonated ominously as I reviewed the backgrounds of my new colleagues, noting that just about all of them had their terminal degrees from Harvard or Columbia. These people knew, some were even trained by, Sorokin, Parsons, Merton, virtual "gods" in the field at the time. How could a kid from a high-delinquency area of Cleveland, a graduate of Ohio State no less, possibly compete with the products of such luminaries? The summer of 1963 was filled with high anxiety and second thoughts for me. Thankfully, my former teacher and friend, Sy Dinitz, reminded me of a simple truth that helped ease my fears: "Remember, Frank, they put their trousers on one leg at a time, too." And, that turned out to be true. Their academic pedigrees notwithstanding, my new colleagues turned out not to know much more than I did, had the same problems getting research funding as I did, published no more than I did, and were no better teachers than I was. With few exceptions, they also were friendly and helpful colleagues. Since then, I have attempted to remember this lesson by paying little attention to where a person trained and more attention to what he or she has accomplished as a teacher and scholar.

Dick Stephenson, my new collaborator at Rutgers, turned out to be a wonderful sociologist and an even better human being whom I quickly grew to respect and admire and from whom I learned a great deal. For the next two years we observed scores of guided group interaction meetings amounting to hundreds of hours. Afterwards, on the drive from Newark to New Brunswick, we would compare notes, offer interpretations of what we had seen and heard, discuss research strategies, and, in general, stimulate each other's thinking about our scholarly work. For me, it was an enriching experience, just as collaborating with Ben Pasamanick and Sy Dinitz had been earlier. Each was more experienced than I, and in most cases more knowledgeable about the research process and the subject matter we were exploring. At first, Stephenson and I attempted to jointly write the manuscripts growing out of our work, but soon discovered we could be coauthors but not cowriters. After a discussion (or several) of the ideas we wanted to present and the manner we wanted to use to express them, one of us had to take the lead on a paper and write the first draft, then submit it to the other for revisions and rewriting. We developed a system of trading work back and forth like that until we were both satisfied with the product. That method worked quite well for us, and I am now convinced that it is the only way coauthorships can be successful.

That doesn't mean it is easy, however. Even though most of us learn to accept criticism of our work from anonymous reviewers, it is often more difficult to have a collaborator reject our ideas, rewrite our prose, or correct our grammar. It is easier to take criticism from a stranger than from an intimate, and a research or writing collaborator is like an intimate, someone whom we expect to accept us as we are, who is sensitive of our feelings, who sees value in who we are and what we do. Perhaps there is a bit of embarrassment, even resentment, in being exposed as less than perfect in the eyes of those with whom we are intimate. Scholars who find it difficult to accept criticism from colleagues or who are unwilling to compromise, even subordinate their own ideas, will be happier working alone.

The guided group interaction research affirmed my belief in the need for criminologists to be in the field, to meet and talk with their subjects, to learn the intimate details of the lives led by those whom we label as delinquents or criminals. Although I was not trained as an ethnographer, nor have I ever written an ethnography, I am convinced of the value of this type of research in order to learn the nuances of what we study and the context in which behavioral decisions are made. I was surprised to learn how much had changed about delinquency and delinquents between the time I worked in a detention center and the time I spent at Essexfields. Much of the argot I knew, for example, was unknown eight years later, although regional differences also contributed to this. To understand what the boys were thinking and saying about their lives and their behavior, I had to learn a new vocabulary, one that I would not have been exposed to had I not submerged myself into the group culture. Although I have used my share of questionnaires administered anonymously to respondents, their utility is quite limited in understanding the processes involved in becoming a delinquent or in changing delinquent behaviors.

## Somebody Has To Do It

At the time, it was a typical pattern for academics to change jobs several times before settling into a tenured, life-time position. Often, significant salary increases and promotion in rank were achieved only by moving. While this had obvious implications for one's upward mobility, it also served to broaden one's experience and contribute to his or her professorial maturation. Changing jobs exposed the professor to departments of various size, to different regions of the country, to new colleagues, to unique situations regarding academic administration, and to a variety of other circumstances and events that served to provide a more universal perspective on academic life. I have always subscribed to this pattern of upward mobility and professional development, believing that those who stay in the first job they accept after receiving their degree tend to become parochial in outlook, unaware of life beyond their own small academic world. Within reason, changing departments is healthy for the individual and for higher education. My own move to the University of Delaware in 1967 was for more money, higher rank, and expanded opportunities, the classic trinity of academic mobility.

At the time, I had opportunities to move to larger, more established departments, but without the unique challenges of the University of Delaware. It was a small department, only eight members, that wanted to grow larger; the university was establishing a new graduate program in sociology; and criminology was to be one of the department's areas of specialization. I would be in on the ground floor of this development, one of the senior members of the faculty shaping the future of the discipline on the campus. These enticements were more important than the salary and rank because they made a good offer an exciting offer. Having already taken a number of jobs "just for the money," I realized the need to be excited about what I was doing, to feel a part of an important development. I've used that as a criterion for what I have been doing ever since.

Two years after I arrived at the University of Delaware, the department chairman resigned unexpectedly and I was asked to become chair. With only six years experience as a faculty member, I didn't feel prepared to assume an administrative role. I was also worried about how this would influence my scholarly career because I could see that it would consume a good deal of time. The dean dismissed these concerns by saying that "somebody has to do it" and I was as prepared as anyone else. He also reassured me by saying that I could make the job into just about anything I wanted, as long as I didn't spend too much money and kept the faculty reasonably happy. He didn't say anything about keeping the administration happy, an oversight on his part that he would soon come to realize.

Being a department chairperson is one of the most important and most difficult jobs in university administration. Caught between the faculty and the university administration, the chairperson often feels the pressure from both sides, representing each side to the other while trying to retain the trust and the confidence of both. As the leader of the unit, the chair is expected to serve as a role model for the faculty by teaching well, doing research, publishing, engaging in service, doing, in effect, all those things on which faculty members are judged. At the same time, the chair serves as counselor and advisor to undergraduates, graduate students, staff members, and faculty colleagues. I am convinced that department chairs should be trained in counseling psychology so they are better trained to handle the many personal crises that occur among a department's constituents. To make matters worse, faculty members are typically independent nonconformists who have an opinion about everything and want to talk about it at some length. Because most departments have limited resources, the competition for these scarce resources is sometimes intense, usually out of proportion to the magnitude of the resource's value. At times colleagues are unable to get along, carrying their personal animosity into department meetings and allowing it to influence their positions on departmental matters. No wonder some wag once declared that chairing an academic department is like "herding cats."

These possible difficulties notwithstanding, chairing a department can be a worthwhile, fulfilling experience, as it was for me. With the help of my colleagues, it allowed me to implement a number of principles of governance emphasizing greater faculty participation in decisionmaking, steer the teaching and research emphases in the direction of relevant social issues, recruit a number of faculty members who helped reshape the department, and bring greater visibility to the department and the university through our dynamic growth. Chairs can do these important things and derive great personal and professional satisfaction from them. Not allowing the "herding cats" issues to overwhelm the joyful aspects of the job is the key to success.

I turned out to be the Minnie Minoso (baseball fans will remember that he played major league baseball in four different decades) of chairing, spreading 16 years of service as department chair over four decades.

During that period, a small department was turned into one of medi-um/large size, a doctoral program was started, highly visible faculty were recruited, and the department's reputation grew, especially in the areas of criminology and criminal justice. Equally important, Delaware became known as an attractive place to be because of its supportive environment for teaching and research. In order for a department chair to be able to achieve these goals and foster such an environment, a great deal of time and energy are necessary, time and energy that can't be directed towards one's own scholarly work. Unless one is truly satisfied by helping others achieve success, this can be difficult to accept, and usually leads to an early exit from the chair. A department's most productive scholar is usually not the best candidate for such leadership because productive scholars seldom want to give up their time and energy for administrative service.

For a job that demands so many skills—planning, supervisory, fiscal, interactive—it is surprising that so little training goes into preparing someone to do it successfully. Typically, a university asks a successful teacher or scholar, even someone who is both, to become chair of a department, assuming that teaching and/or research scholarship has prepared the designee to be able to administer an academic unit. Most chairs have had no management training, and universities seldom provide opportunities for them to learn such skills. Admittedly, few of the chairs I have known would have availed themselves of the opportunity for such training if it were provided, apparently feeling constrained by both time and ego. Miraculously, we seem to muddle through reasonably well, although one might not believe that by hearing the complaints about chairpersons voiced by their faculty over a drink at professional meetings.

## Working With Students

Although most of us who earn doctorates in sociology and criminology teach, few of us have ever received any formal instruction in teaching. Because the Ph.D. degree is a research degree, few departments make any formal attempt to teach graduate students how to convey the knowledge of the discipline to students in a classroom. Nevertheless, graduate students are expected to teach, often as teaching assistants first, and then on their own in a classroom. The lucky ones receive some supervision during this process, and on a few occasions departments may offer them non-credit courses on instructional techniques. Graduate students usually learn to teach by emulating favorite instructors of theirs, a practice they carry over to their first professional teaching position. Once in their first job, many of them become too busy building a scholarly career to spend much time improving their teach-

ing. Although universities pay a great deal of lip service to the important role of teaching effectiveness in the institutional reward structure, teaching often continues to play a secondary role in determining
pay increments and promotion and tenure. And, that's too bad. Undergraduates deserve better, because they are the reason most of us are
employed and, unless we are employed by a research institute, we
have a strong obligation to students.

Graduate students wishing to teach sociology and criminology
must make it a priority to receive adequate opportunity and training in
the art of teaching. This means, first, to be convinced of the value of
good teaching, and then to take every available opportunity to develop
teaching skills. Good teachers are made by showing concern, observing others, trying new techniques, and asking for criticism, from our colleagues and our students. Adhering to the anachronistic custom of not
inviting colleagues to observe our teaching only perpetuates bad teaching. It seems ironic to me that we allow, even expect, our scholarly work
to be reviewed and criticized but will seldom permit colleagues to
observe our classes and offer evaluations. Improving our ability to
teach effectively is beneficial for our departments and our discipline, and
is essential for the intellectual development of our students.

In the past 30 years, criminology and criminal justice have been
attractive subjects for undergraduates, attracting large numbers of
them to our classes and to the major. Many come for the wrong reasons,
though, thinking that they'll be entertained with details of the under-
side of culture, or that the subject matter will help them achieve a career
in criminal justice, usually law enforcement. Criminology and criminal
justice programs, especially those located in colleges of arts and sciences,
should not be pre-professional in nature, oriented towards preparing students for the job market by teaching particular skills. There are training academies that do that quite adequately for those who do select
employment in the criminal justice area. Instead, such programs ought
to teach broad principles of social behavior based on the theory and
research of various disciplines devoted to understanding human behavior. In most four-year institutions, courses more appropriate for training academies are disappearing from curricula, to be replaced by those
concerned with the theory and analysis of crime, the behavioral characteristics of offenders, the role of law in the process of justice, and the
operation of various elements of the criminal justice system. Quite
clearly, no one discipline can address all of these issues, providing students with what they need to know to understand crime and justice.
Therefore, the study of these important social phenomena must be
interdisciplinary, using perspectives from sociology, economics, psychology, history, and other social and related sciences to attain the most
comprehensive picture possible.

The academic and interdisciplinary nature of contemporary criminology/criminal justice education does not mean that these programs should not or cannot prepare students for careers in criminal justice. Rather, it is a recognition that the best way to prepare students for these careers is to provide them with broadly based educational experiences that enhance their ability to assume diverse professional roles. Those entering criminal justice careers, for example, need to know more about the dynamics of human behavior than crime scene investigation, which can be learned eventually at an academy if the student chooses a policing career.

Criminology and criminal justice should be seen as just another option within an array of academic options for the undergraduate, equally rigorous, equally demanding, equally intellectual. Just as few anthropology majors believe they'll graduate and be employed as anthropologists, or history majors as historians, so criminology and criminal justice majors should not believe that their major will prepare them to be criminal justicians. Like anthropology or history, their major should provide them with intellectual skills they can adapt to many kinds of employment or life situations. Programs in criminology and criminal justice must recognize that fewer than one-half of their graduates enter criminal justice careers, while the remainder attend graduate or law schools, or assume positions unrelated to criminal justice. As long as these programs are offered as general education options, it is incumbent upon them to recognize that they serve these three important groups of student constituents, and to educate those who will go on to careers in criminal justice as well as those who will not. The best way to do that is to offer a curriculum that is theory- and research-based, that is interdisciplinary, that is rigorous, and that emphasizes communication and critical thinking skills. When the academic community is convinced that criminology and criminal justice programs do that, they will achieve much greater respect and approval within the academy.

On the other hand, most undergraduate students would probably be better off if colleges and universities abolished majors. Most undergraduates are too inexperienced to make the choices we ask of them, and often end a four-year education knowing little about subject matter that would enrich their lives and enhance their career options. Instead of concentrating in majors, students would gain more from sampling various disciplines, being exposed to ideas they might otherwise avoid and getting a broad knowledge of the many intellectual pursuits available to them. For me, the real objectives of a college education are to teach the person to read, to write, to speak, to compute, and to think critically. Forcing young men and women into majors before they're ready to make such long-term decisions often undermines the achievement of these objectives. The administrative necessity of academic majors will continue to outweigh the real goals of education, however, so our task is to construct concentrations of intellectual experiences that come as close as possible to producing a college graduate capable of assuming a productive role in society as both a worker and citizen.

Students coming to a graduate program usually know pretty well what they want to do and what their career objectives are, although there are occasional wanderers. Because of this, graduate education should be less formal than undergraduate, allowing students to pick and choose among courses, take reading courses of special interest, and prepare for qualifying examinations in both conventional and unconventional ways. My seminars emphasize reading, writing, and speaking, each in abundant quantities. Before the weekly meeting, students are expected to read the assignment, usually consisting of articles from appropriate journals, and be prepared to examine the week's topic in light of the readings. Everyone, including the instructor, is expected to speak, to discuss, to argue, to challenge the others, in order to enhance his or her own insight and to help others develop theirs. Passionate, but civil, discussions are expected. Everyone should be exhausted at the end of the three hours. Two major papers are assigned, both of which are read thoroughly and returned with necessary comments. The final examination is oral, administered in my office to each student individually. Although students seem to dislike this type of exam, it gives me the chance to probe answers, explore areas of weakness, offer advice and encouragement, and make suggestions about content and manner of presentation. An oral final exam gives students the necessary experience of thinking on their feet while under some pressure, learning how to stall for time while formulating an answer, and constructing a response that is organized, concise, complete, and articulate. I've been using this technique in my graduate seminars ever since hearing a candidate for an assistant professorship in our department stumble through answers to questions about his dissertation that he obviously knew well. In addition to making a bad impression on his listeners, it also convinced us that he would not be a good classroom teacher. Needless to say, he did not get the job, and it convinced me to do what I could to prevent our students finding themselves in a similar situation.

Nothing a graduate instructor does is more important than informally mentoring students. Having had influential mentors in Dinitz and Reckless, I know the value of having faculty members show an interest in you and your career. Mentoring, of course, goes beyond advising, an obligation usually assigned to us by the Director of Graduate Studies. We mentor students when we demonstrate our concern for both their professional and personal well-being, when we encourage them to come to us with their problems and concerns, and when we offer them opportunities that may enhance their professional objectives. I attempt to mentor students in a number of ways, including dropping by their office to inquire of their well-being, by having an open door when they need to

talk, by taking them to lunch or inviting them to dinner, and by informing them of opportunities for funding or employment. None of this costs
me anything except a few minutes of my time, and I like to think that
it makes a little difference to the graduate students.

Supervising doctoral dissertations is a more formal way of mentoring students. Because a doctoral dissertation is the culmination of
one's graduate training, it should be a highly personal work, something to which the student is intellectually committed and prepared to
devote a considerable amount of time. In fact, it is highly likely that the
student will pursue the same topic as a post-graduate, perhaps even
extending the very research addressed in the dissertation. For these reasons, students, perhaps with some guidance from a faculty advisor, must
choose their own topic and conceptualize their own problem for
research. Most graduate students who come to me, in fact, have a
research problem in mind and need help only in refining it. After that,
I'm available to offer as much assistance as the student wants in constructing a research design, collecting and analyzing data, and writing
the dissertation. Much of the assistance is in the form of encouragement,
helping solve field problems, talking the student through crises of confidence or frustration, and just being available when needed. Dissertation
advisors should expect to play the roles of expert, counselor, father-fig-
ure or mother-figure, and grammarian at one or several points in the
process. It can be time consuming and even emotionally fatiguing, but
that's alright because that student will forever be known as your student.

One shouldn't get the impression that working with students is only
a matter of your giving valued resources and receiving only satisfaction
in return. That is far from the truth. I have received valuable help from
graduate students with whom I have worked. Many of them have given
me new insights and have kindled my interest in areas that were not of
particular concern to me. In the early 1970s, for example, a particularly
bright and resourceful woman student was quite interested in female
crime, a subject to which I hadn't paid much attention. As my research
assistant on a series of delinquency studies, she was instrumental in our
collecting data relevant to the role of gender in delinquency decisionmaking as well as the differential treatment of girls in the juvenile justice process. This led to a series of papers in which gender was a key
variable and ultimately to an early book on women, crime, and justice.
If it hadn't been for my student I wouldn't have gotten interested in this
area, and I would have been deprived of the opportunity to add to the
developing literature on female criminality. Students have made other
important contributions to my scholarship and to my development as
a teacher, contributions that I can often identify, but some of which have
been subtle and unintended. I know, however, that they have all influenced me and helped shape my thinking.

Viewing graduate student assistants as partners and treating them as collaborators has resulted in their participating in a number of coauthored papers and books. That is another mutual benefit of working with graduate students. I receive welcomed assistance in preparing papers, reports, and manuscripts, while the student is getting valuable experience writing such documents in a nonthreatening, supportive environment. At the same time, the student's vitae is being built with publications that are becoming increasingly necessary to secure even a first position in academia. Helping students develop a competitive set of credentials by providing them with opportunities to publish by using our data, either as sole or co-authors, is an obligation of faculty in research universities. In addition to the necessary role we play certificating the right of graduate students to receive academia's highest degree, we should also put substantial effort into seeing that they find employment in colleges and universities that fit their personal and career objectives. I have always seen one of my roles to be that of fostering their careers. One important way we can do that is by making them partners in our research and published work. It's what two of my graduate teachers did for me, and how can you thank someone for something like that? Simply by doing it yourself for others.

Working with students, sharpening their skills, influencing their thinking, and assisting their careers are the ways most academics leave a meaningful and lasting legacy. For most of us, our scholarly work is relevant for only a very short period of time, mere pebbles on the pyramid of science. If we can remain a footnote, we're doing well. We live through our students, through their achievements, their contributions. We pass on our legacy through them, deriving satisfaction by knowing that we played a role in what they are able to achieve. For me, that has always been one of the joys of being a teacher.

## Interests Change

Some scholars work in the same narrow area of research their whole careers. From dissertation to the final book or article, you can count on their work to focus on one topic about which they have become quite an expert. Others appear to be more restless, less able or willing to concentrate on a single phenomenon or area of interest. I am among this group, although as a young sociologist/criminologist I was advised to stick to one area of scholarship and become known for work in that area. Otherwise, I would be spread too thin, unable to master a particular subject, and not be recognized as an authority on anything. After my brief foray into mental health research, I returned to delinquency and spent the next dozen or so years studying and writing about delinquent behavior. While those years were reasonably successful and I enjoyed my work, my interests were broader than juvenile delinquency and I found myself asking to teach the course in social problems. This seemed to justify reading about family issues, political and economic institutions, poverty and welfare, as well as other forms of social deviance. Social problems seemed to be where I could sample a little of everything. Preparing to teach social problems exposed me to a wider range of literature and to more diverse ideas than had other instructional experiences, and I credit it with putting greater substance and vitality into my teaching. Eventually, this interest led to my publishing several social problems textbooks, and to my general lack of enthusiasm for narrow specializations. Although I am sometimes envious of people who seem to know everything about one subject or another, and I recognize their contribution to scholarship, I know that's not for me and I encourage students and colleagues to branch out, read widely, teach new courses, and even conduct research in previously unexplored areas.

This isn't easy, of course. Simply staying abreast of the literature in one narrow area of scholarship has become difficult as the information explosion continues unabated. Keeping up with the newest developments in all of the subjects covered in a major social problems text can be a full-time job. After publishing three editions of such a text, I found it necessary to share the work with a coauthor who assumed responsibility for half of the subject matter. Under any conditions, keeping up with the literature in one's field requires compromises and short cuts. I read professional books very selectively, relying on reviews to determine what I should read and as substitutes for actually reading a volume (alas, this may be the result of my also reading a number of detective novels, books on baseball, and histories of movie making). Because I cannot possibly subscribe to all journals that might be relevant to my work or my interests, I scan the table of contents of all social and behavioral science journals by reading Current Contents and having student assistants photocopy relevant articles, or, now, printing them from online sources. This practice provides me with wonderful resources, but can become chaotic and overwhelming unless a good file system is maintained. As C. Wright Mills once advised, it is helpful to dump all of our files on the floor once in a while and sort and refile the contents in order to review and reorganize our thinking. Although I don't actually dump the contents on the floor, I do try to go through them often for just the reasons Mills cited. But, no matter what system we use, we can never be aware of everything that exists in the literature that may be relevant to what we are doing, and we should not allow that to paralyze our work. At some point (and each of us must make the decision for ourself, although graduate students often need assistance), the literature search must end and we must build our own work on what we have.

Career trajectories can be influenced by many life-course events, but the most interesting are those that are unexpected and unplanned. After serving as department chair for 10 years, during which I confined most of my research and writing to delinquency issues, I journeyed to Wales to participate in a faculty exchange program. Like most opportunities to spend time in another university, I found this to be an enriching experience that allowed me time to consider what I had been doing and whether I wanted to continue to do the same. It is easier to reflect on our life and work from someplace else, away from routine activities and responsibilities, where we are hardly known and not much is expected of us. By the time I returned to the United States and the University of Delaware, I knew that I didn't want to be a university administrator any longer (although I would change my mind several years later) and that I wasn't interested in more delinquency research. Although I enjoyed being a criminologist too much to abandon that calling, I knew it was time for a change of focus. Before I could seriously consider many options, the decision was made when my colleague Alan Block told me of a situation he had just discovered and invited me to join him in researching the involvement of organized criminals in the illegal disposal of toxic wastes.

Thus began a five-year period of research and writing that was at once the most exciting and the most disappointing I have experienced. It was a new style of research for me, closer to investigative reporting than to the application of experimental designs to which I had been accustomed. Nevertheless, I was convinced that the work must be done and to do it would serve an essential national interest. In addition, I had been reading about organized crime since high school and knew that traditional scientific methods would not apply here. By the time we finished our work, we had chronicled the movement of traditional solid waste companies controlled by crime syndicates into the new and extremely lucrative field of toxic waste disposal. By searching through thousands of documents, interviewing law enforcement officials across the country, and receiving information from a number of the principals actually involved in the business, we documented illegal practices that were polluting land, water, and air and putting entire communities at risk.

In this case, our research did not test a new theory or attempt to understand some mystery that lay deeply embedded in the social order of human life. It wasn't that grand or esoteric, but research doesn't have to be grand to be meaningful, to be relevant, to improve the human condition. Research that allows us to document, to speak with greater certainty about social, political, or economic arrangements that have an impact on our daily lives empowers us with knowledge. And, that knowledge gives us the equipment we need to control our environment and to effect social change. Fortunately, we have a tradition of looking at ourselves, of trying to understand the social, political, and economic dynamics that create our world as it is. Sometimes we don't like what we see, and we begin the laborious task of changing to conform better to our ideals. Research allows us to see ourselves as we are, to understand the consequences of our actions or inactions, to devise a strategy for getting us closer to where we want to be as a society. Research into illegality and corruption, like the toxic waste disposal work Block and I did, uncovers previously unknown practices that few people would condone. Once there is public awareness, the probability of change increases dramatically. For someone like me, who has always been interested in social reform and doing research that "does good," few professional experiences can be more satisfying than believing that his or her research findings have a positive impact on a social problem.

That appears to have been the case with our toxic waste disposal findings, but not without some personal cost. Within days of the publication of the book reporting our work, Block and I were sued by Waste Management, Inc., then the nation's largest waste hauler. They claimed we had libeled them and asked for a $60 million judgment, a figure that made the publisher extremely nervous. Fortunately, the publisher had insurance and we were defended by competent counsel who was confident of our vindication when the case went to trial. But, the process was costly, and after 16 months of depositions, interrogatories, meetings, and other legal maneuvers, the insurer insisted on a settlement when Waste Management proposed one that did not involve a financial judgment. Although we defended the correctness of our position and felt compromised by the settlement, we were ready to have the ordeal end. Unless one is involved in a situation of this type, it is difficult to imagine the time it takes and the emotional strain it creates. Despite this, the book had some impact on the environmental movement and upon legislation that was developed in several states. For a time, we even became mini-folk heroes for a number of citizen action groups around the country, having taken on the combined evils of organized crime and the huge waste companies, and living to tell about it! And tell about it I did by addressing dozens of groups around the country for the next few years. That, I believed, was my civic and professional responsibility, and well in keeping with the service expectation of university professors.

By the late 1980s, however, I had grown weary of such high visibility and controversial research, a condition that was enhanced by my distaste for litigation and threatening phone calls. Realizing I didn't like the heat, I decided to get out of the kitchen and return to safer ground, doing what I had done for the first two decades of my career. I returned as chairperson of the department and served an additional six years. During that time, my colleague, Jim Inciardi, started The Center for Drug and Alcohol Studies in our department, bringing together a group of researchers who shared an interest in substance use and abuse. Coincidentally, I, too, had an interest in drug use, having published a book on youth and drugs some 20 years earlier. Doing drug abuse research seemed like a logical next step in my career, because it allowed me to do more traditional scholarship while believing that the results of the work might make a positive contribution to a national problem. Since then, my empirical work has been in the Center, focusing on therapeutic communities and the way in which they impact members to effect behavioral change. This is not unlike the research on guided group interaction I did earlier and is consistent with my long interest in the interaction between social and individual factors in crime causation and behavioral change. More recently, I have undertaken a longitudinal study of the post-court experiences of clients who are processed before the rather new and heralded drug courts.

Much of the evaluation or applied research I have done was undertaken largely because I believe it has the potential to make positive contributions to solving a serious social problem. It also is a reflection of my values. After all of the discussion of value free research that went on in graduate school, I quickly learned that it is an impossible objective to achieve. Value judgments are exercised every time we choose to investigate one problem rather than another, or use one methodology rather than another. I chose the problems that I have researched because I believed, and continue to believe, that delinquents can be changed, that illegal toxic waste disposal is dangerous, that substance abuse is harmful, and that options for dealing with drug users should be expanded. As a trained social scientist I am able to determine the group and personal consequences of social conditions and behaviors, but the judgment as to their desirability or harmfulness is the product of my value commitments. Others with different opinions may come to contrary conclusions about what is desirable, and they have as much right as I do to let their values dictate the issues they study and the questions they ask. The only obligation each of us has is to be objective in our methods and honest in our presentation of findings. In fact, healthy debate about the efficacy of social conditions and the legitimacy of proposed solutions to social problems advances the disciplines of sociology and criminology and contributes to a necessary examination of public policy.

## Looking Back

The field of criminology has changed a great deal since I entered it as a graduate student, and most of the changes have been for the better. Obviously, it is much larger, thanks in considerable part to the development of criminal justice as an academic and intellectual endeavor. From only a handful of programs specializing in criminology or criminal justice in the late 1960s to more than 1,500 such programs by the end of the next decade, the speed of criminal justice's growth has to be considered unparalleled in the history of higher education. All across the United States, young men and women began declaring their interest in the study of crime and the justice process, often pursuing their post-graduate studies in the same or closely related fields. Thousands of faculty jobs were created as new departments sprang up and established social science units expanded their crime related courses. More women were attracted to the field once dominated by men (with a few notable exceptions, such as Mabel Elliott, Ruth Cavan, and Eleanor Glueck) as interest in female crime increased and as social science disciplines in general were seen as hospitable places for women wishing to pursue careers in teaching and research. The growing number of criminology scholars increased the membership of the professional associations, changing their format and often their politics. The first American Society of Criminology meeting I attended was in 1967 at the NYU Law School, where the 100 or so members of the audience sat in one room for the entire day as the panels of presenters changed in front of them. By 1981, the annual meeting attracted more than 1,000 participants for the first time. Today, the annual meeting accommodates close to 3,000 participants who may choose among hundreds of panels.

The growth of the discipline may also be seen in the number of journals now offering scholarly articles in criminology and criminal justice. More noticeable, though, is the changed nature of such scholarship. The increased statistical sophistication of all of the social sciences is also evident in criminology. It is now difficult to read our journals without some knowledge of path analysis, structural equation models, or hierarchal loglinear models, often used to justify the rotation of one variable and to reach conclusions that are just as baffling as the statistic. Whether it is the result of the inordinate pressure on young scholars to publish or their fascination with advanced statistical techniques, journal articles are becoming increasingly incomprehensible to all but the most knowledgeable readers. Pity the poor practitioner who wants to understand more about crime and tries to read our journals. It appears that we have become so obsessed with being scientists that we have ritualized the method while losing sight of the ultimate objective of our work. Criminology will be best served when scholars pay as much attention to theory development and a qualitative understanding of the process of criminal decisionmaking as they do to statistical contortions of often mundane data.

The recent history of criminology reveals a dynamic era of great growth and scientific sophistication, but with few theoretical advances that have made significant contributions to the etiology of crime. Perhaps that is because, despite our disclaimers, we continue to look for a silver bullet that will allow us to comprehend a complex phenomenon that is the product of the interaction of multiple social and personal variables. In addition, why should any one explanation account for a social construction, crime, that has variable meanings? Instead, the future of theoretical criminology should focus on understanding why unique individuals respond as they do to opportunities and stimuli within a particular social context. This requires our demonstrating the interaction among structural conditions that are favorable to crime and delinquency, the process by which deviant reactions are learned, the motivation for such learning within a conducive environment, and the differential interpretations of these factors by the individual. After all these years, I still want to know what accounts for the good boy in a high-delinquency area. Sociologists and criminologists have addressed all of these issues in the form of social disorganization, differential association, strain, and self-control theories. All are partial explanations in need of integration into a comprehensive explanation. Providing this type of integration and developing the type of research support it will require is a formidable challenge for young men and women entering the field of criminology, but one that is achievable and worthwhile, and exciting to contemplate.

Stimulating challenges and unique opportunities are available in every generation. I was fortunate to begin a career in higher education at a time when colleges and universities were starting a period of unprecedented growth. This was especially true for sociology and criminology, benefitting from the War on Poverty and then the Law Enforcement Assistance Administration for an increase in student interest and governmental support. It is also true that the rapidly rising crime rate assisted those of us wanting to study illegal behavior and its consequences, just as today's national fixation on drug abuse is a boon to drug researchers. In addition, it was also a time when new ideas heightened debate within the field and added a sense of urgency and emotion to otherwise routine scholarly intercourse. Although I never considered myself a radical or critical criminologist, a number of my positions have been altered by listening to their arguments, and the discipline has benefitted greatly from the intellectual stimulation such arguments have provided for many of us.

Being a teacher/researcher is a career I would recommend unequivocally, especially so in the field of criminology. Our research problems are important ones that tend to disrupt society and often cause human suffering. They need to be addressed, and we can derive both professional and personal satisfaction from doing so. If, like me, one wants to do scientific detective work that may contribute to the amelioration of a social problem or alleviate some small measure of human misery, then a career as an academic criminologist is an excellent choice. Where else can a professor do all of this and meet such interesting people?

Being a professor also involves a lifestyle that I find particularly rewarding, although not necessarily easy. Like most of my colleagues, I work a great deal, being accused by family members of being a workaholic (it's interesting that my father worked longer and harder at his blue-collar occupation, yet no one referred to *him* as a workaholic; perhaps the word hadn't been coined yet). I teach two courses each semester, direct dissertations, serve on numerous university committees, and have one or another research project going at all times. Although I tend to be a highly structured person with a predictable routine, the attraction of my job is its flexibility. Aside from a few obligations that must be addressed at set times, being a professor allows me to work at my own speed when I want to. I can write in the morning, at night, or over the weekend, and no one cares as long as I accomplish what I'm obligated to do. That type of flexibility, coupled with the academic year calendar, is a benefit I wouldn't trade. It is liberating; it makes me feel I'm in control of my destiny; it permits me to be creative when I'm capable of it, not on some artificial work schedule. Even better than that, though, is the freedom of thought and expression that is part of the professorial role. Faculty members choose their own research topics and are expected to present their findings to the scientific community no matter what they are. This freedom and responsibility to present the truth makes academics something akin to the conscience of the society, sometimes a heavy burden to carry. At the same time, it may be considered a privilege that is extended to few other members of society.

For many of us in academia, writing is an important and necessary part of our job, and one that is often difficult because it requires time, discipline, and the ability to cope with loneliness. I have usually had the time and discipline to write, but the third ingredient has been lacking at times. Writing is a lonely business, done in isolation, without human distractions. It requires shutting family members, companions, colleagues, and others out of your life for some period of time in order to concentrate all of your attention on what you are creating. It means literally closing the door on our children, spouses, friends, and students; refusing to answer the telephone; turning down invitations; becoming a social isolate for some period of time. While I have always found this part of writing troubling, it has become more so as I age, probably because I now find more satisfaction in friendships, companions, and conversation than in the past. As compensation, I now do my professional writing only during the workday, in three or four hour blocks of time. Never a fast writer, it now takes me even longer to complete a manuscript, but it is a small price to pay to avoid the pall of loneliness and isolation that once made writing so onerous.

Life as a professor/researcher is not all work, however. One of the most pleasant experiences of my career has been my involvement with professional associations. I have been active in both the American

Sociological Association and the American Society of Criminology since early in my career, attending annual meetings, serving on committees, and holding elective office. This activity has given me the opportunity to meet colleagues from around the world, to learn about the scholarship of others, to participate in informal conversations about research and teaching, and to help determine the nature and direction of the discipline. In addition to being a symbol of professional commitment, active participation in the associations exposes us to opportunities that may otherwise be unnoticed or unavailable. Young scholars should be encouraged to become active in the professional associations by making it known to the officers that they want to serve on committees, or participate in organizing national or regional meetings. As with most other things in life, the person who waits to be called often isn't. Learning how to advocate for oneself without being labeled a self-promoter may be tricky, but it is an important skill to master.

I continue to encourage undergraduates to consider graduate education, especially in sociology and criminology. Many exciting career opportunities exist in these related fields, not the least of which is college and university teaching and research. I have never regretted the career choices I made more than 40 years ago, and even knowing what I know now, I would probably make the same choices again. Socially significant research remains to be done, social policy continues to need empirical testing, and additional theories of human behavior are yet to be conceptualized. There is much for future generations of criminologists to do. Perhaps one will even offer a better explanation of the good boy in a high-delinquency area.

## Selected Bibliography

Scarpitti, F.R. (1965). "Delinquent and Non-Delinquent Perceptions of Self, Values, and Opportunity." *Mental Hygiene*, 49(July):399-404.

Scarpitti, F.R. & A. Block (1986). "Casinos and Banking: Organized Crime in the Bahamas." *Deviant Behavior*, 7:301-312.

Scarpitti, F.R. & A. Block (1985) *Poisoning for Profit:The Mafia and Toxic Waste in America*. New York, NY: Morrow.

Scarpitti, F.R. & S. Datesman (1975). "Female Delinquency and Broken Homes: A Reassessment." *Criminology,* 13(May):33-45.

Scarpitti, F.R., S. Dinitz & B. Pasamanick (1967). *Schizophrenics in the Community: An Experimental Study in the Prevention of Hospitalization*. New York, NY: Appleton-Century-Crofts.

Scarpitti, F.R., S. Dinitiz & W. Reckless (1962). "Delinquency Vulnerability: A Cross Group and Longitudinal Analysis." *American Sociological Review*, 27(August):515-517.

Scarpitti, F.R. & J. Landis (1965). "Perceptions Regarding Value Orientation and Legitimate Opportunity: Delinquents and Non- Delinquents." *Social Forces*, 44(September):83-91.

Scarpitti, F.R., E. Murray, S. Dinitiz & W. Reckless (1960). "The 'Good' Boy in a High Delinquency Area: Four Years Later." *American Sociological Review*, 25(August):555-558.

Scarpitti, F.R. & A. Nielsen (1997). "Changing the Behavior of Substance Abusers: Factors Influencing the Effectiveness of Therapeutic Communities." *Journal of Drug Issues*, 27(July):279-298.

Scarpitti, F.R. & R. Stephenson (1974). *Group Interaction as Therapy*. Westport, CT: Greenwood.

Scarpitti, F.R. & R. Stephenson (1968a). "Argot in a Therapeutic Correctional Milieu." *Social Problems*, 15(Winter):384-395.

Scarpitti, F.R. & R. Stephenson (1968b). "Negro-White Differentials in Delinquency." *Journal of Research in Crime and Delinquency*, 5(July):122-133.

Scarpitti, F.R. & R. Stephenson (1968c). "A Study of Probation Effectiveness." *Journal of Criminal Law, Criminology and Police Science*, 59(September):361-369.

# 5

# Learning How to Learn and Its Sequelae*

Joan McCord

High school in Tucson, Arizona, left me thinking that education was a matter of learning how to repeat what others wrote. Fortunately, at Stanford, I had two lucky breaks that taught me otherwise. The first was in a philosophy course that challenged me to think critically about what I read. The professor assigned a series of incompatible theories. When we realized that, being incompatible, they couldn't all be right, we were forced to rethink our earlier conviction concerning each. What a lesson that was. Thirty years later, I returned to Stanford and let Professor John Mothershead know that his course had made a tremendous difference in my life; it had turned me from an acceptor of received opinions into an independent and skeptical thinker.

The second lucky break came in the form of an extraordinary professor who agreed to give me a tutorial course. He agreed on condition that I would read Spinoza, a notoriously difficult project. Having practically no background, but loaded with enthusiasm, I agreed. The reading was dense; the weekly sessions downright painful. Each week, I reported on the sections I had read and what they seemed to mean. Professor Davidson asked for more. Why had Spinoza made that specific argument? What issues were relevant to the questions it addressed? Had the argument been made by others? He conveyed the clear impression that reading the text, even carefully reading the text, was not enough. I remember no compliments, no recognition of effort spent, nothing but a careful exposure of what it means to master a topic. His teaching, I believe, put me on track to become a researcher in a broad and multi-disciplined field that investigates justice.

William ("Bud") McCord and I had been friends since high school. We went to Stanford together and were married as undergraduates. We

*I thank my son Geoffrey Sayre McCord for his careful editing of this manuscript.

decided on academic careers together. That decision was easy once we had been given the sensible advice to talk with people who occupied positions we envisioned ourselves as having in about 10 years. "Don't ask their advice," Professor Cowley said, "but talk with them about their daily routines. Ask them what they enjoy about their jobs. Then decide which lifestyle best fits you." We talked with business leaders in a variety of specialties, with lawyers who had become partners in firms, and with well-established bankers. These people were successful and most of them enjoyed what they were doing, but we found— hands down—that what the professors did was what we wanted to do. We also agreed that I would support Bud while he got his credentials before going on for my own.

After graduation from Stanford, Bud enrolled at Harvard to study with Sheldon and Eleanor Glueck and I got a position teaching children in Concord, Massachusetts. Classroom teaching provided an important opportunity for me to learn more about children. Occasionally, I used my sixth graders to experiment with theories about learning. The experiment I remember best involved teaching children what to value. At the beginning of the year, I asked the class to list their subjects in order of preference. Almost all the 30 children ranked arithmetic at the bottom. So arithmetic became my target. I instituted an Arithmetic Club. It would be open only to those who got 100 percent correct on an assigned paper. (Because I gave individualized assignments, everybody had a chance to join.) Members of the Arithmetic Club were given a special privilege: They were allowed to do weekly arithmetic homework which I would grade. At the end of the term, the class reevaluated their subjects. Confirming a theory about using rewards to shape preferences (based on my interpretation of some work done by Leon Festinger), arithmetic had moved upward for all the students and it had become a favorite for most. This classroom experiment exposed the folly of common practice in using homework as punishment, a practice that sends the message that learning is painful, rather than a privilege.

The classes also proved useful for pre-testing the measurement instruments Bud and I intended to use in our work for *Psychopathy and Delinquency* (1956). One of the tests, designed to measure aggression, involved a dog. The children were to identify the dog's preferred solution in a variety of problem situations, one solution being aggressive, one ameliorating, and one withdrawing from the situation. Because we knew some of the delinquent children to be tested would be illiterate, we used pictures showing the situations and each of the choices. Before giving the test the first time, in my Concord classroom, I had rated the children for their aggression. To honor our own dog, we referred to the one in the test we had designed as "Chumley," asking for each situation, "What would Chumley want to do?" An example is a picture showing Chumley's family displaying a new baby to an unhappy dog.

The attached choices asked: "Does he want to bite the baby (picture)? Does he want to go off in a corner to show how badly he feels (picture)? Or does he want to make friends with the baby (picture)?" Almost all the children picked the friendly choices for just about all the situations, with no differences between the most aggressive and the least. Two months later, I reintroduced the test, giving the dog a different name. Same situations and same pictures. This time the children were asked, "What would Rover want to do?" It was Rover's family bringing home a new baby, having his bone stolen by another dog, seeing a birthday cake on the kitchen table, etc. Although the children had not differed in their perspectives of Chumley, with all finding him to be friendly, they differed in their assignment of preferences for Rover. The more aggressive ones indicated that Rover would want to bite the baby, fight the dog who took his bone, and take the birthday cake. We learned the importance of a name for attributing personality. We also had constructed a test that could be used for differentiating more aggressive from less aggressive children.

One of my aunts introduced us to Ernst Papanek, director of the reform school in upper New York State that took seriously delinquent boys from New York City. With Papanek's permission, Bud and I spent one summer working with and studying delinquents at Wiltwyck. In a reform school without bars, milieu therapy sought to change children by altering their environments. Papanek believed that using punishments would teach the children to use force to gain what they wanted. As an alternative, he manipulated the environment so that the children could learn the consequences of what they did without being punished. They were taught to repair damage. Their classrooms were models of compassion, as the specially trained teachers learned to cope with high degrees of maladaptation.

The whole day for each child was a part of his therapy. Cooks, for example, helped by teaching the children how to make pastries. Each child at Wiltwyck had a small plot of ground on which to grow flowers or vegetables. The boys were also taught to fight with gloves rather than fists. Floyd Patterson, the heavyweight boxing champion, was a graduate and returned annually to coach the boys. In the evenings, counselors retired to their quarters to read and play ping pong. I acquired a lifetime passion for ping pong. Much more important: I learned not to use punishments (i.e., the intentional giving of pain to control behavior).

Harvard had summer scholarships in Education. I was able to "test out" of most of the education courses and use the scholarships to take courses in philosophy. Once Bud received his Ph.D., I quit teaching in Concord and obtained a research assistantship at Harvard, working for a group of social scientists at the cutting edge of their fields. Eleanor Maccoby and Harry Levin were studying child development, using interviews with mothers and doll play with the children. I "coded" the doll inter-actions, which involved marking on a sheet of paper what the child did with dolls that represented a boy, a girl, a mother, and a father. John and Beatrice Whiting were developing codes to check theories of child development against a broader diversity of customs than can be found in the United States. I coded reports on discipline for the Human Relations Area Files housed at Yale. Wesley Allensmith set up experiments to identify and then study children easily led by temptation. In one, children were told they could get prizes by hitting a hidden target with a beanbag. They were also told that it was against the rules to look behind the cloth to see the target. Through a one-way mirror we could identify which children nonetheless peeked, and the studies then explored how those children differed from others who obeyed the rules. Although I didn't work for him, Roger Brown was also at the Laboratory of Human Development. Brown was studying the influence of language on children's thought. Every noon, John Whiting stirred up a pot of soup in the kitchen, where faculty and students ate together. Whiting, director of the laboratory, had one clear rule: lunch conversation was to be about research. Students generally listened while the faculty talked. Listening to the discussion provided the most intense tutorial I have ever attended.

Most of the work for Sears, Maccoby, and Levin's *Patterns of Child Rearing* was done at the Laboratory of Human Development. They had used a questionnaire that involved detailed reporting by the mother about how parents treated their children and each other and how the children behaved. I still recall—and this was in 1955—the lunch in which Eleanor Maccoby described what they had learned about the relation between a mother's discipline and her child's misbehavior. I asked my first question: "How do you know that the mother's report is accurate?"

I had my doubts. Perhaps these came from having overheard my mother's frequent criticisms of me to her friends, criticisms that seemed to me unfair and inaccurate. Subsequent studies, by me and others, supported the skepticism.

My first son was born in December, 1956. The pleasures, for me, of parenthood are beyond description. Though I hated being pregnant, I loved caring for Geoffrey. A fellow teacher at Concord had a baby the year before, and because both of us were convinced that punishments were unnecessary, we discussed alternative ways to teach our infants how to act. My work at Wiltwyck, too, contributed to a commitment to rear my children without using punishment.

Years later, I wrote about the theoretical grounds for that commitment in two articles: "Unintended Consequences of Punishment," published in *Pediatrics Supplement*, 1996, and "Discipline and the Use of Sanctions," published in *Aggression and Violent Behavior*, 1997. I hope the detailed explanations to be found in these articles will help many parents create comfortable nonpunitive environments in which to rear their children.

In the summer of 1957, I was offered a small sum of money to evaluate effects of the Cambridge-Somerville Youth Study on crime. Richard Clark Cabot, who had been one of Sheldon Glueck's professors, designed a randomized control study to test the idea that providing assistance to families of young boys in distressed neighborhoods would reduce delinquency. Each boy was matched to another with similar backgrounds, family structures, and parental behaviors. They also were matched in terms of such characteristics as early aggressiveness, intelligence, and physical strength. One boy in each pair was placed in the treatment group while the other was simply left to his community. The treatment program included tutoring, counseling, coaching in social skills, medical help, and leisure activities. Because of the matching, aggressive and non-aggressive kids were in both the treatment and the control groups.

Evaluation of the program back in 1948 had failed to find the anticipated benefits, and Gordon Allport believed that was because the evaluation had been carried out too soon. We tracked the records of the randomly assigned treatment and control boys and coded their case records on a variety of measures. *Origins of Crime* (1959) reported the results, which again failed to find anticipated benefits from the treatment. We did not even consider the possibility that the treatment might have been harmful!

The case records for the Cambridge-Somerville Youth Study were written with exquisite detail. Cabot, who had been president of the National Conference on Social Work in 1931, wanted to improve the practice of recording information so that case records would be more useful for designing treatments. He hired recorders to transcribe information about contacts between social workers and their clients within hours of the encounters. The case records included information about conversations and other interactions among family members. Such encounters typically took place about twice a month for more than five years, filling several hundred pages of narrative reports. I wanted to use the case records as a source of information about socialization and especially as a way of exploring the impact of child-rearing techniques.

Bud and I successfully applied for funds to code the case records for evaluations against independent information found in records of alcoholism and of crime. The result was *Origins of Alcoholism* (1960). This was the first longitudinal study of alcoholics and, because we learned about characteristics that preceded alcoholism, it enabled us to test which of them might be causal. The work benefited hugely from my training with Eleanor Maccoby. She had taught me to define variables carefully and avoid building evaluations into the coding scheme. The earlier codes, those used in *Origins of Crime*, reflected the categories used by the Gluecks. After 1957, all work based on the Cambridge Somerville Youth Study case records used the redesigned coding scheme. Eleanor had also taught me to worry about reliability, so we tested reliability of ratings by having more than one person code a randomly selected group of case records and used only codes that attained a reasonable degree of reliability.

By Autumn of 1957, I was a full-fledged student in philosophy, with a Josiah Royce Fellowship at Harvard. Concerned to bolster my knowledge, I convinced the teaching assistant in Quantitative Logic to tutor me in exchange for my doing his grading. I was reading Descartes and Hobbes, Hume, and Locke while struggling with Hilbert and Ackermann. A.I. Meldon, J.L. Austin, and W.V.O. Quine were lecturing, and Wittgenstein's *Philosophical Investigations* excited us all. H.L.A. Hart gave a seminar to which all our professors came to argue. It was a wonderful time and place to be learning.

Around that time, my husband was offered a position as Assistant Dean of Humanities and Sciences at Stanford. He loved teaching at Harvard, but he was enticed by the opportunities at Stanford. Although I had been offered, and wanted to accept, a Teaching Assistantship with Roderick Firth in Ethics, we went to California, and I returned to empirical studies as a Research Associate at Stanford.

We rented, for 99 years, a plot of land on Stanford grounds. My cousin Ellen designed our new house, checking the blueprints with her architect father, and I supervised the building. Ellen later became a Senior Editor at *Architectural Forum* and wrote pioneer articles about the relationships between buildings and their occupants. The house was a perfect environment for us, with Bud's study off a private patio and away from noise, and mine within sight and hearing of the play area for our children. Shortly after we moved in, our second son, Robert, was born.

In 1961, we joined 80 Stanford students to spend almost a year in France. Stanford owned a building in Tours that included dormitories and classrooms. We had a small apartment, and I struggled to learn French, attempting to imitate the accents I heard from kids in the parks as I supervised my children playing. In the summer, we lived in a beautiful village, Croix-de-Vie, on the Atlantic coast. With only outdoor plumbing and two young children, living was complicated. But daily shopping brought me into contact with friendly merchants who were willing to listen to my dimly comprehensible French. Their willingness to converse helped me to understand a culture in which relaxation and discussion took precedence over earning money and being successful.

When we came back to California, I received a Stanford Wilson Fellowship to study philosophy. I returned to a field that continues to be the foundation for my thinking. Donald Davidson, Patrick Suppes, Jaegwon Kim, and Richard Jeffrey were the faculty from whom I learned a great deal. Davidson was working on problems linking reasons to actions and puzzling over issues in the philosophy of language. Suppes was in the process of converting set theory to methods for teaching arithmetic to young children, so that his course in logic included a clear exposition of Peano arithmetic as well as first order predicate logic and the axioms of set theory. Kim brought out the relevance of Plato and Aristotle to contemporary issues in philosophy. And Jeffrey conveyed the thrill of discovering Russell's Paradox at the foundation of mathematics, the Lobatchevski interpretation of one of the axioms in Euclidean geometry, and the role of transformations for understanding physics. The department had a "pro-seminar" in which first-year graduate students were required to produce a paper in order to exhibit what they knew. The faculty took the opportunity to show how little we knew by asking tough questions. Although the process was difficult, it helped teach us high standards.

I write about my education hoping it communicates the sense of adventure and the pleasures and challenges of learning. Some of this, it seems to me, is denied students when courses are too easy and are designed primarily to help students "feel good about themselves." But back to the autobiographical story.

I was combining being a student with raising my sons, though I had stopped doing research in sociology. I loved my studies and I was doing well. Soon, I began to think about having an independent career that would grow out of my love of philosophy. Yet shortly after the second semester began, Bud began drinking heavily and became abusive. Bud and I had written extensively about alcoholism, in part because both of his parents had been alcoholics. We had noted, in *Origins of Alcoholism*, that our work would be justified if it contributed to prevention of alcoholism. And both of us believed for a while that our work had indeed saved him. I hoped that Bud's attacks might end when he saw that my independence would not reduce my love for him. To this day, I do not know whether to consider alcoholism as a disease for which one should not be held responsible. I do know that Bud objected to me taking on an independent career. He convinced my family and some of our friends (who were his colleagues) to urge me to drop out of school. Not wanting to be in the middle of a domestic argument, the Stanford philosophy department withdrew its financial support for me. This was 1963. I sometimes wonder whether women today realize how different it is both to have support from other women and to have a legal system that allows for their independence. (I grew up at a time when women could be fired from teaching positions if they became pregnant, when airline hostesses could be fired if they got married, and when it was legal to tell women that they need not apply for a position because a company or university was interested only in hiring males.)

There is little worth writing about here except to say that sometimes divorce is the best option. Years later, I mentioned feeling guilty because

I had deprived my sons of living with their father. Both of them assured me that it had been the right decision. Interestingly, recent research has shown, contrary to popular opinion, that single-parent families are less likely to be damaging to children than are two-parent families in which the parents do not get along well.

Yet the period immediately following the divorce was difficult for me. Needing to support myself and two sons, I could not continue my studies. After a lean year of renting out a spare room in our house, tutoring kids, coaching tennis, and part-time consulting to put food on the table, I obtained a generous fellowship from the National Institute of Mental Health to finish graduate work. The fellowship gave me three years. My original plan had been to continue with philosophy. But I had a good publishing record in the social sciences, having co-authored four books and published 18 articles (some of which had been republished and had therefore reached a wide audience). Several professors counseled that it would be easier for me to find a position in the social sciences, so I decided to take courses in sociology. My sons often accompanied me to class, drawing quietly in the back of the room. I had jumped from being a Research Associate to becoming a student, from being a faculty wife to being a single mother. The shifts made dramatic differences in the way people interacted with me. Prompted by this sad experience, for my thesis, I ran an experiment to study the impact of status.

The experiment had me seen as acting in one of two roles simultaneously. So they would not see one another, a screen separated the two subjects in the experiment at the same time. One believed I was a Professor (with "Professor McCord" on the door); the secretary I hired used the title three times as she spoke about me while leading the subject to the experimental room. The other believed I was a student, with "practice room" on the door and the secretary referring to "Joan, one of the students here" and using just "Joan" to refer to me. I described the study to both at once, so whatever differences were uncovered could not be attributed to differences in my behavior. (In my mid-thirties, I could pass for either a professor or a student.) The subjects were of the same sex and had been randomly assigned to each status. I knew neither the order of entry nor which had been led to believe I was a professor and which believed I was a student.

I was testing a central tenet of sociologists at Stanford: the belief that status mattered a great deal to everyone. I designed a measure of influence that allowed me to use only the subtle pressure of expressing my preference. The task was to select the best sentence from among sets in which one used an adjective, one an adverb before the verb, and one an adverb after the verb. Pretests had shown that without influence, students were equally likely to pick each of the sentence forms in a set. In the experiment, I expressed a preference to both high- and low-status subjects simultaneously. That preference was rotated so that each type of sentence was chosen, though for different pairs. Other people had shown that women were more easily influenced than were men, so I evaluated the task to be sure there was room for influence, that is, that there would not be a ceiling effect. My study demonstrated that status descriptions—in the absence of any behavioral differences—made a difference in terms of influence for males. Yet, contrary to the universality assumption about status, status mattered little in terms of influence to the females. I received a Ph.D. in sociology in 1968.

June 1968 was before there were any legal barriers to discriminating against women, so it was particularly difficult for me to find employment. I wanted to move East, where theater and classical music beckoned, but my few offers came from western schools. Luckily, I had a friend from Harvard days teaching at Drexel University in Philadelphia. He remembered that I loved philosophy and thought that at Drexel I could teach philosophy as well as sociology. After a successful interview, the boys, two dogs, two cats, and I moved to a house just outside of Philadelphia. For a few years, I taught four courses per quarter and barely kept my head above water. Even so, my schedule was flexible enough to allow me to cheer my sons through baseball and soccer seasons. I married my second husband, Carl Silver, in 1970. A specialist in human factors, he delighted in classical music, opera, and fine food. He had courted all three of us, wisely, for my sons and I were good friends and I listened to their counsel.

My earlier work on the causes of alcoholism and crime had been carried out with a sample then in their early thirties. I knew that alcoholism may not develop until later in life and also wanted to use the same sample to learn more about criminal careers. But longitudinal research, research that requires tracing individuals, was expensive and decidedly not in style. It was difficult to convince agencies that the expenses involved would produce enough benefits to make them worthwhile. Since 1970, partly as a consequence of my work, several federal agencies as well as many researchers have come to recognize that if we are to understand behavior, we must come to understand how it develops. That involves learning the sequence of events, which in turn, requires longitudinal studies. Although some knowledge of sequencing can be gained retrospectively, studies of memory have shown the hazards in assuming one should believe what people claim to remember.

After several attempts to get financial support for the study, the National Institute of Mental Health again came to my rescue; this time, with a three-year grant to retrace the former clients of the Cambridge-Somerville Youth Study. As a result of the design, the Cambridge Somerville Youth Study offered an opportunity for a strong test of the possibility that providing families with multiple forms of assistance would be beneficial to their sons. Feedback from the participants indicated that they remembered the program and most believed it to have been helpful. I collected evidence from the courts, mental health facilities, alcoholism treatment centers, and death records.

Drexel, largely an engineering school, was not accustomed to social science research. There were no graduate students in sociology or any of the social sciences. Nevertheless, I managed to pull together a team of enthusiastic and capable researchers, and Drexel personnel included some exceedingly competent support staff. Michael Wadsworth, Jack Block, Jerry Bachman, and Glen Elder, among others, came to my advisory conferences, so I had colleagues with whom to discuss the project. The idea of having such annual conferences came from my Program Officer at NIMH, Tom Lalley, who realized that research thrives on discussions and was kind enough to provide funds to make such discussions possible for me.

My team managed to find 98 percent of the former members of the Cambridge-Somerville Youth Study despite there having been no contact for 30 years. That took some fine detective work by a staff of amateur sleuths. Moreover, we managed to get approximately 75 percent of the men, who were in their late forties and early fifties, to respond either to questionnaires or to interviews. Richard Parente did the interviewing. He traveled throughout the country, tirelessly adjusting his schedule to accommodate others, but unwilling to accept a refusal. Rich was able to put people at ease, and convince almost everyone to let him talk with them. To assure equivalence of treatment, Rich was not informed about which of the men had been in the treatment group and which had been in the control group.

The men who had been in the treatment program were compared with others reared in similar families up to the age when treatment began. Had there been no treatment program, they could be expected to have similar lives. As it turned out, those in treatment died an average of five years younger, were more likely to be recidivist criminals, and more likely to have become alcoholics, manic-depressives, or schizophrenics. The treatment had been harmful! Results of this provocative study have been well scrutinized. They have been published in *American Psychologist* and by the National Academy of Sciences. The most recent report appears in "The Cambridge-Somerville Study: A Pioneering Longitudinal Experimental Study of Delinquency Prevention," published in *Preventing Antisocial Behavior: Interventions from Birth through Adolescence* (1992).

Because the evidence cast doubt on so many social assistance programs, it was initially difficult to get the results published. Yet subsequently, many other researchers have reported similarly negative results from treatment programs that give the appearance of being beneficial. This line of research brought me invitations to speak in Canada, France, England, Sweden, and Switzerland. Recently, Tom Dishion and I pulled together evidence on effects of intervention programs to argue that the problem is related to mutual support among misbehaving young adolescents. The resulting article appeared in the September 1999 issue of *American Psychologist*.

A second major thrust of my research focused on the powerful impact of parental socialization. The studies showed that family interactions, rather than the presence or absence of parental figures, accounted for major differences between criminals and noncriminals (McCord, 1982). Parental conflict and aggressiveness (e.g., using harsh punishments or throwing things when angry) appeared to produce the more serious types of violent crimes (McCord, 1991a). Because the records included information about the parents, I was also able to show that some of the continuity of crime across generations was due to the tendency of criminal fathers to behave in criminogenic ways (McCord, 1991b).

In 1987, I accepted an offer to move from Drexel to Temple University. Shortly after, I became President of the American Society of Criminology—the first woman to have the honor. The presidency was particularly pleasing because my son, Geoff (who is a philosophy Professor at the University of North Carolina, Chapel Hill) came to Reno to introduce my Presidential Address (McCord, 1990). It has also been my good fortune to win recognition for my research, the Prix Emile Durkheim in 1993 from the International Society of Criminology and the Sutherland Award in 1994 from the American Society of Criminology.

Many of my newest projects focus on theory (McCord, 1997) or on methodology (McCord, 2000). Yet just about every topic related to criminology intrigues me. In recent years, thanks to Mark Haller, a colleague who is a historian, I have been reading social history and discovering the degree to which that history enlightens current issues in criminal justice. Effects of that reading appear in "Placing American Urban Violence in Context." (McCord, 1997).

For many years, my interests in criminology have been nourished through reviewing activities. Felice Levine (now Executive Secretary of the American Sociological Association) ran stimulating semiannual seminars to review applications sent to the National Science Foundation's Program in Law and Social Sciences on which I served from 1987 to 1991. I've also regularly been a reviewer for the Office of Juvenile Justice and Delinquency Prevention, the National Institute of Justice, the Center for Disease Control, the Department of Education, and several foreign granting agencies (as well as numerous journals and book publishers). Rarely, in my experience, are there sharp differences in evaluations at the top and bottom of the application piles. The interesting discussions occur in the middle ranges, as reviewing panels try to estimate the contributions an unseasoned applicant might make or the centrality of an issue being addressed by a well-qualified applicant. Rarely, too, have any of the reviewing panels expressed preferences that were not scientifically supported.

At Drexel, most of my students were the first in their families to go to college. The students spent half the year in jobs, through a "Co-op" program. It was a challenge to help them see the value of learning from books. In teaching sociology, I selected books that I found interesting, and then designed activities that they could use to help them see the relevance to everyday life of what they read. One of the more fruitful assignments was tied to Goffman's *Stigma*. Students were asked to talk with a stranger for 10 minutes, then introduce a stigma about themselves and try to continue the same topic of conversation. The students were wonderfully imaginative. One was fixing his car with a stranger watching, commenting, and praising his work. After 10 minutes, the student mentioned that he had learned to be a mechanic "at Holmesburg" (a local reform school). The stranger slammed down the hood of his car and almost broke my student's hand. Another applied for a job and was clearly about to be hired when she handed in the health portion of her application: She had listed "epilepsy in remission." She was pushed out the door amidst much yelling and anger. Another was talking with a stranger while waiting for the train. Her friend stopped by, by design, and said how glad she was to see my student well and out of Byberry (the local mental hospital). Although the stranger had offered to show my student around New York City, she left as soon as she heard the word "Byberry." Another, while changing a tire on the highway, confessed that he was just out of reform school and looking for a job. He was given advice by, as it turned out, a parole officer (a member of the "wise" as Goffman described them) who counseled him not to mention his incarceration when applying for the job. It pleased me particularly to win the University's Lindback Award for Distinguished Teaching.

At Temple, I periodically teach in the Intellectual Heritage program, where first- and second-year students are introduced to classic texts. In addition, I have had the pleasure of teaching graduate students as well as undergraduates. I have particularly enjoyed the handful of graduate students who, as my students, have shared with me the adventures of discovery.

One of the benefits of an academic life is the opportunity to travel. Editing for the Harry Frank Guggenheim Foundation took me to a small town in the mountains north of Rome. A project on the impact of developing democracies took me to Budapest and Prague. My research on psychopathy brought me to Valencia. My work on alcoholism resulted in trips to Tel Aviv and to Moscow just before the Soviet Union collapsed. As Vice President of the International Society of Criminology, I regularly visit Paris for meetings of the Board, and joined those who went to Rio de Janeiro to provide one of the courses sponsored by the ISC. My focus on longitudinal methodology has, over the years, resulted in invitations to Bristol and Cambridge (UK), Voss, Stockholm, Warsaw, Poland; Vienna, Taipei, Groningen, Freudenstadt, and Rhodes. There have been other trips as well, but these stand out. Carl liked to travel and often joined me after my work was finished. Together, we ventured into Egypt and Turkey, Korea and Japan, and drove throughout France and Ireland. Even after Carl was wheelchair bound, we went to Bayreuth, Germany, for the Wagner festival. Carl died in 1998. My son Rob (now President and CEO of the Eastern Technology Council and a venture capitalist) accompanied me for a week in China, where I was giving a couple of talks before going on to Canberra, Australia. In Canberra, I was assigned an office down the hall from the philosophy department, where son Geoff was on a research fellowship.

Writing about my life has forced me to recall events I had not thought about for years. Of course I have regrets, but on major choices, I lucked out. As a career skeptic, I am reluctant to give advice. Yet because the editors of this book requested each author to include advice for the readers, let me draw to a close by complying with that request.

I would urge women to obtain credentials so they can find interesting things to do, activities that will not be heavily dependent on events over which they will have little control. I would not trade being a mother for any opportunity at all, though I recognize that a taste for being a parent is far from universal. I would suggest to anyone considering academe, male or female, that it is better to work on projects you believe to be important than to select with an eye to winning praise or prizes. And I would encourage friends at any time to find fields of inquiry that intrigue them so that they can always experience the satisfactions of learning.

## Recommended Readings

The list is highly idiosyncratic, but I've identified four (maybe five, depending on how they are counted) that ought not be overlooked.

Plato. *Euthyphro* and *Meno* (various editions are available.)

Shaw, C.R. & McKay, H.D. *Juvenile Delinquency and Urban Areas*. The University of Chicago Press, 1942, revised edition, 1969.

Douglass, Frederick. *Narrative of the Life of An American Slave Written by Himself.* (various editions are available.)

Jackson, K.T. *Crabgrass Frontier: The Suburbanization of the United States*. Oxford: Oxford University Press, 1985.

## A Dozen of My Best

McCord, J. (2000). "Developmental Trajectories and Intentional Actions." *Journal of Quantitative Criminology*, 16(2):237-253.

McCord, J. (1997). "Placing American Urban Violence in Context." In J. McCord (ed.) *Violence and Childhood in the Inner City*, pp. 78-115. New York, NY: Cambridge Press, 1997.

McCord, J. (1997). "He Did It Because He Wanted To . . ." In W. Osgood (ed.) *Motivation and Delinquency, Vol. 44 in Nebraska Symposium on Motivation, Vol. 44*, pp. 1-43. Lincoln, NE: University of Nebraska Press.

McCord, J. (1997). "Discipline and the Use of Sanctions." *Aggression and Violent Behavior*, 2, 4:313-319.

McCord, J. (1996). "Unintended Consequences of Punishment." *Pediatrics Supplement*, 98(4):832-834.

McCord, J. (1995). "Crime in the Shadow of History." In J. Hagan (ed.) *Current Perspectives on Aging and the Life Cycle: Delinquency and Disrepute in the Life Course*, pp. 105-118. Greenwich, CT: JAI Press.

McCord, J. (1992). "The Cambridge-Somerville Study: A Pioneering Longitudinal Experimental Study of Delinquency Prevention." In J. McCord & R.E. Tremblay (eds.) *Preventing Antisocial Behavior: Interventions from Birth through Adolescence*, pp. 196-206. New York, NY: Guilford Press, 1992.

McCord, J. (1991a). "Family Relationships, Juvenile Delinquency, and Adult Criminality." *Criminology*, 29, 3:397-417, 1991a. Republished in F.R. Scarpitti & A.L. Nielsen (eds.), *Crime and Criminals: Contemporary and Classic Readings in Criminology*. Los Angeles, CA: Roxbury Publishing.

McCord, J. (1991b). "The Cycle of Crime and Socialization Practices." *Journal of Criminal Law and Criminology*, 82, 1(Spring):211-228.

McCord, J. (1990). "Crime in Moral and Social Contexts." *Criminology*, 28, 1, 1-26. Republished in J. McCord & J. H. Laub (eds.) *Contemporary Masters of Criminology*, pp. 251-276. New York, NY: Plenum Press.

McCord, J. (1989). "Theory, Pseudotheory, and Metatheory." In W.S. Laufer & F. Adler (eds.) *Advances in Criminological Theory*, Vol. 1, pp. 127-145. New Brunswick, NJ: Transaction.

McCord, J. (1982). "A Longitudinal View of the Relationship Between Paternal Absence and Crime." In J. Gunn & D.P. Farrington (eds.) *Abnormal Offenders, Delinquency and the Criminal Justice System*, pp. 113-128. Chichester, England: Wiley.

# 6

# Looking for Meaning in All the Right Places: The Search for Academic Satisfaction

Gary T. Marx

*Life is far too important a thing to ever talk seriously about*
Oscar Wilde

In their invitational letter editors Gil Geis and Mary Dodge suggested that authors for this volume might begin with "the most important piece of advice that I could offer anybody entering the field." If advice-giving is the curse of the elderly class, then I am cursed. I will summarize and expand on some of the major points from previous advice-giving and personal essays (Marx 1984a; 1990; 1992; 1997; 2000) [1] and reflect on some experiences over the last decade.

A detailed career statement up to 1988 can be found in Marx (1990). I was raised in Los Angeles, although I grew up in Berkeley. I attended UCLA as an undergraduate and took a course from Donald Cressey who had been a student of Edwin Sutherland, a central figure in the founding of American criminology. As a moderately rebellious, or at least independent, youth coming into adulthood on the cusp of the 1960s, I was experientially interested in deviance and social control.[2] An adolescent fascination with rebels, whether deviant (as in the films *The Wild One* and *Rebel Without a Cause*) or political, came with ambivalence toward authority and a readiness to ask, "says who?"

My intellectual interest in the field and the related areas of criminology and law and society was sparked by a spectacular course from Erving Goffman my first year in graduate school at Berkeley. I had the good fortune to work with a number of leading scholars. My orals committee was made up of Goffman, Herbert Blumer, S.M. Lipset, Neil Smelser and Joseph Lohman (former Sheriff of Cook County and Dean of the School of Criminology). I clearly recall walking out of that two-hour-plus exam and waiting outside what seemed to be an eternity, while the committee discussed my case. Why was it taking them so long? Were they discussing whether or not to fail me? In fact they were discussing whether or not to pass me with distinction. That honor was an early warning of the unexpected degree of success that was to come my way in the next decade, much of it within the first few years out of graduate school.

Recognition came early and in abundance.[3] Those initial years were a lived fantasy. Because most of the time dreams don't come true, we don't have to confront the question of what happens if they do. Yet that level of success didn't last. I had several years left on my contract at Harvard, but the future there did not look promising. In 1973 I left for a tenured position at M.I.T. For the first time the successes I had come to take for granted weren't there—some grant applications and articles were rejected and the steady flow of invitations and requests that tell us how we are doing slowed markedly. In addition, subsequent successes were less satisfying. This caused me to reflect on the experience and to search for meaning in an academic career.

After a few beers, many productive academics, no matter how successful, will admit that they don't feel sufficiently appreciated and rewarded and that their work has not received the attention it merits (although it is considered gauche to publicly discuss this). That comes with the lectern and is tied to American society's status consciousness and the lack of respect for intellectuals relative to Europe. Perhaps it is found with any competitive endeavor where the standards are not self-evident (e.g., winning a 100-yard dash compared to deciding which book is best for an award).

While it would be disingenuous to deny occasionally feeling that way when a rejection comes along, I feel exceptionally fortunate with respect to professional recognition.[4] The issue for me wasn't not getting enough, but what did academic success and failure mean? What did it all add up to? What was important? What were my goals? What was there in an academic life that gave satisfaction beyond the competitive aspects and that could sustain one in the face of bottom-line bureaucratic challenges and those not sharing academic values?

From this experience of early success and perceived failure, in a 1990 article I drew seven conclusions about success and noted three ways of staying engaged. I came to terms with both winning and losing and was better able, as Kipling advised, to "meet with Triumph and Disaster and treat these two imposters just the same." I developed a perspective that made both failure and success easier to understand and accept. A part of this perspective is awareness of a Woody Allen paradox wherein when we do not have what we want, we are unhappy, but should we get it, it turns out not to be enough.

## Seven Characteristics of Success

*After all how long can one person stay in the spotlight
before the bulb is changed?*

Boxer Jack Dempsey

While it's nice to be cited and invited, success is not all it is cracked
up to be:

1.  It does not last. As Robert Frost observes, "Nothing gold
    can stay."[5] Mark Twain said, "One can live for two months
    on a good compliment." Depending on one's psyche two
    hours or two weeks might also apply. But as a character in
    a Neil Simon play observes, "Nothing recedes like suc-
    cess." With appalling regularity, there is always a later edi-
    tion of a journal or newspaper telling someone else's
    story. Books go out of print and journal articles cease to
    be read. The pages rapidly yellow and are forgotten. The
    1950s song *Make Someone Happy* put it well, "Fame if you
    win it, comes and goes in a minute." People ask what you
    are doing now. Colleagues who know what you have
    done retire, and they are replaced by younger persons
    unaware of your contributions. To make matters worse,
    unlike the natural sciences, sociology and criminology
    are not very cumulative.

2.  You can never be successful enough (at least in your own
    eyes). No matter how good you are, there is always some-
    one better. Whatever you did, you could always have done
    it better and done more, or done it earlier. You never were
    as important or well-known as you thought you were.
    Even the truly famous are not exempt. What is worse, you
    never really get there. As Durkheim observed, in a rapidly
    transforming society you can never achieve enough success.
    When what is at stake is something as open-ended as rep-
    utation, productivity, impact, or accumulation, there is
    no clear limit. With each higher level of achievement the
    definition of success changes such that it is forever out of
    reach. By contrast, failure more often seems limited and
    finite: you know when you have hit the wall.

3.  The more success you have, the harder it becomes to
    reach the next level of achievement. As one moves from
    getting accepted to graduate school, to getting a Ph.D., to
    getting a teaching job, to getting tenure and national
    awards and distinction, the competition gets stiffer, the
    number of slots declines, and the price of success increas-
    es. With each level of achievement the field is narrowed.
    Once a certain level is reached, there is little variation

among participants. Everyone is qualified and hardworking, and there are fewer rewards.

4.  There is a diminishing-returns effect. The satisfaction from external rewards is not as great the second or third time around, whether it be delivering or publishing a paper, writing a book, or getting a grant. Part of the reason may be just the diminution of passion that comes with aging. But repetition does not have the same kick. The sense of curiosity and expectation that accompanies the initial pursuit of rewards weakens once they have been achieved. A meaningful life cannot be constructed out of repetitively doing things to please an impersonal public.

5.  Success may have costly and unintended side effects (apart from the price initially paid to achieve it). There are the obvious dangers of hubris and taking yourself too seriously and the bottomless-pit (or perhaps ceilingless-roof) quality of success. Less obvious is the paradox that success brings less time to do the very thing for which you are now being recognized. In an academic setting increased achievement is associated with increased responsibility. Being well-known brings good-citizenship requests to review articles and books, write letters of recommendation, and serve on committees. Although such invitations are symbolic of success and can be directly or indirectly marshaled to obtain still more success, they can seriously undermine productivity. A virtue of obscurity is greater control over your time and greater privacy. Mark Twain got it right again, "Obscurity and a competence—that is the life that is best worth living."[6]

6.  The correlation between ability, or merit, and success is far from perfect. This is, of course, a central sociological message. Factors beyond merit that may bear on the distribution of rewards include the makeup of the selection committee, what it had done the previous year, timing, the characteristics of the applicant pool, and intellectual, ideological, or personal biases. Even when the selection process is fair, rejections are often more a comment on the scarcity of rewards than on the incompetence of applicants. The major factors here are surely organizational. But the structure and ambiguity of reward situations also make it possible to mask the role sometimes played by corruption. With age and experience you come to feel comfortable judging, and even sometimes doubting the judges. There are enough questionable cases involving tenure and promotion, the awarding of grants, and the acceptance

of materials for publication to make clear the role of non-achievement criteria in social reward. Cynical awareness of this state of affairs need not make you throw in the towel or become corrupt, but it may mean slowing down, putting less emphasis on outcomes, and becoming more philosophical about failure and success. This awareness can take some of the sting out of defeat. It also ought to take some of the pride out of victory.

7.  There is no reason to expect that what you do next will be better, by your own standards, than what you have done in the past or will necessarily bring equivalent or greater recognition and reward. In graduate school and the early professional years this may not be true. You start with little, so each achievement is a milestone and more rewarding than the last. Yet this training effect is short-lived. Career satisfaction in academia and the quality and quantity of productivity are not linear, in spite of the rhetoric of cultural optimism and metaphors of growth. Academics are not like professional athletes, many of whom gradually peak over a period of three to six years and then fall off. For the minority of Ph.D.'s who continue to do research after receiving their degrees, the average pattern for both the quality of their work and the recognition it receives is probably jagged. There may be periods of intense creativity and productivity, followed by periods of reading, pursuing unrelated interests, or laying the ground for the next period of activity. Periods of lying fallow are nothing to worry about (at least if you have tenure). As in agriculture, they may even be functional.

If competitive success couldn't be counted on—either because you failed or because achieving success ceased to be very satisfying, what was left? The mix will vary depending on your situation. In the article on success and failure I discuss three broad practical lessons: (1)value the process of creating as an end itself; (2) develop new professional goals; (3) do not make your career your life. Here I want to expand a bit on sources of work satisfaction involving writing and teaching and the hope that through these one can impact the culture, however modestly.

It is necessary to value the process of creating. Work has to be fun and interesting in its own right, apart from any external rewards. Once you have tenure, if you do not enjoy the research or writing, then it is not worth doing. I receive pleasure from finding partial answers to questions I wonder about and discovering new questions, turning a clever phrase, ordering a set of ideas, and seeing connections between apparently unrelated phenomena.

I work best when I am cranked up and energized and that happens when I feel something strongly and want to figure it out, document it and communicate about it. In my discussion (Marx, 1997) of the mandate to write (#3 Table 1) I consider this in more detail. Writing can be cathartic and help me answer the often-related personal, political and scholarly questions. I am in control of it, and when I write about what I care about it is effortless and deeply fulfilling. As songwriter Gordon Lightfoot has observed, at such times there is no special trick to it, "it's a kind of energy that will not be suppressed." You do it because you have to do it. For example, the level of police abuse I saw when working for the National Advisory Commission on Civil Disorders and the infiltration of a civil rights group I was active in at Berkeley generated indignation and a series of articles and eventually a book on undercover police and the role of social control agents in creating disorder, whether intentionally or unintentionally. My surprise and disagreement with the ejection of whites from segments of the civil rights movement led to an article that sought comprehension that transcended the particular personalities involved by looking at equivalent structures in historical context through comparing tensions between majority and minority group activists during the abolitionist period and the movement to end untouchability in India (Marx & Useem, 1971). I loved research, but contrary to Bob Dylan's song lyrics, the times didn't really change, or at least they didn't change enough from the optimism of the 1960s to the 1970s which saw consolidation and even retrenchment, and contrary to the high promise of social research, most of the changes we did see were not directly tied to our research. In an edited book on muckraking sociology (Marx, 1972) I sought ways that one could both do research and hopefully contribute to social change, not in a social engineering sense, but through effecting the culture with respect to what the facts were and how issues were perceived and analyzed. Concerned both scientifically and politically about the frequent gap between official versions of reality and what may really be going on, I wrote about means for discovering "dirty data" (Marx, 1984).

I don't draw a strong line between writing and teaching. In teaching I try to offer the ideas I am writing about—with the added benefit of getting feedback. Perhaps the most satisfying or enduring aspect of an academic career is the teaching and the friendships that can be formed. Inert words on a page can't offer the excitement of a thoughtful conversation or seeing students improve on work you tackle together, publish their first book, or co-author a paper with one of *their* students. The informal mentoring, the sense of a shared journey of intellectual discovery and being able to pass on knowledge, methods and values is deeply fulfilling. I am amazed to see what my students have accomplished and I have stayed in touch with only a fraction of them. Beyond the majority doing good works in higher education and as popular writers, others are heads of non-profits concerned with police, drug, and probation reform, have founded social movements and held high positions in government. There is something of a sacred family bond between us because of our shared understandings and commitments. I take great pride in their activities and having been their teacher. I feel satisfied with respect to the several thousand or more students who I have had only passing contact with in one course, because I had the chance to educate them about things that matter and to communicate the art of question asking. In the softer social fields, our contribution to students is as much or more about identifying the questions as about the substance of answers.

Editorial work (whether on student papers, reading for journals and publishers, or editing books) has also been very satisfying. This offers a way of keeping up with the literature and of helping to shape fields. I was inspired to become a sociologist partly because of a powerful course on race relations taught by Mel Seeman at UCLA. We used the text by George Simpson and Milton Yinger's *Racial and Cultural Minorities*. The intelligence, richness of information, clarity, balance, humanism, and good sense of that text was inspirational. Given the ways of business publishing and changing academic fashions, the publisher (after several revisions) refused to bring out a new edition. Being able to keep that book alive for yet another generation of students as part of a book series I was editing gave enormous satisfaction.

After you have established a firm sense of your research questions and the intellectual traditions that nourish you, it becomes possible to locate one's self within, and to view one's work as part of, a communal endeavor (including your own students but going far beyond—you will never know most of those in the "community"). This invisible community of scholars can serve as an anchor relative to the past and the future. I take great sustenance and satisfaction in identifying with and seeing the direct lines from Simmel to Park to Hughes and Blumer to Goffman, and in my imaginary conversations with them, knowing that they wrestled with similar issues and that I can build upon their foundations. In that sense, however lonely and internal intellectual work can be, we are not alone. The challenge is to find the appropriate scholarly traditions.

On a hill behind our house we planted a two-foot redwood tree that had been carefully nourished years before from a small container. The tree grows a few inches a year. In several hundred years it will be a majestic redwood. I get great pleasure from imagining that and seeing the daily contribution to it made by rays of sunshine and droplets of water. On a more modest scale it can be the same with academic work across decades and centuries. One need not sit under the shade of the tree he or she plants. It is enough to be blessed to sit under the shade of trees planted long ago and to know those whose lives we touch through writing and teaching, who subsequently touch other lives in an endless idea-chain, may someday sit in the shade of a tree we helped to grow. When scholarship or artistic creation are seen as part of an organic, collective endeavor that endures and transcends the individual, then the daily frustrations or the absence of reward are less bothersome.

## Beyond Success and Failure

In our culture, stories need endings. I don't know the ending to this one, and I may never know it. But I do know how the story evolved over the next decade. The article on success and failure partly summarized above reflected maturity and coming to terms with academic life. It ends on an optimistic note, as I found the appropriate balance between work and life. That balance and career satisfaction deepened over the next decade with more success and greater wisdom and perspective, if at a cost of contradicting the seventh characteristic of success noted above.

In 1988 at the age of 50 with the publication of *Undercover: Police Surveillance in America* my career took off again. The further validation from the external world that *Undercover* and related publications brought—more than 40 favorable book reviews,[7] more awards, fellowships, reprints, translations, testimony and board-serving; publishing widely discussed op-ed articles on surveillance and communications issues in the major newspapers; having one's concepts and ideas enter the culture[8]; numerous radio and television interviews and participation in documentaries;[9] teaching in Belgium, Austria, and China and lecturing throughout Europe; having a double issue of the *Journal of Crime, Law and Social Change* (Block, 1992) devoted to discussing and extending the issues the book raised and with NSF support, organizing an international working group to apply to other countries the model I applied to the United States (Fijnaut & Marx, 1995) was highly gratifying.

With this success I felt a new level of contentment and inner peace. I had become my own person and the person I wanted to be. I learned from Erving Goffman the power of enough role distance for self-respect and to gain an independent perspective, but not so much as to make others uncomfortable or to appear arrogant, and I learned from Max Weber the eternal struggle between the liberating and suffocating aspects of culture and social structure.

From diverse role models I took elements I most admired (intense dedication to scholarship and hard work,[10] engagement with the great social issues of the day, clear writing for multiple audiences with both theoretical and applied concerns, interdisciplinary and comparative perspectives, persistence, independence, risk-taking and a certain cultivated marginality, reflexivity and self-criticism, and honesty, helpfulness and civility with students and colleagues[11]). I avoided those elements I least admired (a one-dimensional life in which work overwhelmed everything else, one-trick theory or method ponies, arcane arguments and misplaced certainty, inappropriate uses of power). I established a recognizable and effective writing and research style and a set of questions around social control and technology that felt right and nourished my soul. I was drawn to issues out of passion,[12] but once there I sought to apply the most rigorous standards of scholarship and writing, often with a mercurial eye to complexity, interdependence, tradeoffs, irony, and paradox.

I hope the perspective on the academic life offered above (and below with my list of 37 moral mandates for aspiring professors in Table 1) provide some guidance to those beginning or re-assessing their careers. There rarely are easy answers and life can't be lived by how-to books. It has to be continually invented and negotiated. That makes it exciting and it encourages you to be clear about your assumptions and the often conflicting values that guide your choices.

Those who work on criminal justice issues of their own choosing from a broad, interdisciplinary, and often critical perspective, generally have a more difficult time than their colleagues whose feet are squarely planted in a single discipline and who quantitatively pursue micro-level questions defined by funding agencies and criminal justice establishments. The success of *Undercover* left me with a number of professional questions which have no fixed resolution, given variation in contexts and value conflicts. However the heightened awareness of the tension between polarities can be positive.

The 12 professional issues noted below are discussed at greater length in Marx (1995).

1.  Is it appropriate for social scientists whose legitimacy and traditions involve ordering micro-empirical measurements with systematic theory to study broad amorphous topics, such as privacy, deception, authenticity, liberty, autonomy, and justice in an interpretive fashion? Wouldn't it be better to start with just one question, replicate prior research, or test a few propositions using rigorous methods and quantitative data? Is it better to know things of lesser importance with greater certainty or to know things of greater importance with lesser certainty? It is paradoxical that a part of our knowledge is awareness of our ignorance, or least of the limits of our knowledge. For many questions we lack firm scientific evidence. This is not only because the research has not been done, but because of the intractability of many problems given history, culture, and consciousness and the weaknesses of our methodologies including limits on human experimentation. Most passionately contested social issues involve con-

flicts over values that can be informed but not adequately resolved by evidence, even if the evidence were unequivocal. When there is a sense of crisis, strident advocates claiming empirical certainty often dominate the megaphone over those whose expertise points toward qualification and moderation.

2.  Even if one opts to focus on a broad topic, should it be approached from a multi- and interdisciplinary perspective, or from a narrower disciplinary base? Given the exploratory nature of my inquiry I sought whatever tools were available. But then as a non-specialist one must confront the issues of poaching. I have chapters in areas in which my formal training goes no further than the sophomore introductory class (e.g., in history and in ethics) and I rely on secondary sources. Can/should we trespass with impunity/immunity in other professional vineyards if we like the look of their grapes? In trying to be all things to all people does one risk being nothing to anyone? Does a book need a disciplinary identity and single point of view? Does breadth have to come at a cost of depth?

3.  What does it mean to "understand" undercover police practices or any criminological topic? What were the goals of my sociological inquiry? What does it mean to be interested in reasons as well as causes, in subjective experiences understood empathetically, as well as in more easily quantifiable objective factors? How can surveys and experiments be supplemented in the search for broad understanding? How can we make use of the truths of novelists and philosophers? What role does wisdom play in the results of sociological research? How does prediction relate to understanding? How does understanding relate to judgment? What is the difference between a social scientist, a journalist, an essayist, and a novelist? What needs to be added to Robert Park's observation that sociology is slow journalism?

4.  Is it possible to balance social science and social criticism so that they are mutually supportive rather than corrosive? We need precision and passion. I don't want my concerns with civil liberties, inequality, and reform to distort my scientific observations—for both intellectual and practical reasons. Scientific understanding should not be sacrificed on the altar of commitment. Yet in this socially important area, I am more than the neutral scientist who just wants the facts (Marx, 1972).

5.  Can the same work make contributions to both social science and public policy? Must one choose between being an uncontaminated basic scientist seeking fundamental knowledge with little notion of how, when, where, or if it will be used; a hired gun seeking normatively based solutions to an applied problem someone else has defined; or a zealous, self-appointed social engineer-moral entrepreneur, peddling your own brand of expert truth and action?

    How does and should knowledge relate to action? Do you have to know why in order to know how? Can academics, with their cross-case knowledge and tenure, who act as Monday morning quarterbacks with no responsibility for the consequences of the actions that practitioners must take, really have much to say that is useful?

6.  Is it possible to write so that one's work is well received by both colleagues and the educated public? In trying to reach for (or at least not exclude) a general audience, one runs the risk of dilution and being labeled a popularizer or even a journalist. Books that are accessible are often suspect in the halls of academe. Yet the trappings of academic respectability—literature reviews, sophisticated techniques, jargon, the assumption of a learned audience, and detached and spiritless writing—are hardly endearing to the average reader.

7.  Was I taken in? Because one of my fundamental assumptions is that things are often not what they seem, in studying persons who are professional liars how far should I go in discounting what they say?[13] Was I conned by some of those I interviewed?

8.  Between starting and finishing the book, my beliefs about the desirability of undercover tactics changed. Rather than seeing them as an unnecessary evil, I came to view their use in the United States under limited and controlled circumstances as a necessary evil. I gained excellent access to the FBI (something I would not have predicted from my days of Berkeley student activism). Does the change in my attitude say something about my openness and intellectual honesty in the face of a very complex situation, or was I co-opted? Is the change partly a strategic ploy, because I want to effect the policy debate and know that a hostile polemic would likely preclude this? How can one balance and maintain a degree of respect/appreciation for our subjects and the sincerity of their beliefs, reciprocity (at least insofar as one doesn't harm them because they are giving something to us with

little in return), with the need to be objective, to be faithful to our moral concerns, and not to be captured by our subjects?

9.   How do you know when you are done? When do you let go? I stopped largely because of the sponsor's expectations, but easily could have spent several more years working on comparative international materials and on literary and film treatments (topics I was later able to write about). I was not quite ready to let go. But I know if I had worked on the book for several more years new topics would have appeared justifying further work, in an endless spiral. In finishing a book on a contemporary topic one risks being out of date as soon as the work is published. As Einstein, in noting the difference between much social inquiry and physical science, observed "Politics is for the moment and an equation is for eternity." Web pages that can be continuously updated may be one answer, assuming one does not get bored with the topic.[14] On the other hand, we are in business partly because there *are* regularities as one becomes more abstract the analytic ability to draw out generic forms and ideal types and to use them in comparative and explanatory fashion is a vital skill.

10.  With respect to book reviews, was it possible to balance the cynicism of the sociology of knowledge perspective with the belief that there really are empirical and normative truths that transcend social settings? Academics cannot claim the degree of disinterestedness or disdain that some artists have for critics (e.g., playwrights who claim they never look at reviews). Given the collective nature of scholarship and its tentativeness, we must learn from each other and any one person is limited in what he or she knows. Yet book reviews are often Rorschach tests revealing as much, or more, about the reviewer as about the book. About half of the the time I could predict at least some of a reviewers' responses by knowing their discipline and politics (e.g., a sociologist of organizations praised the chapter that dealt with bureaucracy and was impatient with the literary quotes while an ethnographer was critical of the bureaucracy chapter finding it abstract and lifeless). It does not follow from this that all views are necessarily equal, whether scientifically or morally, merely because they are socially situated and constructed. Yet awareness of the social construction of perspectives can be a salve for critical reviews, if also a bearer of humility for laudatory ones. It can also make self-reliance easier.

11.  What obligations did I have to promote the book in order to have it be seen and reviewed beyond the confines of a few specialists and friends? Many in the university have a naïve faith that if you do good work it will be noticed. At its worst this optimistic view involves a conceit about how important the work we do is and how eager the outside world is for it.

     The Century Fund financed the study of undercover police and receives the royalties. I was glad to be finished and wanted to move on to other things. Yet I also felt a sense of responsibility to shape public debate and the sponsor desired to have the results widely disseminated. With more than 50,000 books published each year in the United States it is rare that a book speaks for itself. While my identity is as a producer rather than a promoter, I was not shy in calling the book to the attention of audiences, whether colleagues, journal editors, policymakers, or bookstores. Yet I would have much preferred to have been writing or biking.

12.  How to deal with the media such that one gets heard without being diluted? In trying to fit into their format, you must either appear glib and inauthentic or indecisive and academic. The latter is a surefire method for being edited out or not being asked back. I did not enjoy having to fit questions requiring complex answers into the time, space, and sophistication limits of the media format in question. It is frustrating to be told, "Come on, Professor, never mind all the qualifications and hedges, just answer the question "Yes" or "No," or "We only have a minute, can you give us a quick summary of the book?"

There is a difference between helping to identify the right questions and having the right factual and then normative answers. Having the right questions is a first step. I think I have those and I have many of the factual answers, but I am far from the normative and policy answers, although I did suggest a conceptual framework within which to approach them. My initial concern was to identify the issues and encourage public discussion, and only secondarily to offer solutions. Indeed criminological topics are fascinating partly because there often are no easy solutions in the usual sense. But many in the media and policymakers do not want to hear that.

## Go West Middle-Aged Man

*I locked my door as the sun went down said good-bye to Boston town*

                              T. Rush, On the Road Again

My cup was running over as the clock was winding down. I wanted more, but not more of the same. I was ready to spend less energy on my own work and more on institution building. In 1992 I left MIT for a position as Chair of the Sociology Department at the University of Colorado at Boulder. Most of our friends could not understand how we could leave the cozy life of academic Cambridge after 25 years for a non-elite school in the wild west. However, given the pushes from Cambridge and the pulls to the west, the decision was easy.

My MIT department was then headed by a very smart, domineering, mean-spirited and dogmatic individual who had been on my case for two decades (he was against hiring me and later tried to block my promotion to full professor).[15] His response to the best academic year of my life (beyond the success that *Undercover* was enjoying I had just received a large NSF grant for comparative social control work and had taught a very well-received new undergraduate course), was to freeze my salary because he felt I was not doing enough for the department. Given his narrow definition of the situation he was correct. But those were not the terms under which I was hired—I was not a city planner and had no intention of becoming one. Rather I was a scholar following my muse, something that could not be decided by any organization. The salary freeze was symbolic and I could live with it.[16] But when he sought to rename the department by dropping the title "urban studies" (from Urban Studies and Planning) and focus it even more on professional planning and development questions, I knew it was time to go.

As confirmed Westerners, we had never planned to stay on the east coast and viewed it as a cultural experience. Imagine my surprise when, 25 years later, we were still there. Beyond weather and a more relaxed lifestyle, we wanted to be closer to aging parents and our sons who had settled in the west. I felt under-utilized in a department and institute that tended to value application over reflective and critical thought. My best experiences had been working with graduate students and I wanted more graduate students who shared my interests.

In addition, every four or five years I had made a major change of some kind (either in residence, affiliation, or intellectual activity) and it was that time again. The ever present entropic tendencies and dulling from the familiar must be fought (Marx, 2000).

I also wanted to give something back to a discipline and a way of viewing the world that I strongly believed in and that I saw as endangered. I was not happy with developments in sociology—the turn toward ever greater specialization and compartmentalization of research, the fetish of methods divorced from meaningful content, theories that had little to do with reality and the growing influence of ideologues masking as scholars.

The kind of scholarship I learned at Berkeley was pluralistic (if softly positivist) and civil in spite of deep disagreements, sought the integration of theory and research, appreciated the importance of comparative and historical perspectives and was concerned with human betterment. What is more its practitioners were learned individuals for whom the pursuit of knowledge seemed a calling not a job.

I saw being offered the Chair's position and resources to build a great department as a way to sustain and validate my vision of social inquiry. That approach was and remains marginal to much of the sociological and criminological establishments.[17]

However as blues poet Mose Allison sings, "It didn't turn out that way, it just didn't turn out that way." I loved the mountain biking and the grandeur and visual orgy of the physical setting, including living in an artful glass house built into a mountain, made some good friends, worked with some fine students and helped bring about modest change,[18] But after four years, "happiness was Boulder, Colorado in my rearview mirror."[19]

Put most charitably, Colorado was a learning experience. It was a second-rate institution with a potential to be much better, pushed hard by some faculty, administrators, legislators, regents, and the president to become third-rate. I learned on the job about the power of organizational culture apart from the formal structure of power, about the timidity of administrators and how tenure and fear of lawsuits can protect those who would be better served by some other line of work.

It proved to be a big, wide world containing things hardly imagined in the tradition and resource-rich institutions of Berkeley and Cambridge. As a besieged chair, almost everything I had heretofore stood for and believed in was at some point challenged—the effort to be as objective and empirical as possible; the need to define terms; the need to locate our specific findings relative to the discipline, the literature, comparative and historical contexts and broader issues; the notion that knowledge was possible across observers and that membership in a group was neither a necessary, nor a sufficient condition for understanding; the need to determine faculty rewards by focusing on the attributes of the work and its logic, imagination and originality, not on personal characteristics such as ethnicity and gender and the belief that in a university truth should hold sway and that persons of different views had an obligation to discuss their disagreements in a civil, honest and honorable fashion.

Did I make some mistakes? Sure. I was probably too honest and not Machiavellian enough, even though I specialize in studying secrecy and deception. I forgot the first rule of any good scholar or detective: "The unexamined assumption is the mother of error." Based on my three previous decades in the university, I assumed shared values, good will, competence, and integrity on the part of those I dealt with. I was unprepared for the lack of professionalism I encountered.

There are many aspects to the story—an elected and highly politicized Board of Regents,[20] non-supportive taxpayers who looked with suspicion on the university, a hostile legislature, a controversial (and eventually fired) President who exploited tensions on the campus and in the sociology department,[21] insulated and tired administrators lacking the courage to speak out or to lead,[22] and ethnic and gender politics.[23] But a central theme is summarized in the following question, "How many chairs does it take to change a department?" Answer: "Only one, but the department has to really want to change."[24]

The department faculty, while relatively congenial and socially concerned as individuals, had too many persons who were immobile and professionally isolated, avoided external conflict and were ambivalent toward, or resistant to, departmental change. Even most of those who were supportive of change refused to step forward and play leadership roles.[25] As a result of a hand that remained strong from the grave, the department had failed to create a culture of professionalism and continued to fight decades old department battles, sometimes demonstrating a meanness of spirit that was hard for an outsider to comprehend.

The majority of the faculty either received their degrees from Colorado or had never taught anywhere else. Some had checked out of the academic motel long ago, or never even checked in and a few tried to sneak in. Others, who should have known better, could not resist the siren call of the local culture—a culture that could dampen aspirations, lower standards, engender incivility and, as a colleague put it, turn potentially good minds to guacamole. An antiquated 1960s political drug and cult haze, supplemented by an indefensible, but for many, irresistible, political correctness too often clouded the blue Colorado sky.

This is not the place to analyze that experience. As with many nineteenth-century voyagers, Colorado was a stopping point on a migration further west. I am grateful for what I learned there and for the chance to publicly stand for principle, something that academics with their secret ballots, anonymous reviews and the security of tenure rarely seem to do. Salman Rushdie (1995) has observed that "our lives teach us who we are." Seeing what I was against helped me become clearer about what I was for.

The four years at Colorado caused me to reflect on the kind of cultural climate I would like to see in a department, something that I had previously been privileged to take for granted. Such a climate would honor the 37 moral mandates in Table 1 (discussed at length in Marx, 1997). I also came to see more clearly the meaning and importance of a liberal arts environment and the political and economic threats to it in settings such as Colorado's during the mid-1990s.

## The Liberal Arts Ideal

If there is one message above all others that I would like to pass on to future academics and citizen it would surely be the importance and vulnerability of a liberal arts education. Two of its central elements are valuing knowledge as an end in itself and maintaining a climate of openness and civility in which to pursue that knowledge.

A liberal arts education starts with questions, not answers. It asks "why" as well as "how." It values the search for beauty, as well as the search for usefulness. It instills a love of learning, knowledge, and creativity for their own sake. It inculcates humility and tentativeness in the face of complex and changing natural and social worlds.

Under the best of circumstances learning has a sacred quality. Knowledge is one of the few things in life that is enhanced by being shared. Its value often is not immediately perceived. An education must be viewed as more than a meal ticket bought at a discount, through ever larger classes, greater reliance on poorly paid, less-experienced teachers and untested, quick technical solutions. Mass-produced, bargain goods come with hidden price tags. Modern management techniques and bureaucratic standards offer many advantages, but they must be used cautiously and with full awareness of what is special about education and the pursuit of knowledge. A university should not be run in exactly the same way as a business. Its worth and the quality of its performance cannot be adequately determined by market forces or looking at easily quantifiable measures regarding faculty activity, student demand, or the short-run employability of graduates.

Faculty at Colorado and other state schools are increasingly expected to meet a variety of contemporary goals of an applied nature from diverse constituencies—e.g., change curricula and research to better meet the needs of industry, prepare students for jobs, solve social and environmental problems. Yet a university must not become a giant consulting firm for either the private sector or the state, a trade school, or the arm of a social movement, nor must its mission be solely defined by those who momentarily hold political power. The liberal arts ideal involves much more than short-term or local goals and it encourages us to question our goals, as well as our means. We must ask not only, "What do we owe the citizens of the state today?", but "What do we owe civilization and future generations?"

While education and the correction of social and economic ills may be linked, they are not equivalent. The university's central mission must remain education. The university offers an environment in which the values and empirical assumptions accompanying our beliefs about injustice and social needs can, and must be rigorously examined.

Much of my professional energy has been devoted to developing and applying social science knowledge to social problems. I think we have much to contribute. Certainly as citizens and as recipients of resources from the state we have social obligations. Yet the university needs a degree of detachment (although certainly not indifference) from immediate social concerns. The university cannot solve all of society's current problems. But it can help in the preparation of reflective and well-rounded individuals with the skills and humane values required to live creative and socially useful lives.

A state university that is too removed from public concerns and needs runs the risk of being irresponsible and unduly elitist, not to mention being politically stupid. Yet one that is driven solely by public demands sacrifices the independence and critical spirit that should be the birthright of the intellectual. A university must be a somewhat protected enclave for the pursuit of truth. Yet its truths, while dependent on the work of the individual, cannot be subjective. They must be socially ratified. Its claims to truth must be public and submitted to rigorous peer review.

This brings us to another threat to the liberal arts ideal—fundamentalist political and cultural forces on the campus. A fundamentalist is a person who, whether viewing the world from a secular or sacred lens, says, "I'm right because I know I'm right." The fundamentalist seeks to propagandize, not to educate. He or she never gets off the soap box; his or her concerns are non-debatable and non-negotiable. Fundamentalists are unable to see shades of gray or to appreciate irony. Most important, they lack a sense of humor. They are threatened by calls for rational discussion and analysis and by the initial skepticism of the scientist. They will throw up McCarthyite accusations and look for ugly "-isms" under every rock, rather than calmly examine their own and others' beliefs in light of standards of logic, empiricism, and values.

The variety and abstraction of values and the complexity of the natural world guarantees that there will be disagreements. Conflict within proper bounds can be socially constructive. Wise and gentle persons acknowledge the difficulties in finding the truth and then go on to put forward their best case. But this is done in a spirit of openness and is always subject to revision. That is not the case with the fundamentalist, who is self-excused from any reflective activity that might cause the re-examination of positions.

For those who so choose, revealed truths have a place in private settings such as church or a voluntary association. But a public liberal arts university must require that those who walk through its portals honor the sacred values of free and unfettered inquiry. We must guarantee the freedom to ask questions and to express unpopular views.

Ideally a university is a community held together by trust and a shared commitment to professionalism and respect for the truth. Within the university, claims must be argued on the basis of logic and empirical evidence, not by personal attacks on those with whom we disagree. In doing this we have an obligation to put forward our arguments rationally and civilly.

Academic freedom requires that no topic be beyond the bounds of inquiry and that research topics be open to all regardless of their personal characteristics. Yet this freedom must be exercised in a responsible manner with respect to both content and form.

Civility requires that we listen to others with whom we disagree in a shared spirit of understanding. The fundamentalist is prone to behave in exactly the opposite fashion, offering rhetorical behavior that includes: (1) sweeping generalizations divorced from concrete examples, (2) deceptive and selective arguments, (3) argument by name-calling and demonization of opponents, (4) reliance on solipsistic and transcendental justifications, and (5) the failure to listen to what those they disagree with say. As humans and as scholars, language is our most precious possession, and in a university of all places it must not be debased, however strong one's feelings or noble one's cause.

## Movin' On

*'Cause movin' is my stock 'n trade*
*I'm movin' on*
*I won't think of you when I'm gone*

Gordon Lightfoot
"For Lovin' Me"

I am glad to have helped protect the flame of Erasmus amidst the destructive prairie winds of the cost cutting, self-aggrandizing politicians who sought to further bureaucratize and control the university and the politically correct fundamentalists. Those nourished and protected by the ideals of the Renaissance and the Enlightenment must be ever vigilant for the waters are indeed filled with sharks.

After a few years as chair at Colorado it was easy to agree with the view of leadership offered by an Italian politician, who, when asked, "Is it very difficult to lead the Italian people?" Replied, "No, just useless." Given the cornucopia of limitations at multiple levels, it seemed prudent not to anticipate the imminent arrival of a great sociology department at Boulder. Camelot fails again. Once champagne turns to vinegar it never turns back.[26] I was embattled and in danger of becoming embittered. Life is too short for that and besides anger destroys your judgment. Deep in my genetic and cultural code has always been a willingness to walk. As Wallace Stegner knew at such times it is best to keep rollin' west.[27]

Table 1
**37 Moral Mandates for Aspiring Sociologists and Criminologists**

1. Develop the habits of critical thought, evaluation and observation.

2. Write with clarity, logic and vigor.

3. Write everywhere, all the time, on everything.

4. Have a fresh argument.

5. Write books, don't only read them.[28]

6. Take short cuts.

7. Learn how to be an effective public speaker.

8. Don't be scriptocentric.

9. Disaggregate and aggregate.

10. Be wary of scholars bearing over-broad generalizations.

11. Be wary of "Jack Webb-Badge 714 'Just the facts ma'am'" academics.

12. Avoid the dangers that can arise from rigidly taking sides in doctrinal debates over theory and method.

13. Diversify. Don't stay a specialist in one area too long.

14. Be problem and interdisciplinary as well as discipline focused.

15. Be wary of scholars denying the desirability and possibility of scientific approaches to understanding crime and criminal justice.

16. Treasure and develop the unique position of your discipline as both a scientific and humanistic undertaking. Should you choose not to straddle the fence, be tolerant of those sitting elsewhere.

17. Know what the questions are.

18. Be bold. Take risks!

19. Cultivate marginality.

20. Have short and long range plans and goals.

21. Life and scholarship are about unfinished business and process.

22.  Create real and virtual communities.

23.  Actively look for mentors and role models, as well as anti-role models.

24.  Seek out those who are more knowledgeable, clever and/or successful than you are.

25.  Learn to "meet with Triumph and Disaster and treat those two imposters just the same."

26.  Don't be selfish! Give of your time and your thoughts to others.

27.  Be proud to be an academic.

28.  Tell it like it is. Speak truth to power and others.

29.  Believe in the sociology of knowledge and use it responsibly for insights.

30.  Learn to deftly walk back and forth between the point of view of the actor and the observer.

31.  Know the difference between a scholar and a fundamentalist.

32.  Avoid the exclusionary notion that you must belong to a group in order to study it and that individuals have some special obligation to study groups they belong to.

33.  Don't join the thought-police or spend an undue amount of time looking for any possible evidence of racism, sexism, classism, homophobia, or ageism on the part of your peers.

34.  Be aware when you are operating as a scientist and trying to be value-free and when you are a more explicit political actor.

35.  Have fun! Enjoy what you do!

36.  Have a sense of humor!

37.  Keep the faith! . . . Know that both principles and ideas matter and that the individual can make a difference. Believe that knowledge is better than ignorance, that knowledge is possible, and that empirical and scientific knowlege about human and social conditions can result in the improvement of those conditions.

# Bibliography

Block, A. (ed.) (1992). "Special Issue: Issues and Theories on Covert Policing." *Crime, Law and Social Change*, Vol. 18: Nos. 1-2.

Bradbury, M. (1976). *The History Man: A Novel*. Boston, MA: Houghton Mifflin.

Ellis, J. (1997). *American Sphinx: The Character of Thomas Jefferson*. New York, NY: Vintage Books.

Fijnaut, C. & G.T. Marx (1995). *Undercover: Police Surveillance in Comparative Perspective*. The Hague: Kluwer.

Marx, G.T. (2000). "Famished Ardor: Some Reflections on Sociology and Travel and a Trip to China." *The American Sociologist*, Vol. 31:3.

Marx, G.T. (1997). "Of Methods and Manners for Aspiring Sociologists: 37 Moral Imperatives." *The American Sociologist*, Vol. 28:1.

Marx, G.T. (1995). "Recent Developments in Undercover Policing" in T. Blomberg and S. Cohen (eds.) *Law, Punishment and Social Control: Essays in Honor of Sheldon Messinger*. New York, NY: Aldine de Gruyter.

Marx, G.T. (1990). "Reflections on Academic Success and Failure: Making It, Forsaking It and Reshaping It" in B. Berger, *Authors of Their Own Lives*. Berkeley, CA: University of California Press.

Marx, G.T. (1988). *Undercover: Police Surveillance in Comparative Perspective*. Berkeley, CA: University of California Press.

Marx, G.T. (1984a). ""Role Models and Role Distance: A Remembrance of Erving Goffman." *Theory and Society*, 13:646-662.

Marx, G.T. (1984b). "Notes on the Discovery, Collection and Assessment of Hidden and Dirty Data" in J. Schneider and J. Kitsuse (eds.) *Studies in the Sociology of Social Problems*. New York, NY: Ablex.

Marx, G.T. (1972). *Muckraking Sociology: Research as Social Criticism*. New York, E.P. Dutton.

Marx G.T. & M. Useem (1971). "Majority Involvement in Minority Movements: Civil Rights, Abolition, Untouchability." *Journal of Social Issues*, Vol. 1971.

Orwell, G. (1970). *A Collection of Essays* New York, NY: Harcourt Brace.

Rushdie, S. (1995). Interview. *New Yorker*, 12/25/95.

Stegner W. (1987). *The American West as Living Space*. Ann Arbor, MI: University of Michigan Press.

## Endnotes

[1]   These and related papers are available on my web page at mit.edu/gtmarx/www/garyhome.html

[2]   In the *Four Quartets* T.S. Elliot observes, "In my beginning is my end." The earliest entry in my "permanent record" in the Los Angeles City School System, "he had trouble at various times talking out of turn and not taking direction well.... For awhile as a discipline measure he was put back into morning kindergarten, desired effect not accomplished" by the first grade "...would not adjust or conform, he busts his stitches at first opportunity . . . particular troubles on playground, fighting etc." and by the second grade an escalation of the sanctioning, "constant source of irritation and trouble...kept after school, sent to office, denied privileges."

[3]   I taught at Berkeley the first year and then moved to the Department of Social Relations at Harvard. In retrospect, given today's markets and procedures the job process seems unreal. I applied in late September, submitting my book manuscript and some articles and by early November was offered a bountiful job without the bother of a job interview or talk. I never dreaded those and welcomed the chance to make my case. I just wanted the ball as basketball player Larry Bird used to say. My book *Protest and Prejudice* sold well, was timely, of interest to academics and the reading public and contributed to knowledge and social change. Bayard Rustin, the major strategist of the civil rights movement, wrote the introduction. I received coveted fellowships and awards that usually went to older scholars, funding agencies came and offered to support my work. There was also media attention, reprints (an article on religion and protest was reprinted at least 20 times that I am aware of), election to the august executive council of the American Sociological Association, editorial service on the boards of leading journals, tenure offers from Columbia and others schools that I parlayed into a promotion, work for national commissions, identification in the student course evaluation as one of the best lecturers at Harvard and more writing, speaking and consulting invitations than I could respond to.

[4]   With time I sometimes felt it was their loss (e.g., for a residential fellowship or an article they would be unable to publish). I also knew I could always come back again and that there were other places to apply. At the same time one must learn from rejections about both substantive improvements to an application or article and how to better "game" it next time.

[5]   In "Provide, Provide" he further writes, "The witch that came (the withered hag) To wash the steps with pail and rag Was once the beauty Abishag, The picture pride of Hollywood. Too many fall from great and good for you to doubt the likelihood."

[6]   There is no doubt variation here by personality type and career stage. Now as a Professor Emeritus living on an island, I find myself whipsawed between Twain and Greta Garbo's line in *Grand Hotel* (as well as in her life), "I want to be alone" and Jefferson's observation that remaining close to home for five years had an ill effect on his mind and that withdrawing from the world, ". . . led to an antisocial and misanthropic state of mind, which severely punished him who gives in to it." (Ellis 1997).

[7]   While there were occasional criticisms of the book for being too conservative or liberal, too academic or not theoretical or tightly enough organized, too indecisive, and failing in places to offer documentation or to cover particular topics, I was very surprised that among a highly varied group of reviewers there were no negative reviews.

8    Consistent with Andy Warhol's observation about everyone needing a few minutes of fame, it is satisfying to see one's name in print and to be quoted, an adult version of "look ma, no hands." Being quoted in a *New York Times* editorial or in the lead story is thrilling (especially initially), but it was no less thrilling to see my ideas in another *Times* editorial or to hear concepts I have used such as the surveillance society, surveillance creep, covert facilitation and the maximum security society used in the media *without* attribution. While hardly a power behind the throne, there was satisfaction in being the voice behind the speaker. If the cause is just and the words well put, it's ok to be the organ grinder making the music while the monkey gets the attention. I first learned that 30 years ago after a presentation for Vice President Humphrey. Later I heard him use my ideas almost verbatim without attribution in a speech. An important way that academics can effect change is through impact on the culture and climates of opinion. Of course if colleagues steal your ideas that is a different matter.

9    Being driven in that elegant limo to Night Line or Good Morning America is a great feeling. Yet fortunately there are always humbling little reminders that help keep hubris at bay. For example a month after what I thought was one of the best interviews I had ever done, I received the following message, "Hi, this is Lisa from ABC 20/20. The piece we interviewed you for is on this Friday. Unfortunately, you're not in it."

10   Above all this involves focus and laser directed intensity to one's scholarly concerns. There is some truth to the stereotype of the absent-minded professor, although that being-in-a-daze mental state, (or "somewhere else" as my sons used to say when I was obviously tuned out even though physically present) may apply to any deeply engaging activity involving intense preoccupation and concentration. This need also works against leading a balanced life. It sets academics apart from those not so engaged.

11   A style that could be "critical without being curmudgeonly." Yet as I learned at Colorado to those less secure and perceptive, or caught up in a pc feel-good world, this can be misunderstood and threatening. If all one is concerned about is being liked, not challenging others, and bolstering egos perceived to be fragile, then honesty is hardly the best policy, even if it is the morally compelling one.

12   The passion-objectivity and knowledge or art for its own sake vs. its social usefulness tensions can not be avoided. Hemingway observed, "If you want to send a message, call Western Union." In contrast George Orwell (1970) writes, "It is invariably where I lacked a *political* purpose that I wrote lifeless books . . ."

13   The same question ought to apply to readers of any account such as those in this volume. Freud observed that biographical accounts may lead to "lying, concealment, to flummery" and a study of middle-aged men reports that the chance of their accurately remembering events from adolescence is no greater than chance.

14   More generally web pages are a wonderful way of combating the short-shelf life and inaccessibility of academic writing which is often widely scattered over time and place.

15   I mention this not to fight old battles but to remind future academics that they must be prepared to encounter unreasonable people in positions of authority and often be able to do little about it, beyond waiting for them to move on. Their power, secrecy and the interpretive, elastic and conflicting nature of the values that serve to justify actions offer enormous room for bad behavior masked by high sounding motives.

[16]  A bigger issue was the salary compression which can happen if you stay in the same place too long and don't play the game of threatening to leave in order to obtain significant raises.

[17]  Space precludes more detailed consideration. I never thought of myself as a criminologist. Rather I was interested in the question of social order and change and that led directly to issues of norms and control, as well as to an interest in race relations and mass behavior. My interest was not in criminological phenomena *per se* but in the window they offered into broader questions about rules and power in society. I do not follow the criminology literature the way real criminologists do, or should. I came to criminology because that was where a major market and lots of data were to be found. In spite of a record that might qualify me, I am not a fellow of the American Society of Criminology, although I have been nominated several times. I have consistently been rejected by NIJ over the past 15 years, including the proposal for my undercover book.

   While by education, work, service and recognition I have been toward the center rather than the periphery of the American Sociological establishment, that is not the case for the fields I work in. The study of deviance and social control, criminology and social problems are less prestigeful and often seen as less intellectually respectable, dirty, atheoretical and too applied. Such work has not been prominent at elite institutions since the golden age at the University of Chicago. Having spent most of my career in an interdisciplinary department, using a variety of methods and approaches to study a wide range of topics and seeing myself as a social studies person rather than exclusively as a social *scientist* or a humanist was also marginalizing. Specialization is one key to making it, although not necessarily to wisdom or authenticity.

[18]  For example four very strong appointments, new policies and procedures, redefined and more rigorous undergraduate and graduate programs, national and international graduate student recruitment, increased research funding and beginning to redefine the local culture which through attrition and dilution grew weaker.

[19]  This paraphrases a song by Mack Davis about Lubbock, Texas. However I would not claim that "the only good thing about Boulder is the road east and west," rejecting Dr. Johnson's quip that "the only good thing about Scotland is the road south." There was too much that was wonderful about the local and regional setting of Boulder, including the world's best hardware store, and too many good faculty and students for that. There were times, however, when my favorite T-shirt, an image of the city with the words, "Boulder, Colorado 3 square miles surrounded by reality" fit in both senses.

[20]  I should have known that something was wrong at the start when the head of the Board of Regents, a retired Air Force General, tried to block my appointment on procedural grounds, stating that the citizens of Colorado did not need a sociologist from Berkeley. There were other signs that I ignored—although a relatively rich state, Colorado was 47th among the states in proportional funding for the university. A colleague from an ivy league school I spoke to (brought in the year before I came as an outside chair in another department) resigned after only a year, complaining of over-bureaucratization and micro-management.

[21]  As this relates to sociology see the Denver Post, P. 1A Sept. 10, 1995 and my op-ed articles in the Boulder Daily Camera, Feb. 26, 1995 and July 1, 1995. Among other things the President overturned the strong recommendations of four university committees to deny tenure to a sociologist.

22    Many in the administration, for example, were inbred and long ago burned their bridges to regular academic work. Whether out of career ambitions (show that you can keep the lid on things and don't offend any constituency, especially if you are a Dean on the short list to become vice-chancellor), character defects or fatigue, they tolerated incompetence, public mendacity and deceit on the part of some faculty and followed more than led. They were intimidated by the Regents and legislature who seemed always to be investigating the university. The sociology department was investigated several times and always exonerated. This was a direct rejection of those who made frivolous charges, misused grievances procedures and engaged in misinformation, disinformation, slander, defamation and violations of confidentiality and other university rules without suffering any penalties, things that a strong and principled administration would not have tolerated. The administration's perspective seemed to be, "if you ignore it, it will go away." Too often there was, in poet Czeslaw Milosz' words, "a conspiracy of silence," in which, "one word of truth sounds like a pistol shot."

23    To take several examples, in an ostensibly open search, a candidate with an exceptional publication and teaching record who *towered* above the competition was not hired because the candidate was deemed to lack the appropriate ascribed characteristics. In a similar case, a candidate for another position with an even stronger record was hired away from an elite school, but only after a bitter internal fight. The dean acted as if he was doing me a favor in supporting the hiring of the superior candidate. Nor did the administration much want to support change when it became clear that there were political costs. Promotions were granted in several very weak cases and early tenure denied for one of the strongest cases I had ever seen.

24    The department offered great material for a satirical academic novel, were it not so sad and poignant and for the suffering of those involved. At least one such novel has been published and another is unpublished. The department was founded by an individual with broad ranging intellectual interests who was literally born on the campus. He did not have a Ph.D. and had little interest in advancing the discipline. He took pride in his anti-professional orientation and his vision of a department seemed to be that of a salon. He is said to be the central figure in the novel by Bradbury (1976).

This environment involved more than the garden variety of skeletons that can usually be found in academic closets. The department specialized in criminology, although with its history of drugs, alcoholism, mental illness, sexual escapades, violence, a professor claiming a fraudulent Ph.D., embezzlement and the falsification of student records etc., it might have profited most from self study.

25    The lack of stronger and more consistent support from many faculty members was a major disappointment. Perhaps it is not surprising that some resented the mandate of an outside chair brought in as one administrator put it, "to clean up the mess in sociology." The mess was so bad a few years before that serious consideration was given to closing the department. One faculty member went on television complaining that what was wrong with the university was my salary and light teaching load. Others who supported change were conflict shy and didn't want to get involved, or were too busy with their personal lives.

In contrast to the usual pattern in which assistant professors lie low, my strongest support came from the two exceptionally strong assistant professors I was able to hire, in spite of opposition. They have since left the department in disgust for much better jobs and environments. Their departure along with mine and another stellar colleague led some graduate students to believe that rats were deserting a sinking ship. While I didn't much like the metaphor, there is a kind of justice in the fact that in such situations, highly qualified individuals often have other options and the luxury of avoiding the necessity, as the man sings of, "making the best of a bad situation." Given the systemic limitations and supports, nothing much has changed and the ship bobs on in the same seas.

[26]   Vinegar of course has its uses and as Erving Goffman used to say, it's all data anyway. In time I came to agree with the interim chancellor brought in to clean up the bigger mess in the university system, who after we had both left, told me that the Colorado scene during that time period was best viewed as another chapter in the absurdity of the human condition. That chapter continued after our departure— the vice chancellor was stopped for driving under the influence, a new president brought in to save the system resigned under a cloud of suspicion involving the awarding of a lucrative contract to a female friend and three members of the sociology department were arrested.

[27]   He writes being free to move on ". . . is associated in our minds with escape from history and oppression and law and irksome obligations, with absolute freedom, and the road has always led west." (Stegner, 1987).

[28]   As originally written I said write books don't read them. That was the only imperative that generated disagreement and was said partly in jest. Given the common belief that the young know too little of the non-contemporary literature in their own fields, let alone related fields and perhaps an overall decrease in writing quality with the proliferation of outlets and the increased centrality of publishing to reward, one might add another imperative to "read more and write less." As with marriage and guns, perhaps a license should be required for academics to write. But, if you are hungry, there comes a time to fish rather than to cut bait. The scholar's obligation to know the literature can never be fully achieved and should not be an excuse not to write. Another more curious justification (not intended here) was offered by a colleague who rather meekly told me he had not read my article on a topic he had just published on because, "I didn't want to be accused of stealing your ideas."

# 7

# Ignoring Warnings, I Became a Criminologist*

Jackson Toby

Shortly after I came to Rutgers in 1951 as an assistant professor, John Winchell Riley, then chairman of the Department of Sociology and Anthropology, invited me, along with other members of that small department, to a dinner party in his New York City apartment. Jack and Matilda Riley were friendly with many important people in the sociology field, and a few, such as Donald Young, then the President of the Russell Sage Foundation, were at that party. I was flattered that this distinguished elder statesman deigned to chat with me. "What field within sociology do you intend to specialize in?" he asked. "Criminology," I replied. He sighed avuncularly. "An interesting field. No grant money in it though. Have you considered medical sociology?" As it turned out, Dr. Young was wrong about grant money in criminology, but in 1952 he was being realistic. Neither private foundations nor government agencies were making substantial grants in criminology, and he knew that professional advancement usually depended on grant-supported research.

I stuck to criminology despite Dr. Young's warning; I had already made a major professional commitment to the field. I had completed my dissertation at Harvard in 1950 under the supervision of an unlikely criminological mentor, Talcott Parsons. But, as the title made clear, the dissertation was concerned with a criminological topic: "Educational Maladjustment As a Predisposing Factor in Criminal Careers: A Comparative Study of Ethnic Groups." I had investigated why second-generation Italian-American boys had higher delinquency rates than second-generation Jewish-American boys and called attention to the different cultural resources for legitimate social mobility in the traditions from which these youngsters came. I thought I had discovered a way to reduce crime: develop public policies to increase educational achieve-

*The editorial assistance given me by my daughter, Gail A. Toby, greatly improved my manuscript.

ment, thereby reducing the incentive to take illegitimate paths to success: delinquency and crime. I called this approach developing "a stake in conformity."

In 1957 I published "Social Disorganization and Stake in Conformity: Complementary Factors in the Predatory Behavior of Young Hoodlums" in the *Journal of Criminal Law, Criminology and Police Science*. Although the concept of a stake in conformity was not original—Francis Bacon had written of "hostages to fortune" four centuries ago, the notion that a "stake in conformity" is a bulwark against criminality was new, and criminologists began referring to it. I suspect that my coining of the phrase, "stake in conformity," was what led to a startling telephone call in 1959 from Dr. Pendleton Herring, the then-President of the Social Science Research Council. I knew who Pendleton Herring was, but I had had no previous contact with him, and I had no reason to think that he knew of my existence. He asked me whether I could come to lunch a few days later at the offices of the Council. Because this seemed tantamount to a call from God to climb Mount Sinai, I stammered an agreement. He added that Dyke Brown, Vice-President of the Ford Foundation, would join us. I never heard of Dyke Brown and had had no previous contact of any sort with the Ford Foundation.

The day came; I took a bus to the Port Authority terminal in New York and walked to the offices of the Social Science Research Council. I expected to be taken to a restaurant, but Dr. Herring asked me if it was all right to have sandwiches in the office. Of course I agreed. We chatted for five or ten minutes until Dyke Brown arrived. He was a tall, handsome, enthusiastic man. I learned that he was a lawyer and in charge of the Public Affairs Program at the Ford Foundation. We talked for nearly an hour, mostly about delinquency and crime, which neither Brown nor Pendleton Herring, a political scientist, knew much about; they asked questions and I did my best to answer them. I was baffled as to why I had been invited. Lunch over, Dyke Brown shook my hand and rushed off to a meeting, saying that he enjoyed our conversation. After he left, I do not recall that Herring cleared up the mystery of my invitation, although he may have mentioned that the Ford Foundation was considering a new program in delinquency prevention.

Within a week I got a telephone call from Dyke Brown. He invited me to come to lunch at the Ford Foundation. There I met other staff members of the Public Affairs Program, including David Hunter, by profession a social worker; David was the Director of the newly established Youth Development Program. Shortly thereafter I was invited to become the regular consultant to this program, reporting to David. Eventually I learned that the Board of Trustees of the Foundation had voted to establish a program to "do something" about adolescent delinquency and gave the responsibility for operating this program to Public Affairs, that is, to Dyke Brown. Why did they thrust this responsibility on an initially unreceptive vice-president, already busy trying to improve the efficiency of government bureaucrats and the expertise of elected officials? One of the trustees had gone to a dinner party in Westchester; next door, some adolescents were having a raucous party. Streams of uninvited friends and acquaintances crashed the party; the noise was deafening and the behavior worse. The trustee vowed to bring the problem of youth misbehavior to the attention of his colleagues, and he persuaded them at the next meeting to start a small grant program ($5 to $10 million per year) to seek solutions to the problem of youth misbehavior.

Because neither David nor Dyke (nor the other members of the professional staff of Public Affairs) had expertise in criminology, they decided that they needed a consultant to help them evaluate proposals for programs to prevent delinquency or to rehabilitate delinquents. The Ford Foundation had been a generous supporter of the Social Science Research Council. Hence it seemed reasonable to ask Pendleton Herring to help them recruit a criminologist close enough to their New York headquarters to come in one or two days a week and advise them.

I was 34 years old in 1959 and had been promoted to associate professor of sociology with tenure the year before. I had to decide whether it was in my career interest to accept the offer. It paid $50 a day; I had a wife and two young children, and my salary from Rutgers was modest. On the other hand, I wanted to become a full professor, and the time required would be an obstacle to completing research projects I was working on and to writing for professional journals. Yet the glamour of working for the Ford Foundation made the offer too tempting to refuse.

At first I read proposals that David had solicited from people he knew or that came in unsolicited as soon as the word got out that the Ford Foundation was making grants in the delinquency field. I would write long memoranda explaining why I thought they were good or bad. Usually I thought they were unlikely to produce the preventive or rehabilitative results for which the money was being requested. But gradually my role expanded. I became, in effect, a part-time staff member. I went on site visits to San Francisco, Salt Lake City, Cleveland, Chicago, Syracuse. In the summer of 1960, someone suggested that we ought to know about delinquency control programs in European countries that might provide insights into what we should try to promote in the United States. So David, Dyke, two other academic consultants recruited for the task, and I made a whirlwind tour of Sweden, Denmark, Holland, and England. We talked to dozens of criminologists, sociologists, social workers, and psychologists; everyone seemed willing to make time for representatives of the Ford Foundation. We also observed programs, including youth prisons. (I found to my surprise that some Swedish and Danish prisoners knew enough English to speak with me without translators being present. The Cockney speech of English prisoners was harder to understand.)

My role expanded in another direction. I was permitted to promote ideas of my own. I am particularly proud of two of these ideas that passed staff review and were sent up to the Board of Trustees and received funding. One was to establish a small grants program for young scholars: 100 grants of $2,500 each. My plan was to identify senior scholars who would use the money to subsidize the dissertation research of their graduate students. One administrative person at the Foundation opposed such a program on the ground that, regardless of its potential to develop people who could contribute to the objectives of our program, screening small grants would cost as much in staff time as making grants of a million dollars. My rejoinder was that we would not screen the individual grantees. We would award two grants each to eminent senior scholars and let them give the grants to whomever they had confidence in. Many of these grants went to people who made no contributions to criminology then or later. But some—to Travis Hirschi and to Delbert Elliott, for example—were superb investments.

Although Dyke and David overruled the administrator and supported the small grants idea, the objector had a point. Henry Heald, the president of the Ford Foundation at the time, was stingy about staff expenses. He wanted to show the Board of Trustees that Foundation money was being spent efficiently; his measure of efficiency was to keep the ratio of staff expenses, including salaries, to funds awarded to grantees low. Whatever the merit of this measure of efficiency in theory, in practice it meant that the staff never had enough time or enough subordinate personnel to investigate proposals thoroughly or to find out later how they worked out. What would happen often was that an idea would capture the fancy of one or all of the Youth Development staff without providing us with the opportunity to scrutinize its practicality. For instance, the director of the San Francisco office of the American Friends Service Committee asked us for help in establishing a program for delinquent gang members called Youth for Service. An ex-gang member had become a Quaker; he claimed that other gang youths were just as interested in working on socially worthy projects as in fighting. The American Friends Service Committee bought this ideologically congenial idea, and we supported it with a couple of hundred thousand dollars. It seemed to work for a few months—until the reformed gang member returned to his old ways—and then disappeared.

Looking back on the three years I spent as a consultant to the Youth Development Program and asking myself what I accomplished for the field and for my own professional development, I recall both achievements and failures. One of the larger grants that I actively promoted—to Thorsten Sellin and Marvin Wolfgang to finance the construction of a scale for measuring delinquency—resulted initially in the publication of a criminological classic, *The Measurement of Delinquency*, and ultimately in the establishment at the University of Pennsylvania of a fairly large institute dedicated to criminological research.

As for my own professional development, the relationship with the Ford Foundation was a mixed blessing. On the positive side it stimulated me to look at delinquency and crime comparatively. There were amazing similarities between young offenders in the Netherlands, England, Sweden, and Denmark, and those I had known in the United States. But there were differences, too. I later traveled to New Zealand to compare Maori crime there with black crime in the United States and to Japan to see why this highly industrialized country had such low crime and delinquency rates. Furthermore, I enjoyed meeting everyone who was anyone in the field and receiving red-carpet treatment wherever I went. I learned a lot from talking with them and finding out first-hand what they were up to.

But one downside of trying to ameliorate problems instead of merely studying them was the temptation to become overly optimistic, to act as though money and ideas and hard work could soon achieve substantial progress in controlling delinquency. Maybe so, but perhaps progress is more likely when grant-givers are wary of quick fixes. Theologian Reinhold Niebuhr wrote, "Certainly nothing that is worth doing can ever be completed in the life of one generation." All granting agencies ought to keep this in mind. Like the Ford Foundation, the National Institute of Justice and the Office of Juvenile Justice and Delinquency Prevention, to name only a few granting agencies, ordinarily make grants for two or three years at most. This practice limits the chances of dealing effectively with deep-rooted causes. I bought into this misleading optimism when I worked at the Ford Foundation. Another downside of my career as a busy consultant was that my own research and my family life suffered. It is not possible to do everything.

When Dyke Brown and David Hunter left the Ford Foundation, the Youth Development Program was disestablished, and I returned to Rutgers to become chairman of the Sociology Department. I tried to recruit some of the top-notch criminologists I had met while at the Ford Foundation to build criminology at Rutgers, and I thought at first that I was succeeding. Daniel Glaser had accepted an appointment as professor of sociology and planned to come as Director of a newly formed Institute for Criminological Research. He taught a graduate seminar during his two years at Rutgers (1968-1970) while working as Associate Commissioner in charge of research for the New York State Narcotics Control Commission. I became temporarily, I thought, the Director of the Institute for Criminological Research in 1968 while waiting for Glaser to come to Rutgers full-time. But for personal reasons unrelated to Rutgers Glaser decided to relocate to California, and I found myself the permanent Director of the Institute.

This unsought position compelled me to learn how to write proposals and obtain grants, mostly from the federal government, some from private foundations. Over the 25 years that I remained as Director (until 1994), we raised several million dollars for more than two dozen projects. One of our earliest was the evaluation of the effectiveness of a juvenile court program that sent adjudicated delinquents to residential treatment programs instead of to correctional institutions. One of our most recent projects was the evaluation of three boot camps for juvenile delinquents that were used in lieu of correctional placements. Neither project could claim success. It is very, very difficult to change people, even adolescents.

The *New York Times* began to publish op-ed pieces in the late 1960s or early 1970s. I did not, at first, think about writing for a general audience, but in January of 1973 I decided that I wanted to throw some cold water on the widespread liberal mantra that all it took to rehabilitate delinquents was money. I sent off an op-ed piece to the *Times* that I called, "How Can Society Defend Itself against Incorrigibles?" It was much too long; I didn't know then that the target length for op-ed pieces is 750 words. Nor did I realize how difficult it is to write a coherent piece that addressed a public-policy issue within such limits. I probably wrote it more to express myself than because I thought it was going to be published in the *Times.* But it had two things going for it. It was a heterodox opinion, and the op-ed page was created to air a wide range of opinions. Second, the op-ed page editor at the time, Harrison Salisbury, was interested in delinquency. When he returned from Soviet Union after many years of reporting from Moscow, Salisbury worked on a series of *Times* articles dealing with youth gangs in New York City (published in 1958 as *The Shook-up Generation*).

Yet I was startled on the morning of January 15, 1973, to find my article on the op-ed page of my morning paper. Well, not exactly the article as I had written it. The title had been changed to "Open-ended Sentence"; and some of my favorite paragraphs had been cut out completely as well as adjectives and adverbs here and there. But my name was on it and although the change in title had elevated a minor point into the central theme of the article, I was pleased when Rutgers colleagues and friends I had not heard from in years called to congratulate me.

It is not possible to do something for the first time twice. Once I had published an op-ed piece, writing such articles became a realistic possibility. In 1977, I published two more op-ed pieces in the *Times.* I published another one in 1978, one in 1979, one in 1980, three in 1981, three in 1982, and two in 1983. Then, in 1983, I published an op-ed piece for the first time in a newspaper other than the *New York Times.* I was invited to contribute a piece to the *Los Angeles Times* summarizing a chapter I had written for James Q. Wilson's book, *Crime and Public Policy*, which appeared that year.

Publication in the *Los Angeles Times* made me realize what should have been obvious: that many large-circulation newspapers had op-ed pages. I decided to try to write for other newspapers. Over the course of the next 27 years I pursued this quixotic effort to enlighten the American public, publishing in total more than 35 op-ed pieces in large-circulation newspapers: the *Wall Street Journal*, the *Chicago Tribune*, and the *Washington Post*, as well as the *New York Times*, the *Los Angeles Times*, and some smaller newspapers. Not everything I wrote was published. I probably have 30 or more op-ed pieces in my files that editors rejected, usually because they were not topical enough but sometimes because they had already been written about by others. My own titles have never survived the editing process. Most of the time I feel that my title was better than the headline given it by editors, but sometimes they make me envious. I had given the article I wrote for the March 2, 2000, issue of the Washington *Post* a stodgy title; "Cakewalk to College" was a big improvement.

In 1978, I read the 350-page monographic report to Congress, *Violent Schools—Safe Schools*, which described a victimization study of 31,373 students and 23,895 teachers in 642 junior and senior high schools. I experienced an epiphany. I realized that the thrust of my Ph.D. dissertation, that educational maladjustment led to criminality, missed a connection; educational maladjustment ought to have led to school violence first. I began to do research, to publish articles, and to give papers at professional meetings about the causes and the consequences of school violence.

The subject of school violence had been largely ignored by criminologists as not real criminality and by education professionals as irrelevant to basic educational problems such as low reading scores. My first article on school crime, "Crime in American Public Schools," appeared in 1980 in the public policy journal, *The Public Interest*. I used data from the Safe Schools study to describe the nature of the school crime problem and then analyzed what I regarded as its sociological causes. One of the causes, I believed, was the continuing legal and social pressure on adolescents to remain in school until high school graduation. Because some kids inevitably grow disenchanted with school for subcultural as well as idiosyncratic reasons, their frustration in schools is predictable. One outcome of such frustration is violence against both teachers and fellow students, not a situation conducive to positive learning. This being so, I concluded that dropping out of school was not an unadulterated disaster for society and sometimes not for the individual student. Compelling highly alienated kids to remain in school does them little good and disrupts the learning environment for more educable children. I wrote several articles explaining this point, including "Of Dropouts and Stayins: The Gershwin Approach," published in 1989 in *The Public Interest*. (The title of the article used 15-year-old dropout George Gershwin as an instance of a successful life after dropping out of high school.) This article solidified my reputation as a reactionary but also gave me 15 minutes of fame; Jane Pauley interviewed me on NBC's "The Today Show" and Charlie Rose interviewed me on CBS's "Nightwatch."

The Columbine High School murders in the middle-class suburb of Littleton, Colorado, perhaps the most well-publicized case of school violence in the world, forced me to rethink my theory of the causes of such violence. I had developed my theory based essentially on inner-city schools with high concentrations of ethnic minorities; I had cited compulsory attendance laws as unworkable and counterproductive in this environment. I wondered whether an entirely new theoretical approach was needed for middle-class suburbs. Then I asked myself an obvious question: If Eric Harris and Dylan Klebold were so miserable at Columbine High School, why didn't they simply drop out? Why did they feel trapped? Not for the same reasons that black inner-city kids reading four or five grade levels below their classmates felt imprisoned. Yet social and cultural pressures imprisoned them just as firmly. The stigma of dropping out of high school was so unthinkable as to have led these two students to prefer murder and suicide. But in the torrent of words commenting on the murders at Columbine High School I heard only psychobabble about teasing by jocks and, against the evidence, negligent parents. I wrote an article explaining that middle-class suburban kids can regard school as hell and suggesting that what was needed was to make dropping out a legitimate interlude, not an irrevocable disaster. Legitimating dropping out may make eventually returning to school more likely when the youngster realizes that he or she needs more education. But if I had thought that the extension of my theory to suburbia would convince the world to recognize the dark side of preventing dropping out at all costs, I was wrong. Neither colleagues nor the media paid the slightest attention.

That is not quite true. On April 29, 1999, I received an intriguing e-mail message from Professor Peter Reuter of the University of Maryland.

> I would like to talk with you about the possibility of participating in a conference that Mike Timpane and I are chairing from July 23-25 in Wye, Maryland. The conference is part of a RAND project, sponsored by the Office for Safe and Drug Free Schools. Its objective is to examine what the federal government can do to create safer and less drug-ridden schools. It is not primarily about curricula but about how federal programs can change school behavior. We would be interested in exploring with you the possibility of commissioning a background paper on what leads schools to adopt programs and policies that enhance school safety.

Apparently Professor Reuter and Dr. Timpane had read a paper I had written the previous year in *The Public Interest* that set forth a variety of ideas, some old, some new, to improve the disciplinary climates of secondary schools. I was flattered to be invited, and I agreed to prepare a background paper for distribution in advance to the conferees. Even though I had been reading, thinking, and doing research for years on the subject of school violence, I was unaware of the large grant program—an average of $500 million per year—that the Office for Safe and Drug Free Schools in the Department of Education had been running for more than a decade. It was a *grant* program, not a research program. What it did was distribute to a majority of the 15,000 school districts in the United States grants to do whatever they thought might help to curtail violence or drug abuse. Some of these grants were quite large; most were very small. Spread over more than 10,000 school districts, a political necessity for a program that required Congressional reauthorization every year, $500 million does not go very far.

But one of the questions that the conference was supposed to address was whether these grants were helping to reduce school violence or drug abuse and, if not, why not. Articles had appeared in the *Los Angeles Times* and other newspapers showing that some of the school districts had used the funds in ways that seemed remote from the purposes of the program, e.g., to hire a magician to entertain students. While Senators and Representatives agreed that school violence was bad, as was drug abuse, they wanted to be convinced that the annual $500 million appropriated to combat it was being well spent by the Department of Education. A grant to the RAND Corporation to finance a conference to rethink the program seemed like a prudent investment.

The conference was convened at the Wye Plantation, where President Clinton had hosted a conference the previous year on mid-East peace attended by Arab and Israeli officials. It was a posh setting for the small conference: only about 30 people. Some of the attendees were officials of the Education and Justice Departments, some superintendents of school systems, some from academia, and some from intervention programs that claimed to be reducing school violence or drug abuse on the part of students. There were three invited papers besides mine; all four were distributed in advance to participants—along with background material about the Office for Safe and Drug Free Schools, Congressional testimony, and published articles commenting on the program.

I had a chance to open a discussion of my paper by making some of my points informally; reading it was presumed to be unnecessary because everyone had had a chance to see the full text. I decided to emphasize what I thought was the most appealing idea in the paper: introducing adult supporters of teachers into high schools.

> There are already hints of the usefulness of increasing the presence of conventional adults in high schools. For example, Chicago's DuSable High School, an all-black school close to a notorious public housing project, demonstrated the practicality of offering the opportunity for repentant dropouts from the neighborhood to enroll as regular students. A 39-year-old father of six children, a 29-year-old mother of a 14-year-old

freshman at DuSable, a 39-year-old mother of five children hungered for a second chance at a high school education. They accepted the school district's invitation to return to DuSable High School because they had come to believe that dropping out a decade or two earlier had been a terrible mistake. Some of these adult students were embarrassed to meet their children in the hallways; some of their children were embarrassed that their parents were schoolmates; some of the teachers at the high school were initially skeptical about mixing teenagers and adults in classes. But everyone agreed that the adult students took education seriously, worked harder than the teenage students, and set a good example.

These adult students were not in school to bolster the authority of teachers. That was just a byproduct of their presence. Apparently, it is harder to cut classes or skip school altogether when your mother or even your neighbor is a fellow student. For instance, the principal at DuSable High School observed one mother marching her son off to gym class, which he had intended to cut. Most school systems shunt adult students into special adult school programs or G.E.D. classes, partly because work or child-care responsibilities make it difficult for the late awakeners to the value of education to come during the normal school day. But especially in inner-city high schools, much can be gained by encouraging even a handful of adult dropouts to return to regular high school classes. Teachers who have a serious adult student or two in their classes are not alone with a horde of teenagers. They have moral support for the academic enterprise.

The notion of introducing conventional adults into public schools in supportive roles has many precedents: graders to assist teachers in providing feedback on homework, mentors, tutors, crossing guards, volunteer or paid teacher-aides in the lower grades. Why am I touting adults as *students* as a more promising approach? True, I do not have research evidence in support of my suggestion, but, on the other hand, research evidence for the beneficial consequences of adults in these other roles is weak or non-existent. I recommend bringing adults into classes as students because I find it plausible to believe that, properly selected to screen out predators, they would influence youngsters in their classes by what they do and how they behave rather than the usual relationship between adults and children, where adults are *telling* children what children ought to do. Of course, the effectiveness of this hypothesis should be tested systematically; the question is whether it is theoretically compelling enough to be worth testing.

After I finished, I looked for comments pro and con. I did not anticipate what happened: silence. I had apparently misjudged the expectations of the conference. Assuming as I did that existing interventions had little effect on school violence or drug abuse, I thought that what was needed were new approaches. So I offered some. The three other papers met a somewhat similar fate. Thoughtful though they were, they did not offer practical solutions to the issue that had called the conference into being: how to spend $500 million a year to solve, or to appear to solve, problems the causes of which were poorly understood. I never saw the final report on the conference, although more than a year has gone by since it ended. I don't envy the people who, in writing it, had to try to portray the outcome as constructive.

In September 2000, I started my fiftieth year on the Rutgers faculty. Perhaps it will be my last. Although in good health, I am considering retiring from regular teaching—and writing the books and articles I have promised myself to write. In fact, unfulfilled writing commitments weigh on my conscience. If I retire next year, I do not expect to spend much of my time tanning myself on beaches.

Looking back, should I have followed Donald Young's advice, or was I right to ignore it? Was becoming a criminologist a mistake? When one grows old, it is difficult to avoid regretting the many mistakes one has made over a lifetime, both personal and professional. No, becoming a criminologist was not one of them. It has been gratifying to try to solve the difficult intellectual puzzles of criminology: why people commit crimes and whether society is any good at persuading them to stop. It has been somewhat less gratifying but still enjoyable to try to convince undergraduates who want to understand "the criminal mind" that the criminal mind is not so different from the minds of the rest of us. Yes, I would do it again.

Do I have any advice for young people who are contemplating becoming criminologists? Criminology is a vast and changing field, and there are many niches within it. Consequently, giving advice runs the risk of being irrelevant. Nevertheless, I have learned a few lessons that may be useful. First, it seems to me that a criminologist who wishes to do academically respectable research should be deeply rooted intellectually in an academic discipline. I have always considered myself a sociologist first and a criminologist second. It is true that nowadays there are schools of criminal justice and departments of criminal justice; they present a temptation to regard oneself as a specialist in criminal justice rather than in sociology or psychology or law. I think that losing a strong disciplinary identity diminishes creativity. It is more difficult to maintain a disciplinary identity when one is employed in such a school or department, but it is possible—and ultimately beneficial to one's career.

Second, it seems to me that a *comparative* emphasis enhances our understanding of crime: comparative ethnically, by gender, by race, by country, by age, by type of offense, by type of offender. I sometimes point out to my students that, if the inmates at Trenton State Prison offered to hold office hours to explain why people commit crimes, it would be a waste of time to go to listen to them. Why? Because they only know about their own motives, not how their motives differ from those of people who don't commit crimes. Those differences they can better learn about from a criminologist who *compares* offenders with non-offenders.

## Selected Publications

The editors requested "a selected dozen-item bibliography of what each writer believes are his or her most important publications." Here is Professor Toby's response:

*Some recent articles*: "Medicalizing Temptation," which appeared in the Winter 1998 issue of *The Public Interest*; "The Criminalization of Deviance," in the *Encyclopedia of Sociology*, 2nd edition, Vol. 1, pp. 523-527 (2000); and "Schools and Crime," in the *Encyclopedia of Crime and Justice*, revised edition Vol. 4, pp. 1365-1370 (2002). I tend to think highly of articles I have recently written; it takes a while for the glow to wear off.

*Some polemical articles:* "The New Criminology Is the Old Sentimentality," *Criminology*, Vol. 16, February 1979, pp. 516-526; "Going Native in Criminology," *The Criminologist*, Vol. 11, May-June, 1986; "U.N. Hands Cuba a P.R. Coup," *Wall Street Journal*, August 27, 1990. I am particularly fond of the shortest article I ever wrote: "Going Native in Criminology."

*My efforts to educate the general public*: "Worst Thing about U.S. Prisons Is the Other Prisoners," *Wall Street Journal*, June 10, 1986; "Studying Suicide and 'the Nerve of Failure,'" *Chicago Tribune*, July 31, 1987; "Are Police the Enemy?" *Society*, Vol. 37 (May/June, 2000), pp. 38-42. I am always surprised by how little response is evoked by articles published in newspapers with daily circulations over a million.

*My more scholarly articles*: "Is Punishment Necessary?" *Journal of Criminal Law, Criminology, and Police Science*, Vol. 55, September 1964, pp. 332-337; "The Socialization and Control of Deviant Motivation," in Daniel Glaser, ed., *Handbook of Criminology*, Chicago: Rand McNally, 1974, Chapter 3, pp. 85-100; "Where are the Streakers Now?" in Hubert M. Blalock, ed., *Sociological Theory and Research*, Free Press, 1980, pp. 304-313. Professor Blalock, then the President of the American Sociological Association, initially thought from my title that my article was frivolous. (He had invited me to read a theoretical paper about deviance at the annual conference.) After reading "Where are the Streakers Now?" he decided that it was what I claimed it was: a serious analysis of the causes of deviance.

# 8

# My Life in "Crim"

John Irwin

When I entered college in 1957 I had no intention of studying sociology or criminology, nor of becoming a criminologist. At the time, I had enthusiastically taken up surfing and had some romantic notion of being an oceanographer, thus combining my new passion with a future vocation. But my peculiar pre-college biography and other interests steadily veered me toward the social sciences and then criminology. Mainly, between the ages of 17 and 27, I had been a thug, a drug addict and then—after being convicted of armed robbery—a convict.

After two years at San Francisco State I transferred to finish my B.A. at UCLA—closer to the warmer waters of Southern California. There I became less and less interested in math, physics, and chemistry and more drawn to anthropology and sociology. I began considering changing my major to "soc" or "anthro" in which I thought I might obtain a Ph.D. and a teaching job. I sought the advice of Donald Cressey, the chair of the combined Department of Sociology and Anthropology. I revealed to him my nefarious biography and my interests in becoming a professor in sociology or anthropology and asked him if he thought that, given my disreputable past and damaged legal status, there was much chance of getting a job at a university. He assured me that I would be able to and told me the story of a criminologist who was at that time applying for a teaching position after serving a prison term and who was probably going to succeed (which he did). Cressey, who was a highly respected criminologist, not only encouraged me to continue studies in sociology, but to consider criminology as a specialty and to begin by taking his course in criminology.

It was not only my deviant past that caused me to be more interested in criminology than physical science and math, which had been my academic fortes. It was also my intense curiosity about the lives of people I encountered, particularly people who were different. From the time

I was a teenager, I was fascinated with the different "trips," "scenes" "lifestyles"—or whatever you want to call them—of groups of people I encountered—hot rodders, weedheads, thieves, dope fiends, convicts, and surfers. (Not only was I interested in these activities, I joined in and *this* got me into a pack of trouble.) This fascination for different walks of life drew me to anthropology and sociology. It also informed my sociological perspective and therein influenced my career in criminology.

My initial interest in sociology was broader than just criminology, but my criminal and convict background kept pushing me toward crim. It started in Cressey's class. In about the middle of the semester he began a series of lectures on the "inmate social system" and delivered the latest theory developed by Gresham Sykes and Sheldon Messinger.[1] In brief, this theory was based on the idea that prisoners' behavior was regulated by the "convict code" and by prisoner leaders who appeared to be in opposition to the administration but in fact were actually in complicity with it. The way it worked was that the code and the leaders called for other prisoners to "do their own time," that is, not object to or interfere with the activities of the leaders who received special privileges in a trade-off for maintaining control. When I heard and read these ideas they did not ring true. They missed the mark on two issues. First, the convict code was not indigenous to the prison, but was a prison adaptation of the "thief's code." I knew this because I had been thoroughly imbued with the thief's code in my early training as a thief. "Do your own time" was the prison adaptation of the thief's primary dictum, "never inform on a fellow thief." The inmate social system theorists also failed to recognize that the most powerful figures in the prisons in the 1930s, 1940s, and 1950s, which is the era Sykes and Messinger were focused on, were "right guys" who were most often carriers of the thief's code.

After class I started expressing my disagreement with the inmate social system ideas to Cressey. At first he encouraged me to give them a chance to sink in. But the more I heard the more I was convinced they were wrong. He finally told me to write my ideas, which I did in an outline. He began to see what I was getting at and we started to interview ex-convicts, some of whom had been my friends in prison. They were part of the drug-addict rehabilitation program, Synanon, located in Santa Monica, a program with which both Cressey and I had already had some contact. Our efforts resulted in our writing "Thieves, Convicts, and the Inmate Culture," published in *Social Problems*.[2] This article changed the thinking on prisoner social organization within criminology and initiated my identification as a criminologist.

While I was still at UCLA, Lew Yablonsky, a young criminologist who had just published his book on youth gangs—*The Violent Gang*, replaced Cressey who had left to teach at Cambridge University for a year. I studied with Lew and we became close friends and wrote an article togeth-

er on the "New Criminal."[3] When I approached graduation, Lew recommended me for a Woodrow Wilson Fellowship, a one-year stipend for
graduate studies.

I received the fellowship, which stipulated that I must pursue graduate studies in a different University. I was accepted by the University
of California, Berkeley, Department of Sociology and there fell under the
tutelage of Herbert Blumer, Erving Goffman, and David Matza. I forgot
criminology for awhile and concentrated on learning sociology. My
special interest was deviance, and more particularly deviant "subcultures." After my first year, Goffman sent me back to Los Angeles for the
summer to study surfers, in whom he had an interest. (This study and
my general interests in subcultures eventually led to the publication of
my second and favorite book—*Scenes.*[4]

In my three years taking courses and studying for exams at Berkeley, I acquired three sociological positions that shaped my future work
in criminology. The first was a basic theoretical perspective on social
behavior which was combined with a method of doing research. I
learned these, the perspective and the method, directly from Goffman, Blumer, and Matza and through my reading of Max Weber, George
Herbert Mead, and Alfred Schutz. Following the tradition of the "Chicago School," Goffman advised his students to get out into the world and
observe people in natural settings. He emphasized attention to the
fine details in the patterns of social interaction. Blumer, Matza, and the
writings of Mead and Schutz taught me that human beings are not
"objects" that merely react to exterior forces but are authors of action,
are humans who reflect on themselves, transcend circumstances and act
in purposeful fashions. In planning and executing their actions, they are
guided by values and definitions that they acquire in their interaction
with others. This process and the shared subjective meanings are the
essential ingredients of social life and the dominant forces in shaping
individuals' behavior.

Studying social phenomena, then, requires connecting with human
subjects' meaning worlds. We, as fellow humans, are uniquely equipped
to immerse ourselves into others' subjective worlds. In the first place,
we penetrate their meaning worlds by learning their "language," which
is the vehicle of shared meanings. In a manner that we do not fully understand, language carries bundles of meanings that are gathered in experiences with others. The eminent English language philosopher, Ludwig
Wittgenstein, who painstakingly explored the relationships among language, meaning, and behavior, offered the analogy of family resem-
blance to describe how meanings of a word or concept cling together.[5]
Just as we see resemblances in the faces of people who are related even
though we cannot pinpoint exactly why they look much like each
other, we "understand" the meanings of words. The point is that we
acquire this understanding in our collective experiences and commu-

nication. An "outsider," by commingling and communicating with members of a social world, can learn the group's shared meanings. Also, by communicating with an individual over a period of time a researcher can learn the unique set of meanings this person carries and employs in action.

To fully grasp others' definitions and meanings, a lengthy period of immersion into their world is required. Research usually does not provide enough time to do this, so we have to rely on long, open-ended interviews and other qualitative strategies such as "focus groups." Though imperfect, these approaches are better at providing understanding of humans' meaning worlds than standing on the outside and developing quantitative procedures, such as questionnaires that attempt to squeeze the research subjects' definitions, understandings, and meanings into the researchers' quantifiable categories.

Another human skill that we can employ to understand the behavior of human subjects is the process Max Weber called "verstehen" in which we place ourselves in others' situations and abstractly see the world from their viewpoint.[6] Once we have some grasp of others' definitions and understandings, we can imagine ourselves in their shoes and to some extent come to see "their side." With varying degrees of exactitude, we do this to get by in our daily lives. For instance, in most urban locations in the United States (New York City being a notable exception) when urban dwellers start to step off the curb in front of an approaching car, they wait until they catch the eye of the driver and for the driver's subtly delivered message—maybe just a slight change in facial expression—that indicates to them that the driver sees them and is going to wait for them. Then they cross. They accomplish this because they share a set of definitions and meanings related to the situations of drivers and pedestrians and can place themselves at that moment in the driver's position and understand his or her intentions. Evidence of the operation of this process is in the experience of a foreigner who does *not* know the particular country's meanings on this issue and would not dare step onto the street on such a slight and subtle assurance.

I came into conflict with Goffman over this approach to social life because he thought of himself as a positivist—an objective observer of social behavior and he purported to avoid studying subjective states of mind. A friendly disagreement we had after I had completed my PhD reveals our differences on this issue. On a ski trip Goffman and I argued whether one could accurately study subjective states. He asked me, "How do you find out what is on other peoples' minds?" I answered that one way was to ask them. Later that evening I was looking out the window and watching a few scattered snowflakes descend from the sky and commented, "I wonder if it is going to snow?" Goffman retorted, "Why don't you ask the snowflakes?" I responded, "That's the point, you don't recognize the difference between a snowflake and a human being."

I learned "appreciation," another feature of my sociological approach, from David Matza. As he argued in his book, *Becoming Deviant*, the student must suspend his or her moral judgments and get inside the thinking of subjects to understand human behavior, particularly deviant behavior.[7] One must learn subjects' definitions and morality—not accept them, but learn them. This is only accomplished by pulling close to research subjects. Invariably, achieving an understanding of their behavior through this approach leads to the discovery of their essential humanness. They operate with values, sentiments, fears, and aspirations; have intelligence; and are kind and loyal to other people, maybe not all other people, but at least people to whom they are close. In other words, they are much like us.

Another important aspect of the sociological orientation I acquired in graduate school was a strong conviction that a value-free social science was an insidious myth. My studies of Max Weber and C. Wright Mills, and the influence of Matza taught me that researchers' values invariably obtrude into the collection and analysis of data. The choice of what researchers study is greatly influenced by their values. More importantly, what they discover is also colored by theirs or their sponsors' values. For example, James Q. Wilson and Richard J. Herrnstein reviewed existing research on crime and offered a theory suggesting that crime in America had nothing to do with the general economic and political arrangements in our highly stratified society, but was the outcome of criminals' genetic predispositions or faulty upbringing.[8] Critics of their book, *Crime and Human Nature*, point out that they blew little bits of evidence out of proportion and misused and selectively reported other evidence linking crime to individual and inherited characteristics.[9] It is apparent that their politically conservative agenda corrupted their research and analysis.

There is another more complex and significant way that values enter or should enter into the study of human beings. When we operate from the perspective that human beings are actively engaged in meaningful behavior, it follows that in order to understand them we must draw close to them, immerse ourselves into their meaning worlds and learn their definitions and value orientations. In doing this we are compelled to take their values seriously and, unless we "go native," to negotiate their values with our own. It becomes difficult to dismiss others as merely pathological beings who must be controlled, changed, or eliminated (incapacitated). We learn and appreciate their personal problems, which we, as astute social scientists, see, or at least should see, are related to their social, political, and economic situations. Consequently, we are persuaded to seek solutions to their problems that take their viewpoints and aspirations into account. This forces us to search for solutions that are democratic and humanistic. Appreciation, therein, leads to humanism and promotes continual search for universal human values.

Positivism, under the mantle of "objectivity," too often leads to politically conservative solutions that support the status quo or repressive policies—such as the punishment binge that has been unleashed on non-white and lower-class people over the last 20 years. Usually these repressive policies are made possible or are suggested by misunderstandings of subjects, in this case lower-class and non-white "offenders," that have been generated by social scientists pursuing objective, value-free research methods. Studies employing qualitative approaches and a humanistic, phenomonological perspective, such as the classics *The Hobo, Street Corner Society, Tally's Corner, The Cloak of Competence, Stations of the Lost* (and I humbly include my own, *The Felon*) invariably suggested solutions to the social problems the authors studied that are more humane and have a greater chance of working for the general good, which, after all, is our calling.[10]

Finally, my graduate training was influenced by C. Wright Mills' instructions in *The Sociological Imagination* that we must not be seduced by the convoluted vagaries and platitudes of "grand theories" nor waste time deciphering or producing jargon. I learned to keep my eye and mind on social phenomena and to describe and analyze them with concepts and terms that were understandable to the people living involved.

After I had completed all my course work, passed my qualifying exams and was ready to begin my Ph.D. dissertation, Sheldon Messinger, who was the assistant director of the Center for the Study of Law and Society at Berkeley, encouraged me to join a study of parole in California that was being administered through the Center. I decided to participate in the study and write my dissertation on something related to parole. The administrators of the Center were able to obtain permission for me to conduct research in the California prisons, interview prisoners and parolees, and review prisoner files. This, given my ex-convict status, was no small matter and was accomplished because of the Department of Corrections' temporary openness to research and the influence of the administrators at the Center, particularly Philip Selznick, the Director.

My study, as I wrote in the introduction to *The Felon*, which resulted from this research, "expanded to encompass the extended 'career' of the felon" and brought me back and firmly connected me to criminology. In the first place, the book was well received and my reputation as a promising criminologist was established. In addition, something very personal occurred that permanently attached me to issues related to crime and punishment. In returning to the prison and interviewing and interacting with convicts and parolees I re-immersed myself in their social worlds, empathized with them, understood their plight, and comprehended the ill-conceived and unjust practices involved in incarceration and parole routines. I acquired a basic insight that stemmed from my sociological perspective and served as the underlying theme of my analysis of the prison and parole experiences of felons. Many of the cruel, arbitrary, and ineffective practices I discovered in my study resulted from the fact that the overseers in the prison and parole systems misunderstood the perspectives and action of the felons and attributed to them evil motives. Likewise, the convicts and parolees committed stupid and counterproductive acts because of their misunderstanding of the perspectives and motives of their overseers. For example, in studying parole I discovered that most parolees intended to "straighten up their hand," that is live a life that according to them was not one of intolerable and self-destructive deviance. They agreed that "ripping and tearing," that is running amuck, stealing, using hard drugs, particularly heroin, and hurting other people was unacceptable. But smoking a little marijuana, living with a woman, hanging with their friends, many of whom had jail or prison records, would be impossible for them to avoid and should be acceptable. However, the parole rules were written from a relatively puritanical point of view—the parolee "must avoid association with former inmates of penal institutions . . . and with individuals of bad reputation;" "may not possess, use, or traffic in any narcotic drugs;" "must maintain gainful employment;" and "must not leave the county of residence without permission of the parole agent." Agents, being somewhat more realistic, usually attempted to enforce a less stringent set of rules, but they also believed that parolees should refrain from deviant practices, such as smoking marijuana, "shacking up" with a woman, and leaving the county without permission. This difference in points of view was a disruptive factor in parolee-agent relationship and resulted in many "violations" (returning the parolee to prison for violation of parole conditions).

After the publication of *The Felon* my identity as a criminologist was affirmed. My continued interest in the study of crime, criminals, and incarceration was established, and a commitment to work to change the unjust and cruel punitive practices I had come to understand was formed. I had obtained a teaching position in the sociology department at San Francisco State College and there, except for a couple of breaks to do research and then to teach for an academic year at Hunter College in New York, I stayed until I retired. I would have accepted a job in a bigger university with a lighter teaching load, but my continued commitment to surfing restricted my choices to California and my disreputable reputation as an ex-convict and a general pain in the ass among my colleagues for my outspoken criticism of conventional criminology probably damaged my chances of getting a job in the few institutions I would accept. All things considered, San Francisco State University was right for me. Located in liberal San Francisco, the college had the most tolerant and radical atmosphere of all the colleges and universities in the state. And it had the city with its deviant scenes and political activities, even an ocean (very cold water, however).

Through the 1970s and 1980s I kept busy. I learned to teach. This meant not just passing on all the material I had learned, but getting students to think critically about ideas, those they had learned before and those they were encountering in college. I presented them with concepts and insights on subject areas, such as crime, criminal justice, and urban life—which were my specialities. But more important to me was cultivating their skills at distinguishing fact from fiction and recognizing rhetoric, dogma, and sloppy logic.

I continued studying prisons and jails and wrote three more books on imprisonment.[11] (I slipped in a book on my other sociological interest—deviant scenes.) All of my research started with some form of participant observation. When it was possible, I found some way to "hang out" with the people I was studying in "natural" settings. This was of course easy with surfers. I was a surfer myself and the settings were open. In jails and prisons it was more difficult. When I studied the jail, I worked as a volunteer with Prisoners Services in the San Francisco County Jail, which allowed me to circulate freely and mingle with the prisoners. At San Quentin, in addition to conducting lengthy open-ended interviews, I organized a group of prisoner "experts" and met with them regularly for a year. I used this type of group (which would be called a focus group now) many times with very good results. Frequently, the qualitative phase supplied material for or led to quantitative methods, such as questionnaires and statistical analysis of secondary data, e.g. arrest records. But these procedures were always preceded and informed by qualitative material.

In addition to studying imprisonment, I have worked throughout my professional career to reform criminal justice practices. I began while still completing my PhD. At the finish of my dissertation study, I helped the San Quentin prisoners, with whom I had been in contact, to organize a weekend strike protesting their conditions of confinement and the arbitrary practices of the Adult Authority. Then I began organizing prisoner reform groups and eventually The Prisoners' Union. I started Rebound, a college program for ex-prisoners, which exists to this day. I affiliated with the American Friends Service Committee and was invited to participate in their "working party" on criminal justice. In a series of meetings extending over a year and a half, the working party hammered out a set of principles to guide reform of the criminal justice system, resulting in *The Struggle for Justice*.[12] This book, written by myself, Caleb Foote, and David Greenberg, criticized the overextension of criminal law as a tool to solve social problems, the excessively long prison sentences, and the punitive and arbitrary practices of parole authorities operating under the powers granted them in the name of rehabilitation. It inspired a series of other similar critiques and the eventual demise of the rehabilitative ideal as one of the primary purposes of punishment. (Regrettably, it also opened the door for the punitive movement that swept through the system in the 1980s and 1990s.)

All my work in criminal justice—research and reform—was shaped or propelled by the underlying conviction that offenders and prisoners are human beings and, for the most part, rather ordinary human beings. What distinguishes them from free, respectable, "decent" people, is not so much their crimes, but their race, poverty, and disreputability. Criminologists and large segments of the general society were coming to this recognition in the 1960s. Before then, most criminals were thought to be essentially different than "normal" and decent people: members of the dangerous classes, criminal types, mental retards, mesomorphs, psychopaths, neurotics, or sociopaths. Along with other changes that accompanied the civil rights and anti-war movements and the "war on poverty," a general rethinking of the nature of crime and the character of criminals occurred. Criminals were being seen as disadvantaged people, even "political prisoners." Eldridge Cleaver, Huey Newton, and George Jackson even became heroes.

After 1975, when the country was generally rejecting "liberalism," the idea of the criminal type re-emerged. It started with James Q. Wilson warning us in his book, *Thinking About Crime,* that "wicked people exist."[13] Following Wilson, more and more criminologists began developing ideas about a new criminal "bogeyman," variously labeled as the "high rate offender," "career criminal," or "criminal predator." Two slightly different versions of this criminal bogeyman emerged. The soft version was a person who persists in committing property crimes, even after repeated opportunities to live an honest life and after having been arrested many times and having served numerous jail and prison sentences. A harder version is a violent criminal, equally intractable, who goes about his predatory crimes with no regard for other human beings. When he snatches purses from old ladies, he bashes them in the head. When he robs mom-and-pop grocery stores, he unnecessarily beats or murders his victims.

These images, which culminated in the Willie Horton story that played such an important role in George Bush's defeat of Michael Dukakis, were created by politicians fulminating about the crime problem and by the news media that had discovered that crime and violence drew audiences. But criminologists also got on the bandwagon and with few exceptions supplied social scientific theories and data to support the criminal bogeyman idea.

From my close experiences with "criminals," both in my personal life and my research, I understood how wrong these ideas were. I discovered in a study of people entering jail that most were members of the disreputable underclass—the "rabble"—who had only committed very petty crimes, such as drinking in public. I concluded that they had been arrested and held in jail because, in addition to being poor, uneducated, and unemployed or under-employed, they were "detached" and "disreputable." As I wrote in my book on the jail:

> They are detached because they are not well integrated into
> conventional society, they are not members of conventional
> social organizations, they have few ties to conventional net-
> works, and they are carriers of unconventional values and
> beliefs. They are disreputable because they are perceived as
> irksome, offensive, threatening, capable of arousal, even pro-
> torevoluntionary.[14]

I and other researchers have found that, increasingly, just being non-
white is the determining factor in arrest and conviction.

Likewise most persons convicted of felonies and sent to prison are
guilty of nonserious felonies that lack any feature the public abhors.
Their charges involve no use of a weapon, violence, theft of a large
amount of money, abhorrent sexual acts, or sale of drugs. Even the "high
rate offenders" who commit frequent felonies and define themselves as
"outlaws," "dope fiends," "crack heads," or "gang bangers," commit mostly petty felonies. They are, as James Austin and I wrote in our study of
persons going to prison,

> for the most part, uneducated, unskilled (at crime as well as
> conventional pursuits), and highly disorganized people who
> have no access to any form of rewarding, meaningful con-
> ventional life. They usually turn to dangerous, mostly unre-
> warding petty criminal pursuits as one of the few options
> they have to earn money, win some respect, and avoid monot-
> onous lives on the streets. Frequently, they spend most of
> their young lives behind bars.[15]

In prison I knew many persons who had committed monstrous
acts. Even they departed from the popular image of vicious, uncaring
psychopaths or predators. When they committed their crimes either they
were overwhelmed by circumstances or contextual forces or they operated with a twisted morality of their own. For example, Archie Conniff,
who I got to know after he had served 20 years, killed his wife and children in a fit of rage and then tried to commit suicide by slitting his throat.
He lived to regret and mourn his actions for the rest of his life and continually tried to compensate for his crimes through public service. I
recently read a story based on the interview with Timothy McVeigh who
bombed the federal building in Oklahoma City. He argued that he was
repaying our government for the violence it had unleashed previously
on the Branch Davidians in Waco, Texas, and the Weaver family at
Ruby Ridge, Idaho. Both groups had been ambushed by federal agents.
McVeigh stated that he regretted that there were children in the Oklahoma Federal building, but that the government was irresponsible for
having them there. Twisted thinking, but not much more twisted than
the thinking of Presidents Johnson and Nixon in planning and approv-
ing of the massive bombings of Hanoi and Cambodia.

I also know from my studies that crime is not concentrated in the segments of population that receive almost all the attention from the press, most criminologists, and criminal justice practitioners. In fact, the most serious crime in America, in terms of dollars, injury and death, is the crime committed by conventional or "respectable" people whose actions are seldom scrutinized by police. These people, whose crimes include violations of anti-trust laws, tax law violations, fraud, bribery, and pollution, are rarely prosecuted and they almost never go to jail. The crimes of reputable people are not only more costly economically than street crime, but they result in much greater damage to the public's health and the loss of life. Each year there are fewer than 20,000 "traditional" murders in the United States, but more than 100,000 workers die from industrial diseases. These deaths are not the unavoidable result of occupational risks, but are too often the result of actions or lack of actions taken by the managers and owners of industries who have known about the risk of diseases such as asbestosis, and have attempted to deny or suppress evidence related to them.

The most serious corporate crime is pollution, which Gilbert Geis, who for years has tried to shift the attention of criminologists from street crime to corporate crime, suggests amounts to "compulsory consumption of violence by most Americans." Geis further argues that this "damage, perpetuated increasingly in direct violation of local, state, and federal law, shatters people's health and safety but still escapes inclusion in the crime statistics."[16]

My study of the career of the felon, which was my Ph.D. dissertation, my study of the jail, and my own experiences as a convict made me fully understand how incarceration, particularly if it is too long, ill-equips people for living outside. It is not so much that these settings—the jail and the prison—are "schools of crime." More than that, in them prisoners are imbued with the routines of incarceration, their skills required for living outside are progressively diminished or destroyed, and they are handicapped by the legal and social stigmas of the ex-prisoner or convict. Recidivism results more from "prisonization" than criminal personality traits.

Finally, I know from my research and experiences that most convicts, even those who have defined themselves as criminals, aspire to relatively modest conventional lives. While serving their time, they sincerely plan to live what they see as a "straight" life when they are released. This is true even in cases in which the persons had been to prison two or three times and fit the criminological definition of a career criminal. In my personal and professional life, I saw many of these persons come apart after their release and swerve back into crime—not because their true criminal character manifested itself, but because their chances for living a conventional life, which had never been that great, had been further reduced by incarceration.

Given my beliefs on the nature of crime and criminals, what has distressed me most in my 30 years in the profession has been the swing toward excessive punitiveness, which has resulted in increasing the nation's prison population sixfold, abandoning almost all efforts to prepare prisoners for a life after prison, and converting prisons into cruel and dangerous human warehouses at best, dungeons at worst. I entered criminology on the wave of reason and tolerance that swept through the field in the late 1950s and the 1960s. It was only because of these progressive changes that I was allowed to enter the profession and achieve some respectability. Then, after several years of working with great expectations of continuing progress on prison reform, the reaction set in. I was dismayed and depressed by the massive swing towards the excessive use of imprisonment, the abandonment of most rehabilitative efforts and the institution of crueler and crueler prison strategies. I also had to witness many of my colleagues getting on board and helping to justify the imprisonment binge.

Criminologists contributed to the imprisonment binge by their reestablishment of the idea that crime was mainly perpetuated by a few people in the population. These "criminal types" or, using the more contemporary label, "career criminals," it is argued, are fundamentally different than "innocent people" or "decent citizens" and can be controlled only by the threat of severe punishment or by incapacitation for long periods. As suggested above, it started with James Q. Wilson announcing that "wicked people exist" and that "nothing avails except to set them apart from innocent people." Then Peter Greenwood and Allan Abrahamse, in a very influential study, purported to have located a category of criminals they labeled "high-rate" offenders and offered means to identify them so they could be "selectively incapacitated."[17] This began a flurry of interest in locating "high-rate" offenders or "career criminals."

John Dilulio, a student of James Q. Wilson, supplied the finishing touches to the punitive reaction. Dilulio established himself as an "expert" on criminal justice issues through a study of prison administration written from an authoritarian viewpoint, and thereafter was appointed to several key positions in government and private institutions, such as the Brookings Institute. He then regularly fulminated in the popular press on the severity of the crime committed by and the leniency of courts toward career criminals.[18] In effect, he and the other conservative criminologists supplied politicians with a scientific ideology for mounting the imprisonment binge that has changed America into the most punitive country in the world with rates of incarceration that are 10 times those of the other modern, industrial nations.

If it is true that most persons arrested and incarcerated have committed relatively non-serious crimes and most prisoners sincerely desire to stop pursuing criminal lives, then why was it that in the late 1970s, through the 1980s and 1990s, so many criminologists came to different conclusions? It appears to me that they erred for two reasons. The first was a shift in criminological research that increased the distance between researchers and the people they studied. Criminologists began relying more and more on quantitative research methods and lost contact with their research subjects. Instead of close interaction or "participation" with human beings, they relied almost exclusively on questionnaire and "secondary" data—such as police arrest records and prison files. For example, in the research conducted by Peter Greenwood and Allan Abrahamse, samples of incarcerated burglars and robbers were administered questionnaires asking about the types and frequency of crimes they had committed before imprisonment. From their answers to these questions and other data from their records, Greenwood and Abrahamse developed a "high-rate offender" category. In a subsequent study, Greenwood and Susan Turner followed a group identified by this technique and discovered that these supposed high-rate offenders did not continue to commit crimes of the type and rate expected.[19] If Greenwood and his associates had studied the prisoners in the first study more closely, using appropriate qualitative research approaches, they would have learned what is well known among prisoners themselves: incarcerated individuals often make grandiose claims about their criminal past.

Another (and probably more important) reason that so many criminologists abandoned the more liberal notions on crime and the criminal that prevailed in the 1960s and early 1970s was that the government, beginning with the Nixon administration, declared a war on crime and began forcefully promoting conservative theories on crime causation and its control. At that time, conservative politicians saw street crime, that is, crime perpetuated mainly by lower-class and non-white persons, as the perfect issue to divert the public's attention away from other pressing social problems and the Vietnam war. This was accomplished by conducting research through government agencies, such as NIJ and NIMH, and by rewarding academics and other "pundits" who espoused conservative ideas with research grants, participation in federally funded and congressionally initiated studies and commissions, jobs in government agencies, appointments to commissions, and invitations to prestigious government sponsored conferences and assemblies—all perks that greatly enhance academics' normally low prestige and meager professional lives.

Academics who will supply the government with intellectually respectable embellishment for any reactionary political policies are always standing by. These are not just hacks. Some are tenured professors at the country's most prestigious universities. If the university professors are glib and have somewhat flexible commitments to the truth-finding endeavor or have the remarkable human ability to believe what is in one's best self-interest to believe then they can get in on the government awards.

Through its influence over funds and positions, the government helps create a hierarchy of prestige, power, and privilege in the academic community. A class of elites is established and sets the tone for what are respectable ideas and research. Down the ranks other academics who are scrambling for grants and jobs get in line. In criminology, the lower-status academics understood that their careers would be enhanced if they engaged in a more conservative "rethinking of crime" and possibly would be damaged if they continued defending "liberal" interpretations. I witnessed this process in action when I presented a paper on the negative consequences of the ongoing prison expansion at the 1991 annual meeting of the American Society of Criminology. After the session, a close associate, a prominent criminologist who had had the reputation of being a solid liberal—but as I knew, was a perspicacious follower of trends—came up to me and said "John, are you still worrying about those convicts?"

The effects of the influence of the conservative establishment over the rank and file in criminology is clearly revealed in the publications that appear in our journal, *Criminology*. In 1997 I scanned editions of the journal over the preceding two years. For the prior 15 years the unprecedented expansion of the prison populations had been occurring. A major, if not *the* major, research issue for us as criminologists was what was going on in the new crowded prisons which were holding higher and higher proportions of non-white prisoners to the extent that our imprisonment policies were instituting an American form of apartheid. Most educational and vocational training programs had virtually disappeared, the prisoners' mobility and privileges had been drastically reduced, and racial hostilities and violence were escalating. I found articles on crime, crime causation, police work, recidivism, juvenile delinquency, but not one article on prisons or prisoners.

Here at the end of my career, reviewing my experiences in research and social activism, my accomplishments and disappointments, I have learned to cherish one professional virtue above all others: "intellectual integrity." Our primary mission, I believe, is to find the truth, which is not an easy task. We must hone the skills required to see the truth, including a variety of research skills. I have learned that, when it comes to human subjects, empathy, intuition, and appreciation are crucial, as well as a heightened capacity to see through sham, dogma, and illusion. A plethora of hurdles, pitfalls, and diversions get in the way. We carry our own bundle of stereotypes, biases, categories. To reduce their influence on our perception and analysis of phenomena, we must continually search for them, weigh them, attempt to reduce their influence on our observations and analysis, always recognizing that only partial success is possible. One can, though, attempt to make them explicit, so any interpreter of one's "findings" can evaluate for themselves the findings' validity.

The most serious and insidious obstacle to achieving intellectual integrity is self-interest. Human beings operate with an agenda of desires and goals. Their intellectual capacities are directed toward achieving these and one of their particularly devious capacities is to shape perceptions and conclusions about events to further these personal goals. We are all guilty of this and can only reduce the distortions created by it by constant effort to recognize the force and direction of this bias and by consciously working against it.

## Endnotes

1   "The Inmate Social System," in *Theoretical Studies in Social Organization of the Prison*, Social Science Research Council Pamphlet (March 1960), pp. 5-19.

2   (Fall, 1962).

3   John Irwin & Lewis Yablonsky, "The New Criminal: A View of the Contemporary Offender," *British Journal of Criminology*, April, 1965.

4   (Beverly Hills, CA: Sage Publication, 1977).

5   *Philosophical Investigations* (New York, NY: Macmillian, 1965). See p. 45.

6   Max Weber, *The Theory of Social and Economic Organization* (London: The Free Press of Glencoe, 1947).

7   (Englewood Cliffs, NJ: Prentice Hall, 1969) Chapter Two.

8   *Crime and Human Nature* (New York, NY: Simon and Schuster, 1985).

9   See particularly, Leon J. Kamin, "Is Crime in the Genes? The Answer May Depend on Who Chooses What Evidence," *Scientific American*, Feb., 1986.

10  Nels Anderson, *The Hobo* (Chicago, IL: University of Chicago Press, 1923); William F. Whyte, *Street Corner Society* (4th ed. Chicago, IL: University of Chicago Press, 1993); Elliot Liebow, *Tally's Corner* (Boston, MA: Little Brown, 1967); Robert B. Edgerton, *The Cloak of Competence* (Berkeley, CA: The University of California Press, 1967); Jacqueline Wiseman, *Stations of the Lost* (Englewood Cliffs, NJ: Prentice Hall, 1970); and John Irwin, *The Felon* (Englewood Cliffs, NJ: Prentice Hall, 1970).

11  *Prisons in Turmoil* (Boston, MA: Little Brown, 1980); *The Jail* (Berkeley, CA: University of California Press, 1985); and with James Austin, *It's About Time* (Belmont, CA: Wadsworth, 1994).

12  (New York, NY: Hill and Wang, 1971).

13  (New York, NY: Vintage Books, 1975) p. 235.

14  *The Jail*, p. 2.

15  *It's About Time*, p. 137.

16  "Deterring Corporate Crime," in *Corporate Power in America*, ed. by Ralph Nader and Mark J. Green (New York, NY: Grossman, 1973) p. 12.

[17]    *Selective Incapacitation* (Santa Monica, CA: Rand Corporation, 1982).

[18]    See particularly "Crime in America: It's Going to Get Worse." *Readers Digest* (August, 1995):33-37.

[19]    *Selective Incapacitation Revisited: Why High-Rate Offenders Are Hard to Predict* (Santa Monica, CA: Rand Corporation, 1987).

# 9

# Criminologist as Witness

Richard Quinney

We are all witnesses to the life of our times. Witnesses in one way or another to the joys and the sorrows of being human in a particular time and place. We are witnesses to the sufferings around us and within us. And at times we are moved by conscience to observe and report these sufferings. "This thing I'm telling you about, I saw with my own eyes," reports a woman who witnessed a mass killing years ago. Such witnessing comes out of awareness, and is an act of conscience. If actions more physical in nature follow, they do so because there has been awareness and there has been witnessing.

As criminologists, especially, we are in a position to observe the human sufferings of our times. We have devoted much of our lives to observing these sufferings. The subject of our attention, crime, is by definition that of suffering. Crime is the window through which we understand the world that produces crime. We soon realize that there can be no decrease in crime without the ending of suffering. The primary object of our attention is thus suffering rather than crime. We are students of suffering, and we bear witness to suffering.

One's biography as a criminologist can be traced as a journey in witnessing. In the documentary that follows, I have gathered observations from my own life of witnessing as a criminologist. As part of the movement for a critical criminology, my life has been a gradual development in understanding crime and the emergence of the criminal justice system. Along the way, there have been the critical reflections on being a criminologist, on being a witness.

My own development as a critical criminologist—in a collective effort with other criminologists—can be seen as a progression in the life course. In other words, my thoughts and my actions have developed and changed as I have experienced the world—as I have aged. There is no separation between the life of the mind and the life of the one who is doing the thinking. Gathered here, chronologically, are the artifacts of a life that has attempted to make sense of the world while living in that world. These fragments from my writing may be seen as signposts along the way, as stages in the course of bearing witness to the sufferings in the world.

# I

When I began graduate school in 1956, the dominant stance in the social sciences—in sociology in particular—was the acceptance of existing social conditions. Perhaps because of my background, on the edge of two worlds, town and country, I became an observer and critic of the status quo. Some of this background I would later allude to in articles, and I would discuss more fully in my autobiographical books *Journey to a Far Place* and *For the Time Being*. As I studied sociology I became greatly interested in the social problems endemic to the country. Asking, of course, Why? And how could things be different? The United States, in the midst of the Cold War, seemed to be driven more by class, conflict, and inequality than by the consensus suggested in the prevailing social theory and national ideology. I thus pursued a class and conflict theory as I began to write and to teach in a series of colleges and universities.

Clearly, what was defined as crime was a product of the economic and political life of the country. Criminal laws were constructed to protect special interests and to maintain a specific social and moral order. This understanding of law and order was evident in the turmoils of the time: the civil rights movement for racial equality, the protests against the war in Vietnam, and the revolts within universities. At the same time, there was emerging a legal apparatus, called the criminal justice system, to control threatening behavior and to preserve the established order. Critical criminology developed with an awareness of these events and conditions. By many names—radical, Marxist, progressive—a critical criminology was created to understand and to change the direction of the country.

My travels through the 1960s, the 1970s, the 1980s, and the 1990s were marked by a progression of ways of thinking and acting. From the social constructionist perspective to phenomenology, from phenomenology to Marxist and critical philosophy, from Marxist and critical philosophy to liberation theology, from liberation theology to Buddhism and existentialism. And then to a more ethnographic and personal mode of thinking and being. It is necessary to note that in all of these travels nothing was rejected or deleted from the previous stages. Rather, each new stage of development incorporated what had preceded it. Each change was motivated by the need to understand crime in another or more complex way, in a way excluded from a former understanding. Each stage incorporated the changes that were taking place in my personal life. There was to be no division between life and theory, between witnessing and writing.

## Observations

While political freedom is a delicate and dubious matter in all political democracies, it is particularly problematic in the United States. It seems apparent that Americans, as compared to other peoples in representative governments, are especially intolerant of social and political differences. This intolerance is expressed in the denial of various civil rights to certain social and political minority groups, religious groups, racial and ethnic groups, and political dissenters of various persuasions. Numerous criminal laws and rulings have been formulated to handle these differences. Behaviors by political minorities committed out of conscience have been made illegal. In addition to the numerous acts that have been defined as subversive (by the groups in power), recent attempts to express dissatisfaction with nuclear testing, civil defense, military buildups, and racial discrimination have been subject to criminal action. A host of previously existing laws, for example, have been used in suppression of dissent and protest. Demonstrators for racial civil rights and other causes have been arrested on such charges as disorderly conduct, breach of peace, parading without a permit, trespassing, loitering, and violation of fire ordinances. Under other laws, persons have been arrested for refusing to pay income taxes used for military purposes, for not complying with local civil defense ordinances, for picketing military bases, for refusing to register for the draft, and for violating state laws which require the segregation of races.

All of these criminal behaviors share the common element that the offenders are pursuing values out of conscience and conviction different from the values of those groups that are formulating and administering the criminal law. The result, nevertheless, is criminal behavior. Theories of such criminal behavior must include a knowledge of the political process. The politics of crime thus becomes an essential aspect of a theory of criminal behavior. Most important, the politics of crime provides the basis for an explanation of the criminal law and its administration (1964).

The ability of the individual to break with the established order is perhaps nowhere better illustrated than in some forms of deviant and criminal behavior. Protest on a large scale can be interpreted as a desire by persons to find meaning, identity, or a "reality world." Dissatisfaction with present values and norms can produce a response by entire groups of people. Much juvenile delinquency can be seen as a reaction of individuals and groups to situations defined as difficult or undesirable. "Political extremism," some of which may be defined as criminal or may result in criminal offenses, appears to be a conscious attempt by individuals to improve particular situations. Violation of the law may be carried out as a protest against policies and conditions that are regarded by some persons as unjust. Behavior that is defined as criminal may at times be the only appropriate means for achieving desired ends (1965).

[The following is an excerpt from "Dialogue with Richard Quinney," which was conducted by Eileen Goldwyn, and appeared in *Issues in Criminology* (1971).]

*Eileen Goldwyn:* Can you retrace how you came to that position?

*Richard Quinney:* Probably not. As I am forced to look back on it now, it's difficult for me to describe the intellectual sources of what I did then and what I'm doing now.

*EG:* I'm not thinking so much in terms of intellectualism but I can remember feelings just like that because of Berkeley and the events that were going on then. I was for once really on the outside as opposed to being inside of the law and it just made me see it in an entirely different way and I was just curious if there was some occasion when you got that feeling, more than just sort of reading about it.

*RQ:* Yes, well as you say it was more in terms of what was happening outside than what was happening in criminology or sociology. It was more my own relation to the world. It was the time when I began to see many of the injustices around us, and rather than assuming that the law was the instrument of justice, I began to question the law. I think this is one reason that criminologists up until the early 1960s did not consider criminal law. I think that they assumed that the law was good in itself. This is a concern of mine right now, which I plan to continue: How our intellectual tradition has opted for social order rather than for individual freedom and radical change. And I know my training as an undergraduate and as a graduate student really obscured the kinds of things I'm interested in now—I'm just coming out of the training I was forced into. I think certain influences of my growing up, outside a formal education, are more important to me intellectually than anything I learned formally as a student in the late 1950s, or anything that I learned from sociological theory or much of anything that I've learned from criminologists.

Social theory developed as a conservative force in reaction to revolution—the French Revolution, the Revolution of 1848. And these are the theories that we rely on today, theories that support social order, theories that apologize for the status quo no matter what the content of the existing order. I now see the law as a tool to support the status quo. I'm afraid that many criminologists and most sociologists have followed this liberal social theory. This was the reason that up until the late 1960s we looked at the criminal law as an instrument to maintain the existing social order. Now we're beginning to question the law because we questioned that social order. In fact, the idea of social order doesn't have much meaning for us now. What I'm trying to do is to work out a social theory that doesn't rely on the conservative social theory that we learned as sociologists. What I want to develop is a radical social theory, a theory that will liberate us as human beings rather than oppress us. Sociological theories have supported a society that oppresses. Ideas themselves have oppressed us.

*EG:* Can you go into the directions of that theory or are you still just forming them?

*RQ:* Well, for one thing it has to do with changing the model of science. We do not have to accept a traditional model of what a theory looks like, for example. A theory can be anything that helps us to understand the world around us. A theory can be propositions, it can be a poem, it can be a photograph, it can be a word, anything that is visual or verbal that allows us to understand something that's bothering us. This also means that science itself is changing. Rather than following the canons of the natural sciences, the new science will be different and it is uncertain to know what it will look like. In fact, we probably don't have to ask what the new mode of knowledge will look like, because if we do, it will be as oppressive as the old science. The scientific model itself has oppressed us and limited us.

And the role of the scientist is changing, if indeed one is still to be called a scientist. The kinds of questions we ask will be different. Rather than merely asking what *is*—the question that we were taught as graduate students and still continue to ask, supposedly the only legitimate question we are supposed to ask as sociologists is what is—I think we begin to ask what *ought to be* and this I think is another reason we are looking at the criminal law rather than taking it for granted.

The problem, then, is how does one ask a question beyond what is? In other words, how does one ask what ought to be? So, one of the problems I'm dealing with now is *transcendence*—to transcend what is. But in order to transcend what is, one has to ask the question what ought to be. My thesis is that we really haven't understood what is because we haven't been able to ask what ought to be. Whenever I want to have some understanding of the present, I have to deal with the alternative of what things could be like. This, in turn, gives me a better understanding of what exists.

The new mode of thought, and what we're doing with our lives, has something to do with a different model of science, or may not even be concerned with science. It has to do with transcendence, as I said, but it has to do with other things also. It means being *involved* in society rather than standing apart from it. We were taught that we were scholars, men of reason, that it was sufficient to know. The original idea of rationalism was to know because you wanted to act. But in this century we thought that it was sufficient to want to know, and we became impotent in thought *and* action. I think now, because of many things happening around us, we are saying it is not sufficient to know, that we need to act too. So this means if we want to know it's because we need to act, and in our acting we'll want to know. In the case of research from my own standpoint, I think I will only do research that allows me to know something that I want to act upon; otherwise I don't need to do the research. Research doesn't need to be done professionally for the sake of doing it. It has to do something personally to my life and for people around me.

What I'm saying is that the way we live our lives will be political, that what we've done all along in the name of "value free" actually has been political. That theory has been oppressive social theory. We have accepted the status quo and that has been political. We have not acted and that has been a political act. And now we're saying that we will act and we will know and in our knowing, act. I would argue that a theory, then, is as good as its politics. So, it has to do with the way we go about knowing and I'm arguing for a transcendental mode of knowing. And it has to do with acting and being political.

And also it is *personal*. The model that we were trained in taught us to be detached and universalistic. I think now what we are saying and what we are developing is the belief that one can only know through one's own eyes. This is not just happening in sociology; it is happening in journalism and in fiction.

*EG*: So then you could just get away from the illusion that you can have a separation of what your values are and what your conception of reality is?

*RQ*: Yes, that's right. To me it's no longer a question that you have to separate them. It's impossible and even if you could, you wouldn't want to.

*EG*: What sorts of reactions did you get from people within the field? You don't identify your "we" with them necessarily?

*RQ*: I just know what I have to do. I think I've always worked alone to a great extent, which has to do with the way I grew up in rural Wisconsin. Maybe there's some purpose to this. I find that specialization is a very stifling thing and whether or not I intended it or not, I don't think in terms of speciality. I think specialities have been a part of the problem and that if we are going to think in new ways, we have to break out of traditional thoughts and established ways. We have to break out of the disciplines that perpetuate these ideas. We have tended to stick to the traditional ideas because we stick with the established disciplines entrenched in the structure of the university and because of the conservative force of the professional associations (the American Sociological Association included). And it happens that at this point in history the things I'm influenced by the most are not coming from sociology and criminology.

*EG*: Do you have anything as a last word to criminologists that you would want to say about the field of criminology to the people that are studying it now?

*RQ*: I think it should be obvious that my concern really is not what happens in criminology. We are free to ask questions that would otherwise be constricted by a discipline. And if a criminology continues, I think it can only be enhanced by the questions that we ask outside of it. (1971).

# II

In the preface to my book, *The Social Reality of Crime*, published in 1970, I stated that my purpose was to provide a reorientation to the study of crime. It was my intention to create a new theoretical perspective for criminology, drawing from past criminology but informing the new perspective with the sensibility that was forming at the end of the 1960s.

I left New York for a long sabbatical in North Carolina at the beginning of the 1970s. I resigned my tenured professorship at New York University to live and to write away from the confines of the university. I needed time for reflection and time to write about what was happening in the United States—as reflected in the criminal law and the emerging criminal justice system. I began my book *Critique of Legal Order* with a call for a critical understanding of crime and the legal system. With a critical Marxian philosophy, I suggested, we could demystify the existing social order and, at the same time, create a form of life that would move us beyond the exploitation and oppression of capitalism. I offered a critical theory of crime control in American society, and observed that only with the making of a socialist society will there be a world without crime.

During the mid-1970s, I moved back to the East Coast and to the New England city of Providence, Rhode Island. I began working on a book that was about Providence and about my life there, and about the reconstruction of social and moral order. I turned my attention to the study of theology, especially the theology of Paul Tillich, and brought my current thinking into criminology. I pursued the thesis that we all are at the same time products of our culture and creators of it. I quoted Marx's concise statement that people make their own history "but they do not make it just as they please; they do not make it under circumstances chosen by themselves, but under circumstances directly encountered, given and transmitted from the past." My argument was, as it continues to be, that criminology is a cultural production that shares the character of such other productions as philosophy, religion, and art. The criminologist is engaged in a cultural practice that interprets and gives meaning to the existing society. Our productions are located in the class relations of the existing society, and our critical understandings are part of the struggle for a better society. The objective in knowing the world critically is to change it. Criminology is to be more than a reflection of the world; it is part of the process through which the world is transformed.

At the end of the 1970s, I published *Class, State, and Crime.* My purpose was to provide a structural interpretation of the current developments in crime and criminal justice. When I revised the book for a second edition, published in 1980, I incorporated my thoughts on a socialist theology. I argued that our whole being, personal and collective, is defined by the historically specific goals and demands of advanced capitalism. The social and moral problems of contemporary society are the result of capitalist development. The solution to crime and to social injustice is ultimately in a transformation that is fundamentally socialist.

## Observations

I have felt it necessary to reinterpret criminology for more than academic reasons. Much of our criminology lacks a sense of the contemporary. I seek a sociology of crime that fits into our own times. I am, also, explicitly interested in the ideals of justice and individual freedom. When we find ourselves able to examine crime as a human construct, then we can raise questions about the justice of criminal law. It is my hope that the theory of the social reality of crime has the power of forcing us to consider libertarian ideals. I contend that a relevant criminology can be attained only when we allow our personal values to provide a vision for the study of crime (1970).

The purpose of a critical understanding of crime in America is to expose the meaning of law and order in capitalist society. The false reality by which we live, the one that supports the established system, must be understood and thereby demystified. It is through a critical criminology that we can understand how American law preserves the existing social and economic order. Criminal law is used in the capitalist state to secure the survival of the capitalist system and its ruling class.

And as capitalist society is further threatened by its own contradictions, criminal law is increasingly used in the attempt to maintain domestic order. The underclass, the class that must remain oppressed for the triumph of the dominant economic class, will continue to be the object of criminal law as long as the dominant class seeks to perpetuate itself. To remove the oppression, to eliminate the need for further revolt, would necessarily mean the end of the ruling class and the capitalist economy.

Criminal law continues to assure the colonial status of the oppressed in the social and economic order of the United States. The events of the last few years relating to crime, including both "disruption" and repression, can be understood only in terms of the crisis of the American system. Moreover, the oppression within the United States cannot be separated from American imperialism abroad. The crisis of the American empire is complete. The war waged against people abroad is part of the same war waged against the oppressed at home (1973).

Our current understanding of crime—our criminology—is archaic and dangerous. Criminology today serves an existing system that is as obsolete as it is oppressive. Even a dialectic that would allow us to transcend established thought is usually lacking in our theories and our research. We must begin to think and act in terms of a socialist tradition. We must build a body of ideas that will allow us to critically understand crime and the legal order in America. In this way will we not only understand our contemporary experiences but we will be able to change our social world. This is the thought and practice that is appropriate to our age (1973).

The rise and fall of American criminology is at the same time the rise and fall of the frontier. The cowboy, the outlaw, the lawman—all gave rise to a way of thought and ultimately to a myth. Criminology is part of that myth. As the frontier is removed from our mind so is most of our current criminology. Our new dialectic is in the removal of the old myth and the creation of a critical form of theory and practice.

Goodbye, Lone Ranger. (1973).

Once there was a way—or so it seemed—to get there from here. All we had to do was follow our procedures; all would be well. But then we began to understand. It was no longer possible to gain a better collective life under the established order or to comprehend the current reality according to conventional wisdom. Other sources became necessary (1974).

We do not adequately understand our contemporary existence. Our comprehension of the present, as well as of the past, is obscured by our current consciousness—a consciousness developed within the existing order and serving only to maintain that order. If we are ever to remove the oppression of the age, we must critically understand the world about us. Only with the development of a new consciousness—a critical philosophy—can we begin to realize the world of which we are capable. My position is thus a critical one: critical not only in an assessment of our current condition, but critical in working toward a new existence—toward a negation of what *is* through thinking about and practicing what *could be.* Any possibility for a different life will come about only through new ideas formed in the course of altering the way we think and the way we live. What is required is no less than a whole new way of life. What is necessary is a new beginning—intellectually, spiritually, and politically (1974).

In critically understanding (and demystifying) our current historical reality, we are in a position to act in a way that will remove our oppression and create a new existence. Though we are subject to the objective conditions of our age, as human beings we are also collectively involved in transforming our social reality. Our praxis is one of critical thought and action—reflecting upon the world and acting to transform it. We can free ourselves from the oppression of the age only as we combine our thoughts and our actions, turning each back upon the other. Our theory and our practice are formed in the struggle to make a socialist society. This is a critical life (1974).

A Marxist criminology is a form of *cultural politics.* We are creating (producing) a way of understanding and a way of living in the world. Our cultural production is specialized in speaking to other criminologists, but it is also popular as it becomes part of everyday consciousness and action. Although many of us will continue to work within that ideological apparatus known as the university, it is nevertheless one of the forums available to us for dialectical expression of criminological production. Criminology as cultural politics has to be developed and practiced in this institution, as in other (and possibly alternative) institutions in capitalist society. The production of knowledge is a political act (1978).

In a Marxist criminology there is no such thing as a theory that is produced in detached, contemplative observation. A theory without a practice not only makes bad theory but also shuts off the possibility of actual political struggle. On the other hand, practice without theory leads to incorrect action for socialist revolution. The only way to confront the problem is to combine social theory and social practice. The process is a never-ending one, being subject to reformulations of both theory and practice (1978).

In understanding crime and criminal justice we produce a theory and a practice that have as their objective changing the world. The importance of criminology is that it moves us dialectically to reject the capitalist order and to struggle for a socialist society. We are thus engaged in the working-class struggle—producing the conditions for our own development in history. The struggle is shared in common and goes to the core of our being. As the theologian and socialist, Paul Tillich, reminded us: "The most intimate motions within the depths of our souls are not completely our own. For they belong also to our friends, to mankind, to the universe, and to the Ground of all being, the aim of our life." We are in the struggle together, always (1978).

As long as society in the United States is based on the destructiveness of the capitalist political economy, no procedure (civil or criminal) can be appropriate. Programs formulated and implemented within the capitalist framework continue to repress those who are already oppressed. Only far-reaching changes in the move toward a socialist society will help solve the problem of crime.

As we understand the nature of criminal justice under capitalism, and as we engage in socialist struggle, we build a society that ceases to generate the crime found in capitalist society. Criminal justice ceases to be the solution to crime. Socialist solutions are to be found in the nature of the society itself—a society that neither supports nor depends on a political economy of criminal justice (1980).

## III

The time came for me to return to my homeland in the Midwest. In 1983 I moved back to the Midwest. I would teach sociology for the next 15 years at Northern Illinois University. Upon being given the Edwin H. Sutherland award for contributions to criminological theory, I presented my thoughts on being a criminologist—a criminologist who is also living a daily life that includes keeping a journal and carrying a camera to photograph the landscape. My song was "On the Road Again" by Willie Nelson. Along the way, I was beginning to see criminology as the making of myths that necessarily have consequences in the social worlds that we create. Criminology—as part of the making of myths—is as much art as it is science. We are the makers of myths, and because of this, we must take great care in what we think and what we do. And there was the awareness of the passing of time: "Gee, ain't it funny how time just slips away."

One's personal life cannot be separated from mental productions—at least I have found this to be true in my life and work. Life is a spiritual journey. Add to this a sense that absolute reality is beyond human conception, that all that exists is transient, and that human existence is characterized by suffering. With all of this you have the makings of a special kind of criminology. By the end of the 1980s, I placed these thoughts and experiences into my criminology. The essay titled "The Way of Peace: On Crime, Suffering, and Service" presents this criminology—a criminology which assumes that crime is suffering and that crime will be ended only with the ending of suffering, only when there is peace. This is a peacemaking criminology, a nonviolent criminology of compassion and service which seeks to eliminate crime by lessening the suffering in ourselves and in the world.

Finally comes the realization that whatever we may be doing as criminologists, we are engaged in a moral enterprise. Our underlying questions are always: How are we human beings to live? Who are we, and of what are we capable? How could things be different? Whether or not we are educated as moral philosophers, and whatever the nature of our criminology, we operate with an implicit moral philosophy and we are constantly engaged in the construction of moral philosophy. And most importantly we are witnessing to our times. We are witnesses to suffering, to violence in its many forms, to hatred and greed, to inequality and injustice, and to the possibilities of peace and social justice. Witnessing is an active vocation that is grounded in a particular moral stance toward human existence.

## Observations

Of late I have taken to looking at what is very near in my search for the ultimate. How to live daily with faith in a meaningful existence is the contemporary concern. We are seekers in a world where the traditional answers are no longer convincing. We are travelers who desire to reach beyond the material rationalism of the modern age. The sights and sounds along the road have a double meaning. They suggest that we are indeed in the world, but not of it. The traveler is a gnostic—an artist and a theologian—delving into the mysteries held by the land. I travel along these roads to know their secrets, and in so knowing to become part of the landscape (1985).

Is it possible to go beyond the myth of crime—that is, to go beyond the reality of crime? If crime is the dominant myth and reality of the age, and if the age is far from what may be possible, might we not envision a time and a place when and where we could live by some other means and thereby have a different life? It is not that we are lacking in knowledge about crime or anything else—but that we do not know how to transcend that knowledge. Krishnamurti tells us, rightly and wisely, that our lives are conditioned by a knowledge that enslaves us. As criminologists we tend to do little more than explicate, elaborate, and synthesize the obvious. When will we cease to name and begin to live—to live life firsthand? Our task, it seems to me, is to see things exactly as they are and to live our lives accordingly. And to see things as they are requires an openness and an awareness—a mindfulness—that comes with a new practice, a practice that involves not only collective struggle, but also personal stillness. This is a practice that is unclouded by conventional thought, by the illusion of self, by the mythology of crime. This is a journey to the sacred, to that part of our humanity that is beyond all thought—to that part of us that is, in Zen terms, "nothing." With awareness we may go beyond myth to a new creation—to a world, among other things, free from crime. We are traveling into a new territory (1985).

Let us begin with a fundamental realization: No amount of thinking and no amount of public policy have brought us any closer to understanding and solving the problem of crime. The more we have reacted to crime, the farther we have removed ourselves from any understanding and any reduction of the problem. In recent years, we have floundered desperately in reformulating the law, punishing the offender, and quantifying our knowledge. Yet this country remains one of the most crime-ridden nations. In spite of all its wealth, economic development, and scientific advances, this country has one of the worst crime records in the world (1988).

Suffering is the condition of our existence. The forms of suffering are all around us. In our personal lives, there are tensions and anxieties.

Each day we experience the physical pains in our bodies and the psychological hurts in our hearts and minds.

Our interpersonal relations often are carried out in violence of one kind or another, if only in the withholding of what might be offered. We have created societies that are filled with the sufferings of poverty, hunger, homelessness, pollution, and destruction of the environment. Globally, nations are at war and threaten not only one another but all of earthly life with nuclear destruction.

All these human problems, or forms of suffering, are a result of how we have lived our lives, moment by moment, day by day. The threat of nuclear war began as suffering on a very personal level and elevated gradually and systematically to the collective condition. The forms of suffering are symptoms of the sufferings within each of us.

If the social and global sufferings ever are to be ended, we must deal with the suffering of personal existence. What is involved, finally, is no less than the transformation of our human being. Political and economic solutions without this transformation inevitably fail. The solution is very near to us. There is no shortcut to the ending of suffering (1988).

As long as there is suffering in this world, each of us suffers. In being witnesses to the concrete reality, and in attempting to heal the separation between ourselves and true being (the ground of all existence), we necessarily suffer with all others. But now we are fully aware of the suffering and realize how it can be eliminated. With awareness and compassion, we are ready to act (1988).

*Dion Dennis*: Define for us the principle tenets of peacemaking and from where it arose *for you* and to what it is a response?

*Richard Quinney*: I have to recall my own personal journey. There was a five-year period in my life when I was not doing much criminology. In my revision of *Class, State and Crime*, I developed more of a structural Marxism and I put into it some sense of the prophetic. I had gone about as far as I could down that road in relation to criminology. I was looking for something that would help me in my own life. This was a very personal quest and I didn't know if I would ever return to criminology. About five years ago I began drawing from the revival of the peace movement—which is as close as we've come to an active Marxism in American society. I began to use peace studies material and my own sensibilities. I also began to draw more from Buddhism and I developed a personal practice in Buddhism. With that came the notion that peace must be within one's self as it's concurrently developed in the world, that there is no difference between inner and outer. You don't make peace on the outside and then transform the human being to become peaceful. It's a project that must, out of necessity, go together.

*DD:* How would you define peace?

*RQ:* Peace cannot be defined as the absence of war and conflict. It is a sensibility about *how* one lives one's life. It's total *being*. It has to do with the qualities of humility, simplicity, equanimity. Peace involves connection and relation to all that is and the recognition that you are not separate from those you would define as being in opposition to. That you are inextricably part of the system (1989).

Our response to all that is human is for life, not death. What would a Gandhian philosophy of existence offer a criminologist, or any member of society, in reaction to crime? To work for the creation of a new society, certainly. But, immediately, the reaction would not be one of hate for the offender, nor a cry for punishment and death. Punishment is not the way of peace.

Responses to crime that are fueled by hate, rather than generated by love, are necessarily punitive. Such responses are a form of violence, a violence that can only beget further violence. Much of what is called "criminal justice" is a violent reaction to, or anticipation of crime. The criminal justice system, with all of its procedures, is a form of *negative peace*. The purpose is to deter or process acts of crime through the threat and application of force.

*Positive peace,* on the other hand, is something other than the deterrence or punishment of crime. Positive peace is more than merely the absence of crime and violence—and of war. Positive peace is the attention given to all those things, most of them structured in the society, that cause crime, that happen before crime occurs. Positive peace exists when the sources of crime—including poverty, inequality, racism, and alienation—are not present. There can be no peace—no positive peace—without social justice. Without social justice and without peace (personal and social), there is crime. And there is, as well, the violence of criminal justice.

The negative peacemaking of criminal justice keeps things as they are. Social policies and programs that are positive in nature—that focus on positive peacemaking—create something new. They eliminate the structural sources of violence and crime. A critical, peacemaking criminology is a form of positive peace.

Thus our socialist humanism, the attention given to everyday existence, love and compassion, and social justice. Our efforts are not so much out of resistance, as they are an affirmation of what we know about human existence. The way is simply that of peace in everyday life (1995).

I am struck by the apocalyptic vision embodied in much of Western moral philosophy. The notion that there is an ultimate destiny, that history is moving in the direction of fulfillment, and that the better world—the new kingdom—will come with the catastrophic collapse of the old order. Such a notion provides an imperative to make a better world, but at the same time promotes a judgment that impedes the humane living of daily life.

In contrast, Eastern thought, Buddhism particularly, identifies historical change with an increasing of individual awareness. As individuals transform their limited selves into an identification with the larger world, a more compassionate and humane existence is created. And in our own Western version of this mode of thought, Existentialism, the focus is on the living of everyday life. If attention is given to everyday life, the result cannot be other than the creation of a better world. Criminology—as moral philosophy—cannot help but be a part of the major thoughts and trends of the age (1998).

> *Richard Quinney:* More and more I find it difficult to talk abstractly about a subject and that's why I find it difficult in a discussion here to talk about crime. I don't know what I have to say about crime. We talk orally or in our writing about what we did today and what we're thinking and what we're doing.

> *Larry Tifft:* I think crime is about life. You wrote that, and to me that was important in the sense that we're not separate from that. One of the things that interests me is that we're people who are generally very comfortable with the idea that we should collectively respond to crimes, that we have an obligation to collectively respond to tragedies when they've occurred, but people generally don't see that they're part of the social arrangements, the sources, that are collectively responsible for the crime in the first place.

> *RQ:* So much of criminology, criminal policy, or teaching criminology or criminal justice is a "we" and "they" thing, that we're separate. But, if you want to understand crime, understand yourself. You cannot understand the criminal without understanding yourself. It's the same stuff.

> *LT:* You talk about concrete but when I say those kinds of things, people say they're very abstract.

> *RQ:* Now I'm talking very abstractly. So I won't say much more about that. I have to say something about crime, about what the criminal justice system is, and the structure of society and so forth. I suppose when necessary and pressed I will give my views but that's not what I'm enthusiastic about doing. I'm more enthusiastic about telling what I did today. You see, since my life has very little to do with crime, what am I supposed to write about? The criminal justice system? The criminal in prison or on the street? The drug war? I'm not involved in any of that kind of work or life. If I were a prison guard, I could write good criminology I think, or if I were in prison or on the street doing whatever, but I'm not doing that. Buddhists have said that abstract thought is crazy thought; it's not here and now; it's not what you're doing. More and more I find it difficult to talk about pathology.

> *Dennis Sullivan:* But you can talk about suffering though.

*RQ:* I can talk about my own suffering and through that I can connect with other people's suffering. If I can say something about my own suffering, I am also talking about everyone else's suffering, some aspect of their suffering so it's not just egotistical work. People who read my work about my own suffering are plugging in their own [experiences]. It's not my life that is the object of attention but their own life.

*LT:* It struck me when I was taking a Death and Dying class that in our culture we avoid talking about death. People are fearful of death so, to some degree, it is avoided. It's sort of an insight that inside cultures where death is not seen as something inevitable and natural, or talked about, people do not talk about life everyday. The hottest topic is crime and so forth on the news. They're talking about an aspect of life; they're not talking about how we get there, living, so I connect social justice issues with criminal justice issues.

*RQ:* What kind of world could it be where there was not that kind of suffering?

*LT:* Rather than specialized forms of suffering we could simply talk about suffering; rather than types of suffering we could talk about the prevalence of suffering.

*RQ:* We want a better world, not just for my life but for all life. We've thought of ourselves as workers, as ideological workers who try to get across that idea of how things could be. That's why we keep repeating ourselves in criminology. We really don't need much more criminology. We know what we need to know about what is necessary. So we keep on doing criminology for various professional and academic reasons. But we do it, why? To get the message across, right? We keep repeating ourselves about injustice and class structure, about social justice. With each class of students we feel we are countering what's coming over the media, a different ideology or image. That's our work. Our work is a committed work.

*DS:* So you connect suffering with service, a connection you've written about. And for this better world, service would be what?

*RQ:* Well, it's the service to teach, isn't it? If we were employed other ways, our service would be something else or some other kind of work outside of academic service. It's quite a service just to keep the message going, to teach against the common, conventional image of violence that's prevalent in the media, violence begetting violence. In the last two years I've been thinking of this idea—we've talked about it, Dennis—the idea of bearing witness. It's a powerful idea to me. In a way, it's also a way out of the criticism that you are not really doing any good because you are not involved in making policy or enforcing the law or working for this agency. So partly, it's a rationalization out of that criticism, but I also think there's truth to it, in a long tradition of bearing witness to trouble and suffering.

*LT:* You're also a witness to the root of things.

*RQ:* Right, as to what I see as the root of things. I bear witness to that and to how I live it each day. We think we're constructing theories or doing empirical studies but whatever the work is, we are bearing witness to our time. Then the question we can be critical about is what kind of witness are we?

*LT:* We are either dreamers and dismissed or out of bounds. We must be talking about something that's important that others don't want us talking about. I remember taking a European History course a long time ago and the teacher said, "Well, we'll just skip the Middle Ages" and my mind, running as it does, asks, "What happened during that time period such that you really don't want to talk about it or that we really shouldn't be thinking about it?"

*RQ:* From a Marxist analysis, our message doesn't fit in the scheme of things. It's a threat like Buddhism is a threat. We're all concerned about here and now and bringing peace in our lives and I think that's a threat to capitalism. Capitalism depends upon aggression and commerce and much of what we're talking about is antithetical to capitalism's arrangements. But our conviction is that if we keep talking long enough, at least we're on the right side.

*LT:* That's what I wanted to ask you. In your presentation earlier today, you spoke about "doing the right thing" but how do you know what the right thing is?

*RQ:* Well, in the Buddhist tradition, there are various practices, basically meditation and concentration, where one focuses on the here and now There is a loss of ego in that, in that you connect with compassion to others. And with that, one naturally does the right thing. Where in the Western tradition you need a philosophy or a religion to keep people good, and if you don't have some structure with punishments and rewards, as in the case of religion and philosophy, people will go amuck and be bad to each other. Buddhism is so simple that we just can't handle it; we think it has to be complicated in order to be true. The idea is that with the here and now connected to all that is, you go from moment to moment and you do the right thing because it's moment to moment as opposed to operating on some grand scheme that you're trying to impose on the moment. Not being in the moment makes us do the wrong thing, because we're not there. You've got to be there in order to do the right thing (1999).

# IV

As criminologists, we are witnesses to the various forms of violence, to the atrocities, and to the sufferings of many people. As with journalists, photographers, peace workers, and fellow social scientists, we witness and report the sufferings throughout the world. Observations and reports are made of the Holocaust, the ethnic wars, illness and starvation, sexual abuse, and the many other sufferings of being human in the modern world.

The witness obviously is not a neutral observer that a simplistic dichotomy of active agent and passive observer might suggest. The witness is certain to be in the right place at the right time. And once being there, is moved by conscience to actively observe and report what is being witnessed. If actions more physical in nature follow, they follow because first there has been the witnessing. Without prior witnessing, there will be no subsequent action that is wise and appropriate. Witnesses act with clarity and purpose because they have the awareness and conscience of a witness. Ready and with open mind, the witness truly sees what is happening, and knows what further action is to be taken. Without witnessing, any action is unfocused, confused, and little more than a chasing of the wind.

There is plenty for the criminologist to witness. Make your own list of what we as criminologists should be witnessing. My own current witnessing is to the kinds of suffering and violence that are a systematic and structured part of contemporary existence. In fact, the largest portion of violence is structured and is generated by, or committed by, governments, corporations, the military, and agents of the law.

The war at home is against the poor. It is a war that is waged to maintain inequality so that the rich can maintain their position. Whole populations are being held hostage in poverty, sickness, addiction, and brutality against one another—remaining unemployed, underemployed, and uneducated. Prisons are overflowing, and prison construction and operation are growing industries. The rich not only create the war, to secure their position, but also profit from the war. In our own nonviolent actions and protests, founded on witnessing, we take our stand. Which side are you on? is still the relevant question.

Directly associated with the war on the poor, the war to keep a minority of the population rich, is capital punishment. The death penalty—state-sponsored murder—is the final resort of a violent and greedy minority. That so many, the majority of the population when polled, support the practice of capital punishment is all the more reason that criminologists as witnesses are needed to expose, to analyze, and to protest. Someday, I am certain, historians will note that the United States was one of the last nations to continue to violate the most basic of human rights—the right to life. It was one of the last nations to systematically violate the rights of its own citizens.

Everything we do as criminologists is grounded in a moral philosophy. Whatever we think and do, our criminology is the advancement of one moral philosophy or another. And each moral philosophy generates its own kind of witnessing—in the events to be witnessed and in the forms of witnessing. The work in criminology that is historically important is the work that is informed by a moral philosophy. As witnesses, we are on the side of life—a reverence for all life. Such is the way of peace.

## Bibliography

(1999). "A Stranger in Search of Home: A Conversation with United States Criminologist Richard Quinney." *Contemporary Justice Review*, 2(No. 3):309-326.

Dennis, D. (1989). "Richard Quinney: An Interview." *The Critical Criminologist*, 1(Summer):1-14.

Goldwyn, E. (1971). "Dialogue with Richard Quinney." *Issues in Criminology*, 6(Spring):41-54.

Quinney, R. (1998). "Criminology as Moral Philosophy, Criminologist as Witness." *Contemporary Justice Review*, 1(Nos. 2 & 3):347-364.

Quinney, R. (1995). "Socialist Humanism and the Problem of Crime: Thinking about Erich Fromm in the Development of Critical/Peacemaking Sociology." *Crime, Law and Society*, 23(No. 2):147-156.

Quinney, R. (1988). "Crime, Suffering, Service: Toward a Criminology of Peacemaking." *The Quest*, 1(Winter):66-75.

Quinney, R. (1985). "Myth and the Art of Criminology." *Legal Studies Forum*, 9(No. 3):291-299.

Quinney, R. (1980). *Class, State, and Crime*, Second Edition. New York, NY: Longman Inc.

Quinney, R. (1978). "The Production of a Marxist Criminology." *Contemporary Crises*, 2(July):277-292.

Quinney, R. (1974). *Critique of Legal Order: Crime Control in Capitalist Society*. Boston, MA: Little, Brown and Company.

Quinney, R. (1973). "There's a Lot of Folks Grateful to the Lone Ranger: With Some Notes on the Rise and Fall of American Criminology," *The Insurgent Sociologist*, 4(Fall):56-64.

Quinney, R. (1970). *The Social Reality of Crime*. Boston, MA: Little, Brown and Company.

Quinney, R. (1964). "Crime in Political Perspective." *American Behavioral Scientist*, 8(December):19-22.

# 10

# Reflections of an African-American Criminologist

Julius Debro

It was 1962, at San Quentin State Prison in California
Hey Julius, Hey Julius what are you in for?
These were the first words that I heard as I
Entered San Quentin's main yard on my
First day of work as a Group Counselor
For the prison system. I looked around and
Saw two or three of the guys that I grew up
With in West Oakland. My immediate
Thought was how did I survive the ghetto
When so many of my black brothers ended
up in prison.

I have been requested to write about my experiences as a criminologist and to offer some advice to young people entering the field. To clearly understand the advice and suggestions for success in the field of Criminology one must understand the author and his or her thought process. I believe that it is also important to discuss the process of entering graduate school, dealing with graduate school, applying for the first position as a faculty member and dealing with what I call the Politics of the Academy.

I started in the field some 45 years ago as a Counselor working part-time in Juvenile Hall in Alameda County in Oakland, California. My experience is both in the real world where one lives day to day with crime and criminals and in the academy where one talks about how things should be. The most difficult transition is from the real world of courts, police, and prisons to the academy where life is so different. The academy is where we discuss how things should be rather than how they are in the real world.

I have taught at three universities: starting with the University of Maryland, then moving to Atlanta University, and finally at the University of Washington.

I have served as Chair of a Sociology Program, Chair of Criminal Justice, Chair of Public Administration, and Associate Dean of a Graduate School. I have served as Principle Investigator for a grant funded by the Justice Department titled "Criminal Justice Standards and Goals" in which leadership for the grant was divided up between the American Society of Criminology and the Academy of Criminal Justice Sciences. My research funding has amounted to more than $4 million, mostly from the Department of Justice and from the National Institute of Mental Health. My specific areas of interest have been corrections, both adult and juvenile.

Each of the three universities at which I worked was different in size, diversity, and programs. The University of Maryland at College Park, upon my arrival, did not have a Criminal Justice/Criminology program and so my first year was spent in Sociology. My mentor was Peter Lejins who became the first Chair of the Criminal Justice/Criminology program at the University of Maryland. My second stop was Atlanta University which was a historical black university with only a graduate program. It has since merged with Clark in Atlanta and is now called Clark Atlanta University. My last stop is the University of Washington in Seattle, which does not have a full-fledged Criminology/Criminal Justice department but has a program in Society and Justice.

My career has been interesting, to say the least. After I left Berkeley, they abolished the program. While I was at Atlanta University, they abolished the University. At the University of Washington, they have not abolished the University but the state did abolish Affirmative Action which has resulted in fewer minority students entering the university in both the graduate and undergraduate programs.

Each university is different, each city is different, but what they have in common is a faculty and staff committed to education and research. Issues of crime are different in each city, policing is different, and city, county, and state governance is different. Challenges for a minority professor in each of these cities are different. The state of Washington is 85 percent Caucasian but the jails and prisons are more than 50 percent minority. My academic life has been wonderful and there are no regrets but there are some parts of my academic life that I would do differently.

## Early Years

I have lived by the three "R"s ("reading, 'riting, and 'rithmetic") since leaving Mississippi as a young child of twelve years and moving to Oakland, California in 1945. The years in Mississippi were spent in a totally segregated environment where black children could not go into restaurants and sit with whites for meals, could not sit next to a white person on the bus, had to sit upstairs in the movie house and could not drink out of the same public water fountain. Whites could kill blacks and never be convicted. My early schooling was in an all-black school, with black teachers and black staff. And we lived in an all-black neighborhood. Mississippi was and still is the poorest state in the country. My entire life has been shaped by my early background in Mississippi. I have devoted my life to studying African-Americans. I came from a very wonderful family but my parents had limited education. My parents are still living and have been married 74 years. I have one older brother and one younger sister. As children, we lived by the three R's. In the South, we dropped the "w" from writing and the "a" from arithmetic. Today, my three R's are somewhat different because they are Read, Respond, and React.

As an African-American, one is always **reading** about acts of racism which tend to shape your research and thinking process. One is constantly **responding** to questions of race and trying to **react** in a world that is somewhat less tolerant than it was two decades ago when we all thought there was hope for America after the Civil Rights movement. Not a single day in my life goes by in which I am not responding to issues of race and racism. While some may see race and racism as difficulties in day-to-day living, I see it as a challenge. A challenge not only faced by me but one faced by many whites, blacks, Asians, Latinos and Native Americans who have tried over the years to make the road easier not only for me but for all members of minority races. My advice to all criminologists, but especially to minorities, is tempered by my constant exposure to issues of inequality.

To understand issues of race one has to understand how my life has been molded by criminal justice issues in this country. It has been 55 years since my family arrived by train in Oakland from Jackson, Mississippi. My father had migrated to Oakland, California by himself and then later sent for his family. Mississippi was the cradle of segregation, so moving to Oakland was seen by my parents as liberation from discrimination. As a child, I grew up hearing and seeing as well as reading about atrocities committed against black people.

Oakland in 1945 was a city that had very few African-Americans but the few that it did have lived in the ghetto of West Oakland where crime and violence was an everyday occurrence. Our schools were predominantly African-American, so that was little change from our schools in Mississippi. Fighting, stealing, and police responses were routine occurrences in our neighborhood. The police were always being called to some disturbance in the neighborhood. I would frequently have to step over men who had passed out on the streets when I delivered items from the drugstore where I worked as a youngster. It was this part-time job from the local drugstore and my parent's insistence that I attend church every single Sunday that kept me away from the numerous temptations to engage in criminal behavior. As a small child, I developed a tolerance for violence and learned to live in the community without getting arrested as a juvenile. I escaped the ghetto only by accident, not by design.

With this brief background, I will try to offer advice, understanding, and support to persons going into the field. My entry into the field was accidental, but I am convinced that because of my childhood, I was destined to study criminology even though I did not know it at the time of my undergraduate years. I was a political science major with aspirations for law school. I came out of the military with no job. It was September and school had started and I had a year before I could apply to law school. Now, in retrospect, I could not have asked for a better field and as I reflect over 50 years of crime-related work, this is the best of the best.

I came into the field at the most exciting time in the history of this country. In the early 1950s, the United States was just responding to issues of segregation and inequality. There was a mass migration of African-Americans from the South to all parts of the country including the West. The Korean War had just ended and veterans were returning to the United States, most of them with a new sense of purpose and a new sense of tolerance for people of color. I had just finished two years in the military and was back in Oakland, living with my parents.

My entry in the field was through the Alameda County Probation department. The local Juvenile Hall was located in West Oakland near my home. Many of my friends had been locked up as juveniles, so I knew the facility well. I was hired as a temporary Juvenile Counselor and eventually moved up to the position of Juvenile Probation Officer. I worked in the system for seven years before moving to the State Department of Corrections. I spent two years at San Quentin as a Correctional Counselor and then moved to the U.S. Government where I worked for four years as a U.S. Probation Officer out of the San Francisco office. While working at Alameda County Probation, I enrolled in a Master's Program in Sociology at San Jose State. This was an evening program designed for working persons. While in the program, I met two outstanding professors who became my mentors.

Mentoring is absolutely necessary not only in obtaining a degree but in moving in the system. My mentors were people of compassion who had a strong sense of justice and were concerned with injustices committed against the poor and the disadvantaged. One professor was a Southerner who I am convinced had strong racial prejudices but also had a sense of compassion for African-American students. This professor, more than any other, insisted that I stay in school and obtain an M.A. degree even though I was working full time and often did not want to enroll each quarter. His courses were exciting, he brought into the classroom practical experiences of his work in the prison system. He was a scholar who stayed at home each morning and wrote constantly about minority issues. After obtaining my M.A. in sociology, I continued working in corrections but moved to San Quentin State Prison for two years before moving on to Federal Probation where I had the privilege of working with Robert Carter and Leslie Wilkins on research funded by the Justice Department. Bob Carter was perhaps the most conservative of all criminologists on the faculty at Berkeley but was a prolific writer and a person who saw the field as highly exciting. Because of Bob Carter, I applied and was admitted to the School of Criminology in 1966. Carter and Gordon Misner both became great mentors.

Mentoring is more than meeting with students at the student's request. Effective mentoring is becoming totally involved in the student's life from the day he or she enters into the program until he or she has obtained a position. More on this later.

## Preparing for Graduate School

Preparation for graduate school should start in the junior year of an undergraduate program. The student should begin to contact schools recommended primarily by their professors. Many contacts can be made on the World Wide Web where students can locate the college or university, search the department for the name of a professor in the area in which they are interested and contact that professor or contact the graduate advisor in the department for information concerning the program. If the student is fortunate to be attending a school that has a criminal justice or criminology program, then the student should con-tact their favorite professor in their school and inquire about attending one of the professional meetings held by the American Society of Crim-inology, the Academy of Criminal Justice Sciences, or the Western Soci-ety of Criminology. Other disciplines may have courses related to the field and one could attend one of those meetings as well. Most of the national meetings will have sections dealing with entry into graduate pro-grams. Attendance at professional meetings will give you an opportu-nity to meet professors from various schools and assist you in making a decision.

Most schools require that students take the Graduate Record Exam-ination (GRE). The student should inquire about programs that they can enroll in to prepare for the examination. I would recommend enrolling in the Princeton or Kaplan programs for a review. Both are somewhat expensive but well worth the price. I also recommend searching for financial assistance on your campus to assist in paying for the course. Some schools also provide programs for GRE prep on campus.

While professors will tell you that GREs are not that important, do not believe them! GREs are very important and in many cases will make a difference in whether or not you are admitted or, if admitted, whether or not you receive assistance in your first year.

Graduate schools require at least a 3.0 or better grade point average and also a personal statement plus references from former professors. The personal statement is of utmost importance because quite often it may be the deciding factor as to whether or not the department will accept you. Your personal statement should include why you want to get into the program, what your future plans are after graduation as well as a life history, including any hardships that you have encounted prior to entering graduate school. If your grades are marginal, you should explain the reasons for the low grades. Have two or three professors read your personal statement. Ask someone within your department if you can look at a successful folder, especially one that has a great personal statement.

Three letters of reference are also required. Try and get letters from professors rather than friends at work or friends in the community. Letters from professors carry much more weight than those from community people. Search out persons in your university who may be able to make a personal phone call to professors at the university or college of your choice. Request letters of reference from professors in courses for which they hold you in high regard. It doesn't matter about the discipline. What you are looking for are teachers that will say that you can achieve in graduate school. Beware of a professor who will not give you a copy of the letter of recommendation. If a professor refuses to give you a copy, then you may be in trouble. Tell the professor that you would like a copy for your files and that you may use it to apply to other schools.

Some schools have counseling centers that, for a small fee, will send out all of the information to all of the schools that you express an interest in attending. You now can download all of the application information for every school on the Web.

I was fortunate in that I had an opportunity to work on a research project with professors who taught in the graduate school prior to my applying to the School of Criminology at Berkeley. I also had received an M.A. prior to my application to the Graduate Program and had completed my GRE's prior to entering the M.A. program. I came to the School of Criminology as a much older student with a commitment to complete my education and get on with my career. Each person may enter a program at a different level. Prior experience is not absolutely necessary but I highly recommend working in the field for some length of time because it helps you understand concepts in a better way and also helps you to decide on your area of interest.

The disadvantage of work experience is that one tends to apply everyday solutions gained from prior work experience to academic issues. Academic solutions are primarily based on theory and day-to-day working is often based on crises issues. This work knowledge may get you into trouble sometimes in the classroom because you know some theories will not work, yet the professor who has no experience in the field may enthusiastically endorse them.

My suggestion is that students should talk with professors who are in programs prior to applying. How does one know that this is the field that one would like to pursue when there are many more opportunities to go into fields such as computer science, math, engineering, business, and to make more money than in the field of criminology and criminal justice.

Which school to select once admitted to more than one creates a dilemma. Try to visit each school if at all possible prior to acceptance. If you are at the top of the list for those students admitted that year, you may be able to obtain a paid visit to the school. If you are not invited, call the department and speak with the chair or with someone on the admissions committee and request travel funds. In most cases, the school will put you up with students in the program. If you have not met them during your visit, request to meet some of the students. Meet the students in an informal setting away from the faculty. Ask questions about the faculty, about the courses, about mentoring, and about graduation rates. You want to make sure that once you enter the program, you will graduate in a reasonable time. Average time to graduation is important and drop-out rates are important.

Inquire about financial aid. Will there be an opportunity to work as a Research Assistant or a Teaching Assistant? If you are not offered financial support you should look at other schools. If the financial package is not sufficient, let the department know that you have other offers and that they are providing adequate support. Do not cut off negotiations, but let the department know that your needs are greater than what they are offering.

Because most of the research in criminology and criminal justice deals with minority issues but a department may not have minority students or faculty, inquire about the minority population both of students and faculty. Is there a commitment by the department to hire non-white minorities and women? Don't believe the old saying that they can't find minorities or that they left because they had better opportunities. Most minority faculty will depart only because they perceive that the environment is unwelcome or that they are used as showcases and that when tenure opportunities are available they are not considered. How many minorities are on tenure track and how many have tenure are important issues for all students. Schools with a diverse student body and faculty provide better opportunities for learning because that says something about the tolerance level at the university.

Berkeley had very little diversity in its faculty. It had one minority faculty member, no minority staff members, and only one minority graduate student. Needless to say, the graduate student and I shared office space. Issues affecting African-Americans are at the heart of criminology and criminal justice. It is important that there be African-Americans on faculty so that they can be involved in issues that deal with crime and race. It also is important to have someone who understands problems of minority students. The California faculty was a great faculty and provided a great education, but I often wondered how that education would have been enhanced if there had been faculty that looked like me.

## Selection of School

Consult reference guides for rankings of schools or departments. *USA Today*, *The Chronicle of Higher Education*, and professional organizations will have information on school rankings. I selected Berkeley because it was the top school in the country and had a very activist program. The major problem with Berkeley was that, because it was so radical, it had very few research grants on which students could work. Students suffered because they did not have the opportunity to work with principal investigators, or to work with grant monitors, or to learn how to write grants. It is important that you are a part of some project because through that project you learn how to conduct investigations, write grant reports and obtain material that may be a part of your dissertation.

Once the school has been selected, it is now time to began the most serious work. Graduate school is enjoyable, so do not try to work full time and attend graduate school. Try to live within your means so that there is time to spend with faculty and students. While some graduate students would like to obtain fellowships that require little, if any, work, be wary of those kinds of grants because they do not provide opportunities to work as a Research Assistant or Teaching Assistant, positions that should be requirements for graduation. Some of the students you meet will be your friends for a lifetime and they, along with you, may be leaders in programs for years to come. Professors are different in graduate school. You now have an opportunity not only to learn but to work alongside some of the best minds in the field. Socialization is very important in the department. If you are invited to a department party, attend because now you will have an opportunity to mix informally with staff and faculty.

Staff in some cases is more important than faculty. At Berkeley, we had a wonderful lady by the name of Ann Goolsby who was the administrative assistant to the Dean. Ann knew everything about the school and had more information about graduate student problems than the

Dean. As a graduate student, get to know staff. When students needed assistance in any area, Ann would be there to help. When students needed introductions with agencies off-campus, Ann was always available to assist. After 30 years of being away from the school, Ann is still our "rock."

## Preparing for Graduation

Each college or university has required courses prior to taking preliminary examinations. While it is important to do well in these courses, most of them have little to do with passing your written exams. Start early preparing for your exams. Find out which books are on the required reading list and spend time reading those books, in addition to reading for your courses. Inquire about previous examination questions and obtain copies and review those questions along with other students in the department. Try to find a senior professor who will review your answers to questions and provide feedback. Senior professors have nothing to lose in the department and are more approachable than junior professors who must worry about promotion and tenure, and they often try to establish a reputation as being difficult.

Your selection of the dissertation committee determines in large part when you will complete your work. Try to choose someone who has an interest in your topic and who will agree to spend time with you on issues relating to your dissertation. Remember, your primary purpose is to complete your dissertation and get on with your career, not to solve the problems of the world at the dissertation stage.

It is very important that you learn who gets along with whom in the department because you do not want to select a committee that will fight among themselves over issues that have nothing to do with your work. Contact previous students who have completed their dissertation and inquire about committee members, but be careful when listening to students, because they may have biases as well. A committee should be as small as possible; the more people there are on the committee, the more problems you will encounter. I would recommend no more than three persons. If you decide to add an outside person, remember that the outside person will have very little influence in the decision-making process. I would also recommend getting people who are interested in your work and hopefully those at the associate level and above. Assistant professors may not obtain tenure and may not be around by the time you complete your dissertation. Select a topic in which you have an acute interest or choose a topic from a grant that you are working on with a professor. If you work on a grant, you may also obtain publications you can use to obtain a position in the field. Quite often students will leave the university after they pass their comprehensives. This is a big mistake because in most cases it takes much longer to finish the degree because you are into other things. Once the degree has been obtained is when the fun begins.

## Interviewing for the First Position

My first interview was at a prestigious Ivy League school on the East Coast. My graduate school did not prepare me for interviewing nor for teaching. Nothing was said about interviewing techniques in graduate school. I did not receive a teaching assistantship so I did not have to run a class or handle a section. I received a call for a job interview and off I went as an ABD (All but the Dissertation). There are a series of tribal rites that one goes through before the position is offered; these include a rite of passage. I gave a presentation on research that I had been conducting, went out to lunch, and out to dinner and drinks with different faculty members. Faculty members pass you around to other members, then they caucus after you leave and make a decision as to whether or not they should offer you the position. One must be on one's best behavior. Dress is important so one should consult with others about appropriate attire. You will meet students, faculty and staff and in some cases perhaps the Dean. A lesson that I learned is that you should not drink any alcoholic beverages at lunch and should drink only one or two alcoholic drinks at dinner. You are the show and faculty members are evaluating you to see if they want you on the team. You have very little time to yourself during the period that you are on campus. People will meet you for breakfast; students will meet you for lunch and perhaps for coffee, and more people will meet you for dinner. The last person that you will meet before you leave campus should be the Chair and he or she will give you information about the department and the university. I did not know that if the Chair did not mention salary that you should, so after two and a half days, we had no discussions about money. After I returned to Berkeley, a salary was offered which was unacceptable. Do inquire about salary and let your expectations be known to the Chair. Remember that salary and benefits are negotiable, as well as space, equipment, and teaching load. Needless to say, I did not take that position but did go on to interview at the University of Maryland and accepted my first teaching position there.

Read as much as you can about the university and the department that will be interviewing you for a position. You can now look on the Web to find information about each faculty member. Learn their areas, their strengths and, if possible their weaknesses. Find out as much about the department as you can from other colleagues. If there are tensions, you should know about them prior to accepting the position and you must decide if you can live with those tensions. You should know as much as possible about tenure and promotions because your life will depend upon these matters. What's expected for promotion and tenure? What are the publication requirements? Most colleges and universities will not tell you that you need, say, six publications in refereed journals, but they will give you some general indications of what's expected. Will books rather than article publications serve as material for tenure or do you need all journal articles or journal articles and a book? What about publications in minority journals? Do they count as well? How do you count service to community, to school? What about grants and contracts? What is the policy of the university with regard to attending professional meetings? What is the amount of reimbursement? These and other questions should be asked prior to signing a contract. A considerable amount of information can be gained informally by talking to faculty members.

## The Job

Class preparation is most important and it takes considerable time to get ready for classes. One should not take on an enormous teaching load the first year. Try to teach courses that are in your area and where you have considerable knowledge about the subject matter. Do not teach statistics or methods if they were not your strong courses. Oftentimes you will be assigned courses that no one else would like to teach. Negotiate your class schedule and also the times that you are teaching. Do not teach every day because you will need time to write, and you should arrange to have at least one day a week away from the university. If you are on campus daily, you will find that the entire time will go by and you will have accomplished very little in terms of you own work.

My experience has been that faculty members are generally very busy with their own work, and while one may talk about collaborations and collegiality, both rarely exist. Social scientists tend to work alone rather than in small groups. Try to establish specific times for writing. I worked with a professor who stayed home and worked three mornings a week; he was a prolific writer. Publishing is the key to success in the university. Public service is good and so is teaching but the only true evaluation is on the basis of publications. Give yourself sufficient time each week to write and conduct research. Set office hours and stick to them. Students will take up an enormous amount of time and most faculty will enjoy them.

Some universities provide mentors for junior faculty but my experience has been that very few know how to mentor; thus you will be left generally on your own. Which, in some cases, is not all that bad!

## The Faculty Years

I would suggest publishing in an area where you have a strong interest. Most of us have changed subjects because the federal government has provided funding for research in these areas. In my 30 years of teaching, I have seen many commissions established by the federal government. In 1963, The President's Commission on Law Enforcement and Administration of Justice was established and it had a profound impact upon the country. In 1968, Congress passed the Safe Streets Act, which established the Law Enforcement Assistance Administration, which eventually became the National Institute of Justice. Some 30 years later, the Justice Department brought some of us together in a Symposium on the thirtieth anniversary of the Commission and it was sad to see that we had not solved many of the problems from some 30 years prior. Most of us chase dollars provided by the National Institute of Justice or by other agencies of the Department of Justice such as OJJDP (Office of Juvenile Justice Delinquency Prevention). Funds also can be obtained from foundations. Find your area and stick to it regardless of whether or not there is funding.

Tenure is the ultimate career goal of a professor. Usually one has six years from the day that you receive your appointment to convince your colleagues that you are worthy. One has to prepare a year-by-year folder of accomplishments, which includes three areas (i.e., publishing, teaching, and service). Try to obtain as much information from faculty as to expectations. Some schools may not tell you what is expected and it comes as a big surprise in the sixth year when you have to prepare your folder for consideration for tenure. If you do not receive tenure, then you have one year before you are expelled from the club. It is much more difficult, but not impossible, to obtain another position if you have not attained tenure. Most schools will evaluate you after year two, so you do have some feedback as to how you are performing.

Minority professors often have pressure from the community to take on community projects. Also, minority students have so few people of color that you are constantly spending more time with students of color. Both community and students are important, but try to set aside some days each week to stay home and write as well as time in the summer. Most departments are understanding of minority professors and their other obligations, but community service and more students will not help you obtain tenure.

Attend professional conferences, serve on committees from national organizations, and become active in the department and in the university. If invited to social events, attend, if only for a short period of time. Do not, however, lose your sense of purpose. If you see inequities on campus or in the department, become involved.

Once you obtain tenure, if you want to become involved in administration, don't hesitate. Most of my career has been in administration and my only complaint is that there was not sufficient time for publishing. I would recommend that you publish as much as possible before attempting administration because there is very little time left for serious work in one's discipline after administrative meetings.

When I started graduate school in 1964, there were very few minorities. I knew of no Native Americans, only one or two Hispanics, few, if any, Asians, and four African-Americans with doctorates from schools of criminology and criminal justice. The African-Americans were all from Berkeley. Gwynne Peirson, a former police officer from Oakland; Alex Swann from Jamaica; Lee Brown, a former police officer from San Jose; Ben Carmichael; George Napper; and myself. After teaching for many years at Howard University, Gwynne is now deceased. Alex is still teaching at Texas Southern, a black university just outside of Houston; Lee Brown is Mayor of Houston and has been the Commissioner of Public Safety in Atlanta, Houston, and New York City as well as the Federal Drug Czar. George Napper served as chief of police in Atlanta and as Commissioner of juvenile programs for the State of Georgia.

Today, there are many ethnic minorities in the field—but still not enough. As you enter the fields of criminology/criminal justice, try to bring others along with you and try especially to bring more minorities into the field. If we are going to change the face of justice, we must change the face of those who teach about and dispense justice.

# 11

# Looking Back on 40-Plus Years of a Professional Career

Rita J. Simon

After attending the University of Wisconsin in Madison as an under-graduate, and studying at Cornell University for two years as a graduate student, I transferred to the University of Chicago and received my Ph.D. in Sociology in 1957. I spent part of 1955 and 1956 in India doing research on the Indian jury system. In January 1959 I became an Assistant Professor in the Sociology Department and offered a graduate seminar to my former classmates. In the three years that I remained in Chicago after I received my Ph.D., I continued to teach in the Sociology Department and to do research on the Jury Project at the Law School. When I left Chicago and moved to New York after I was married in June 1961, most of my professional time was spent working with Mobilization for Youth at the Columbia University School of Social Work and writing *The Jury and the Defense of Insanity*.[1] I also commuted to New Haven one day a week to teach a seminar on Research Methods to the faculty of the Yale University School of Nursing.

The early 1960s was not the best time for a husband and wife to seek faculty positions at the same university (albeit in different departments). But Julian and I were lucky, and we, in fact, had a choice among three universities. We chose to move to the University of Illinois in Champaign-Urbana. My appointment was a joint one between the Institute of Communications Research in the School of Communications and the Sociology Department in the College of Arts and Sciences. I was given the dubious title of "Visiting Associate Professor" because at that time Illinois was one of many major universities that had a nepotism rule. What that meant was that no wife could have a tenure-track faculty appointment as long as her husband was also a member of the faculty in any department of the university. I accepted the position and the title with the understanding that at the end of the academic year, should my work prove satisfactory, the then-Director of the Institute of Communications Research, Professor Charles Osgood, would join me in an effort to do away with the nepotism rule at the university. We succeeded, and the label "visiting" was dropped from my job title. I was also granted tenure. Four years later I was promoted to full Professor. What enormous changes have taken place in the hiring and tenuring of women faculty in the past 40 or so years.

Today, it is not at all uncommon for spouses to seek and obtain tenure-track positions at the same university, and the bias against married women gaining such positions is a thing of the past. When asked, as I often am, for advice by my married graduate students who are seeking their first university positions whether they should adopt the strategy of searching for and accepting the "best" offer (i.e., the one from the most prestigious university or department, the one with the lowest teaching load, the highest salary, etc.) or for going on the market together and eventually accepting jobs at the university that offers both of them positions, I strongly urge the latter. I believe it is very important not to strain personal relationships and family ties for the sake of "careerism." Now I am not saying one of the two partners should make all of the sacrifices in the name of personal togetherness. I am strongly urging that both parties be willing to compromise on job searches in order to be able to live together. Newly minted Ph.D.s who have ideas, ambitions, and a willingness to work long and hard can get their papers published and make a name for themselves at second-, third- and fourth-rate academic institutions. Tenacity, motivation and, yes, a bit of luck are very important factors.

As a side note, I should add that I was sufficiently upset at the existence of nepotism rules which, in 1963, were widespread at American universities, that I obtained a grant from the Department of Education to conduct a study that resulted in the publication *Of Nepotism, Marriage and the Pursuit of an Academic Career*[2] in 1966 and *The Woman Ph.D.*[3] in 1967. The main purpose of the studies was to compare the productivity of the woman Ph.D. against that of the male Ph.D. and to compare productivity among married and unmarried women Ph.D.s, holding constant major, field, and year of degree. Behind this interest was a desire to answer empirically the following two-part question: Compared to men, how much of a return does society receive from its investment in the higher education of women—as much as it receives from men, three-quarters as much, half as much, or more? And, compared to unmarried women, how much of a return does society receive from its investment in the higher education of women who marry and have children?

We found that about 15 percent of the women who received their Ph.D.s between 1960 and 1966 believed that their careers had been hurt by anti-nepotism regulations. These regulations appeared not to be barriers to entry into the academic market, but they imposed restrictions on conditions of employment, the likelihood of advancement, and the securing of permanent positions and satisfactory salaries. In describing how anti-nepotism rules affected their careers, women were most likely to mention restrictions on their mobility, having to change their areas of interest or specialization, having to accept lower professorial ranks, denial of tenure, and lower salaries.

We also found that married women who claimed they were affected by anti-nepotism rules published more than respondents in any other group (i.e., men, single women, and women with husbands not in academia). The most surprising finding was that married women, including those with children, published more than men and more than unmarried women, controlling for field and year in which the Ph.D. was received.

In 1968 I was asked to serve as chairperson of the Sociology Department, which I agreed to do for two years, before my family and I went off to spend our sabbatical in Israel. In the intervening years since we had arrived at the University of Illinois, I had given birth to three children: David in 1964, Judith in 1965, and Daniel in 1968.

The 1970-1971 sabbatical in which I taught at the Hebrew University was our family's second extended stay in Israel. The first occurred for six months in 1968 when we chose to go there after I received a Guggenheim fellowship and my husband a leave of absence. We both taught at Hebrew University in Jerusalem. We were able to do that one more time in the academic year 1974-1975. After that, our two oldest children got "too old" and insisted, when we wanted to go back on our next sabbatical, that their Hebrew was not good enough for them to be able to keep up with Israeli students in the eighth and ninth grades.

After 1971, my position at the University was divided into three parts: the Sociology Department, the Institute of Communication Research, and the Law School. During some of those years I served as Director of a campus-wide program in Law and Society, and I did a three-year stint (1978-1980) as editor of *The American Sociological Review*.

We remained at Illinois until 1983, when we moved to the Washington, D.C. area, where I once again assumed an administrative position, this time as Dean of the School of Justice at American University. The school faculty was composed of persons trained in sociology, criminology, law, philosophy, social work, and psychology. Although it was considered among the most prestigious units on campus (in terms of faculty research and publications and student evaluations), the Provost, in 1988, dismantled the School of Justice and reconstructed it as a Department of Justice, Law and Society within a newly established School of Public Affairs, of which I served as an Acting Dean for one semester. During my first three years at the School of Justice I also served as the Editor of the newly founded official journal of the Academy of Criminal Justice Sciences, *Justice Quarterly*. In 1989 I was appointed a University

Professor in the School of Public Affairs and the Washington College of Law at American University, a position I still hold.

One of the most important decisions a scholar has to make is what issues, what problems, he or she should study. One of the major criteria I have used and I urge on others, is to ask "Is the issue important and might the research findings make a difference?" In looking back over the issues I have spent a lot of time researching, there are three major ones that I think are especially important and have had a significant impact. One is the research I have done on the American jury system. Beginning with my earliest work when I was a Research Associate with the University of Chicago Jury Project in the 1950s, we showed the competence, seriousness, and the dedication with which jurors went about their task of deciding whether defendants were negligent in a series of civil actions. Our subjects were real jurors randomly selected from jury pools in the Chicago, St. Louis, and Minneapolis trial courts. They listened to recorded trials about which they then deliberated. The jurors were under the jurisdiction of the courts and they reported their verdicts to one of the judges on the trial court bench. The results of those studies demonstrated that jurors understood the role they were expected to play, listened to the testimony carefully, went over the evidence they heard during their deliberations, and arrived at verdicts that were consistent with the law and facts of the cases.

Later, when I studied jurors reactions to the defense of insanity and focused especially on their understanding of the rules of law and expert psychiatric testimony, I was able to report the jurors' competence in distinguishing their own role from that of expert witnesses, and their understanding about various manifestations of mental illness, and when and how it may be directly related to a person's ability to distinguish right from wrong, or to induce behavior that was against the law. In *The Jury and the Defense of Insanity*, I described the jury's competence in discussing the legal, clinical, and factual aspects of the trials they heard. In commenting on the deliberations, I reported the respect the jurors had for the system by how it treated fellow jurors whose views differed from the majority's, by how they reviewed the judge's instructions, and by how they tried to avoid being a hung jury. Later in the 1970s, when I studied jurors reactions to pretrial media coverage and to the similarity between jurors' and judge's operational definition of "reasonable doubt" and "by a preponderance of the evidence," the jury again came through with high marks. My review in the 1980s and 1990s of other scholars' work on the jury confirmed much of my own assessment.

The jury is a wise institution and should be retained. Way back, when the University of Chicago Jury Project first got underway, it did so in part as a response to a growing attack on the system, led largely by members of the appellate bench who felt it was an outdated institution. Results from the University of Chicago project did much to weaken those attacks, and in later years, when the jury has again come under attack, I am gratified to see that my work is among others that are cited in support of the system.

Another body of work that I believe has made a difference is my 20-plus-year study of transracial adoptions.[4] I started that study in 1970 by interviewing parents and their children (adopted and birth) who were between the ages of four and seven years old, and I conducted the last set of interviews with the adult children (adopted and birth) in 1991. We surveyed the families four times—in 1971, 1979, 1983, and 1991. At each phase of the study we reported the problems, setbacks, and disappointments, as well as the successes, joys, and optimism about the future. None of the families disrupted the adoption. The major thrusts of the work show that black children adopted by white families grow up emotionally and socially adjusted, and are aware of and comfortable with their racial identity. They perceive themselves as integral parts of their adopted families, and they expect to retain strong ties to their parents and siblings in the future.

Throughout the study, we also described how the birth children were reacting to the transracial adoption experience. As adults, the birth children now talk about the special window they had during childhood, from which they were able to observe how blacks and whites interact with each other, and how families and communities respond to racial differences. They feel that their lives were enriched by the transracial adoption experience, and that they—like their black brother or Korean sister—have entered a more complex social world than would have been available to them had they grown up in an all-white family.

The findings from this work have been cited in several state legislatures including Texas and California. I have also served as an expert witness in more than 40 cases in which white families have sought to adopt black or biracial children and have been stymied by state and county agencies. In more than 80 percent of those cases, the child was released for adoption. The recourse in most instances would have been temporary placement in foster care or an institution. But the high point of my work on transracial adoption came on August 20, 1996, when President Clinton signed into law a provision that prohibits "a state or other entity that receives federal assistance from denying any person the opportunity to become an adoptive or a foster parent on the basis of the race, color, or national origin of the persons or of the child involved." The statute should expedite the placements of tens of thousands of children currently in institutions and foster care into permanent loving homes. These goals have been achieved notwithstanding the more than 20 years of attack by the National Association of Black Social Workers (NABSW) against transracial adoption. The NABSW claims that "no white family can raise a black child in this racist society." They have referred to transracial adoptions as "cultural genocide."

A third major area of research, and one that I did not initiate but which for almost 30 years has been one of my strongest interests, is women and crime. Shortly after I served on the Advisory Board of the Center for the Study of Crime and Delinquency of the National Institutes of Mental Health, Saleem Shah, the Director, called to ask me if I would be interested in writing a monograph for them on women and crime.[5] Prior to that invitation I had done no work in criminology. I did not know about the availability of any kind of crime data (i.e., arrest, conviction, imprisonment rates). But as I thought about the project, the idea became more and more intriguing, and as I began going through the "literature," I discovered how little empirical work had been done on the topic. I came across the work of Cesare Lombroso, who theorized about why women commit crime.

Lombroso concluded that individuals develop differentially within sexual and racial limitations, and they differ hierarchically from the most highly developed, the white man, to the most primitive, the nonwhite women. According to Lombroso:

> Women have many traits in common with children: their moral sense is deficient; they are revengeful, jealous. . . . .In ordinary cases these defects are neutralized by piety, maternity, want of passion, sexual coldness, weakness, and an undeveloped intelligence.

Lombroso explained that women have participated in such a small proportion of criminal behavior because they lack intelligence. Women who do engage in crime are more masculine than are their conformist sisters. He also claimed: "The anomalies of skill, physiognomy, and training capacity of female criminals more closely approximate that of the man, normal or criminal, than they do those of the normal woman."

In the 1930s Eleanor and Sheldon Glueck studied juvenile and adult offenders and described the women in their study as follows:

> The women are themselves on the whole a sorry lot. The major problem involved in the delinquency and criminality of our girls is their lack of control of their sexual impulses. Illicit sex practices are extremely common among them, beginning surprisingly early and carry in them brain disease, illegitimacy and unhappy matrimony. . . . . When we consider the family background of our women we should rather marvel that a sizable faction of them, by one influence or another, abandoned their misbehavior, than that so many of them continued their delinquencies.

Some 30 years later, Rose Giallombardo, writing in 1966, characterized the woman offender as:

Women who commit criminal offenses tend to be regarded as
erring and misguided creatures who need protection and help
rather than as dangerous criminals from whom members of
society should be protected.

Otto Pollak's book *The Criminality of Women*, (1950) was important because it challenged basic assumptions concerning the extent and
quality of women's involvement in criminal behavior. Essentially, Pollak argued that women have been commended for their drastic under-
representation in criminal activities but, in fact, they do not deserve such
praise. According to Pollak, women's participation in crime has not been
significantly lower than that of men's; rather [1] the types of crimes
women commit are less likely to be detected; [2] even when detected,
they are less likely to be reported; for example, shoplifting, domestic
theft, and theft by prostitutes; and [3] even when crimes are reported,
women still have a much better chance than do men of avoiding arrest
or conviction because of the double standard, favorable to women,
employed by law enforcement officials.

Pollak's work did not stimulate a new generation of criminologists
to reconsider the roles and frequency of women in crime. It did not even
succeed in getting "women" or "females" into the indices of basic texts
on criminology.

In 1967, Walter Reckless and Barbara Kay reviewed the various
explanations offered for the low proportion of female involvement in
criminal behavior and concluded:

> Perhaps the most important factor in determining reported and
> acted-upon violational behavior of women is the chivalry fac-
> tor. Victims or observers of female violators are unwilling to
> take action against the offender because she is a woman.
> Police are much less willing to make on-the-spot arrests of or
> "book" and hold women for court action than men. Courts are
> also easy on women, because they are women. . . .Overlook-
> ing, letting-go, excusing, unwillingness to report and to hold,
> being easy on women are part of the differential handling of
> the adult females in the law enforcement process from origi-
> nal complaint to admission to prison. The differential law
> enforcement handling seems to be built into our basic attitudes
> toward women.

David Ward, writing in 1968, observed:

> It is not surprising that criminology textbook writers have been
> able to cover the available knowledge about female criminal-
> ity in one chapter or less. Our knowledge of the character and
> causes of female criminality is at the same stage of development
> that characterized our knowledge of male criminality some 30
> or more years ago.

With this much as background, I plunged into an assessment of the extent and types of women's involvement in criminal activities in the United States. I discovered the FBI statistics on arrests by types of offense, conviction data by selective states, data on parolees, and prison inmates.

As I analyzed the data I decided that there were two major reasons for writing a monograph on women and crime. One was to organize and interpret the statistics and observations that had been accumulating over several decades in order to assess the proportions of women who have engaged in various types of crimes, and to examine how they have been treated by the police, the courts, and prison officials. The second was to make some prognosis about the future. If one assumes that the changes in women's roles, in their perceptions of self, and in their desire for expanded horizons that began in the latter part of the 1960s will not be abated, either by external events such as a major economic depression or by internal processes whereby women examine their situation and decide that their happiness lies in the traditional pursuits of homemaking, wifely companionship, and motherhood, then we would expect that one of the major by-products of the women's movement will be a higher proportion of women who pursue careers in crime. We would also expect changes in the particular types of crimes to which they will be attracted, and in the roles they will perform within the criminal subculture.

I concluded that as women become more liberated from hearth and home and become more involved in full-time jobs, they are more likely to engage in the types of crimes for which their occupations provide them with the greatest opportunities. They are also likely to become partners and entrepreneurs in crime to a greater extent than they have in the past. Traditionally, women in criminal activity have played subservient roles. They have worked under the direction and guidance of men—their lovers, husbands, or pimps. In most instances, their job was to entice victims, to distract or look out for the police, to carry the loot, or to provide the necessary cover. As a function both of expanded consciousness, as well as occupational opportunities, women's participation, roles, and involvement are expected to change and increase.

But the increase, I reasoned, would not be uniform or stable across crimes. Women's participation in financial and white-collar offenses (fraud, embezzlement, larceny, and forgery) should increase as their opportunities for employment in higher status occupations expand. Women's participation in crimes of violence, especially homicide and manslaughter, would not be expected to increase. The reasoning here is that women's involvement in such acts typically arises out of the frustration, the subservience, and the dependency that have characterized the traditional female role. Case histories of women who kill reveal that one pattern dominates all others. When women can no longer contain their frustrations and their anger, they express themselves by doing away with the cause of their condition, most often a man, sometimes a child. As women's employment and educational opportunities expand, their feelings of being victimized and exploited will decrease, and their motivation to kill will become muted.

A second major objective of this monograph, then, was to examine whether increases in female participation in financial and white-collar offenses had already occurred and, if so, to report how law enforcement officials at various levels of authority, from police to prosecuting attorneys to judges, have been responding and are planning to respond to it.

What I learned, and reported from the data I analyzed, was that in 1972 there were more women involved in criminal activities than at any other time since the end of World War II, and probably before that. I went on to comment:

> But the increase has been in certain types of offenses; theft, forgery, fraud, and embezzlement, not in crimes of violence or in the traditional female crimes, such as prostitution and child abuse.

> As of 1972, 30 percent of all arrests for major larceny were women; 30 percent of all arrests for fraud and embezzlement were women; and 25 percent of all forgery arrests were women. These proportions are not 50 percent, but they are at least twice as high as they are for any other offenses; and if present trends continue, in 20 years women should be making a contribution in white-collar, financial crimes commensurate with their representation in the society. The fact that female arrests have increased for these offenses and not for all offenses is consistent both with opportunity theory and with the presence of a sizable women's movement.

> The prison statistics, which extend back over two decades, do not show a growing proportion of women being sentenced. Rather, a better case can be made for the opposite course. When decisions about whether to grant paroles are considered, women do not appear to have any great advantages. Once parole is granted, however, they are somewhat more likely than men to stay out. The two types of exceptions are women with prior convictions and women with a history of drug usage.

> In sum, the picture today about how women fare at various stages in the criminal justice system is that although one in 6.5 arrests are women and one in nine convictions are women, only about one in 30 of those sentenced to prison are women. These ratios have not changed drastically over the past two

decades, even though these years have seen a women's movement develop and expand, and an increase in the proportion
of women working full time outside their homes.

Having gone through a whole new and exciting learning experience, I then continued writing and thinking about the issues involving
women and the likelihood of their involvement in various types of criminal activities.

In 1979 I joined with Freda Adler in co-editing *The Criminology of
Deviant Women*[6] for Houghton Mifflin, and in 1991 Jean Landis, a doc-
toral candidate at American University, and I wrote *The Crimes Women
Commit, The Punishments They Receive*,[7] published by Lexington
Books.

In the Epilogue I commented that:

> In the 15 years since *Women and Crime* was published,
> women and crime has become a major intellectual and pro-
> fessional specialty. Within criminology and criminal justice, and
> among the subfields within sociology, psychology, and eco-
> nomics, research on women who commit crimes has grown
> into a major area of interest.
>
> Substantively we found that:
>
> [T]he pattern we saw forming in the late 1960s and early
> 1970s has continued. Women's participation in property and
> white-collar crimes has continued to increase. In 1987, 31 per-
> cent of all larceny, 44 percent of all fraud, 34 percent of all
> forgery, and 38 percent of all embezzlement arrests were of
> women offenders. The percentages of women arrested for rob-
> bery (8%) and burglary (8%) also increased but at nowhere near
> the levels for other property offenses. Women's involvement in
> violent offenses did not deviate from the earlier pattern. In
> 1975, women accounted for 10.3 percent of Type I violent
> offense arrests (arrests for what the FBI defines as violent crimes);
> in 1987, women accounted for 11.1 percent of those arrests.
>
> Thus, the overall pattern of women's participation in
> criminal activities has not changed dramatically since 1975. The
> increase observed in the 1980s was for the same types of
> offenses reported earlier: property and white-collar crimes that
> women now have greater opportunities and skills to commit.
> There is no evidence that women have been any more involved
> in organized crime than they were at earlier times or that
> they have become more violent and aggressive than they were
> in the past.
>
> The federal judicial statistics and those available from the
> states of California, Pennsylvania, and New York reveal a pat-
> tern that is consistent with recent arrest data—namely, that
> there has been an increase in the percentage of women
> charged with and convicted of property offenses. For exam-

ple, the percentage of women convicted in federal courts increased by 6.4 percent, from 10.8 percent in 1979 to 17.2 percent in 1987. In 1987, 20 percent of the larceny, and 29 percent of the forgery convictions were of women. In the state courts, women accounted for 23 percent of the larceny convictions in California, 26 percent in New York, and 24 percent in Pennsylvania. In each of those states, women were convicted of less than 10 percent of all violent offenses in 1987.

Women still account for 5 percent of the prison population, and more women than men are housed in medium- and minimum-security prisons (84% versus 71%). But there have been changes in the conditions under which women do time. The vast discrepancies between women's and men's opportunities for vocational training and jobs for pay have diminished. Not only do all women's prisons now offer academic classes, but they also offer a broader range of training in vocations that will help provide female inmates with jobs once they are released from prison. Some prisons also have industries that offer women an opportunity to earn money while doing time.

Perhaps even more dramatic than the improvement in the opportunities for vocational training and industry have been the accommodations available for women to spend time with their children. In some women's prisons, children may visit as often as once a week and stay for as long as eight hours per visit. Some have weekend programs. At least 19 of the state and federal institutions responding to our survey also reported the availability of furlough programs whereby mothers may visit their children at home or in halfway houses. Since some 70 percent of female inmates are mothers of young children, these changes are probably most welcome.

We concluded by noting:

[T]hat women are more represented in official crime statistics today than they have been at any time since systematic national data have been available. Their criminal niche seems to be property offenses, especially white-collar offenses involving small-to-medium amounts of money. Such criminal activities appear to be most consistent with their skills and opportunities.

At the same time I am writing this piece, in my capacity as Editor of *Gender Issues*, I have arranged for a special issue on a comparative analysis of Women and Crime.[8] In the piece I co-authored with my research assistant, Nina Chernoff, we examined crime data for 27 countries from 1981 through 1995 with an eye toward answering the following questions:

1.  Has there been an increase in the overall crime rate for women from 1962 through 1995, and has the increase been greater in the more economically developed countries?

2.  If there has been an increase, did it occur primarily in property and white-collar crimes (i.e., theft and fraud)?

3.  Did the rates of female participation in violent crimes (i.e., homicide and robbery) decrease?

4.  Is there a positive relationship between the status of and opportunity for women in the society and the amount of female participation in property and white- collar crimes in that country?

5.  Is there a negative relationship between the status of and opportunity for women in the society and the amount of female participation in violent crimes in that country?

Briefly, the answers are that there has been an increase in the overall crime rates, but only a slight increase in the female crime rates. The increases that did occur were greater in the more economically developed countries. In examining the four different offense categories (homicide, robbery, theft, and fraud), we found that the increases were higher for theft and slightly higher for fraud than they were for homicide and robbery. The relationship between women's overall crime rates and the countries' economic development were positive and significant. In those countries in which women occupy higher status, as measured by formal years of schooling and percent in the labor force, we found some positive and significant correlations with the arrest rates for theft and fraud. There was some strong negative relationship between female arrests for homicide and their status in society.

Returning to the thesis made originally in 1975, the comparative data also showed that as women become more liberated from hearth and home and become more involved in full-time jobs they are more likely to engage in the types of crimes for which their occupations provide them with the greatest opportunities.

Since 1962 there have been increases in women's involvement in property offenses but almost exclusively in the more economically advanced countries.

The above discussion summarizes 25 years of writing on women and crime. But not only did the invitation from the Crime and Delinquency Center awaken an interest in and a desire to study women's involvement in criminal activities, it also spurred interest in writing about women's role in society more generally.

In 1991, in collaboration with Gloria Danziger, I wrote *Women's Movements in America: Their Successes, Disappointment, and Aspirations.*[9] As we stated in Chapter 1 of the book:

> [T]ells the story of how women's status in American society
> has changed over a time span of two centuries on such impor-
> tant matters as personal and family life, work and education-
> al experiences, and contributions and visibility in the political
> and public spheres. It shows successes as well as failures. It
> looks at the bumps and detours that have been part of Amer-
> ican women's journey from 1790 to 1990. Where appropriate,
> it applauds and celebrates events and acts that have enhanced
> women's status. It does not shy away from indicating where
> women's movements have failed, on which issues they were
> divided, and which goals are still being sought.

Between 1975 and now I have done research and written about
women as immigrants, as rabbis and ministers, as lawyers, as professors,
and as political terrorists. These, and other writings on women's roles,
appeared in a volume titled *Rabbis, Lawyers, Immigrants, Thieves* in
1993.[10] Other chapters included essays on "Married Women and Their
Friends" and "Careers and Close Friendships Among Successful Women."
Ten of the 18 chapters were written in collaboration with sociology graduate students at the University of Illinois, and with law and graduate students at American University. Two of the co-authors were undergraduates, and my daughter is another co-author. Six of the students and my
daughter subsequently completed their Ph.D.s or J.D.s and are working
in their respected fields. As I look over my résumé, I see that I have
authored or edited 13 books with eight colleagues and five graduate students and of the 200 plus articles I have written 40 were co-authored
with colleagues, 43 with graduate students and law students, and seven
with undergraduates. My husband and I jointly authored eight articles, my daughter Judith and I wrote 6 pieces and when Daniel, my
youngest child, was 14, he and I conducted a study of black-white
friendships that we published.[11]

So much for research! What are the lessons to be passed on about
teaching? First, again, a brief biographical summary. Over the course of
almost 40 years I have taught at five universities to undergraduate and
graduate students in sociology, communications, Jewish studies, and
criminal justice, to law students, and to a faculty in a professional
school.

Over the years, and I think with each passing year, I emphasize the
following points even more strongly. The first is the importance of data.
The importance of being able, both as consumers and producers of
research, to distinguish the difference between real and bogus data and
to recognize the difference between opinions, our own, those of others, or even those of "widely respected" people and scientific evidence. Thus, whether I am teaching undergraduates in large lecture classes or conducting small seminars for masters or doctoral students, I
keep repeating "I don't care what position you take on controversial

issues of public policy, e.g., immigration, drug abuse, affirmative action, so long as you are able to defend your position with data."

The most challenging of my teaching experiences involved an introductory sociology class I offered to some 400 students over several years. Not only was the size of the class somewhat daunting, but I envisioned the purpose and goals of a successful introductory course. I set for myself the task of culling the most important ideas and research that had been done in the field as well as laying before the students a sense of what sociology was all about. I believed it was important to excite and stimulate the students so that they would want to take additional, more specialized courses in sociology, and perhaps go on to do research of their own. What, for example, of Max Weber, Emile Durkheim, Karl Mannheim, August Comte, Robert Merton should I discuss and should I have the students read? Also, I included lectures on research design, hypothesis testing, representative samples, and measures of validity and reliability.

So much for research and teaching. I would like now to make a few comments about the role of the editor of an academic journal that I hope will be useful both to young scholars who are just starting on their professional careers and to future editors. Much of what I say here appeared in *Editors as Gate Keepers* that I co-edited with James Fyfe in 1994.[12] The most important advice I can offer to scholars, and especially those who are just entering the publishing world, is to find out as much as you can about all of the journals in your discipline and in allied disciplines: for example, social psychology, demography, criminology, sociology, law and society, and so on. What kinds of pieces appear in those journals? Which journal seems to publish pieces that are most similar in subject matter, method, and/or orientation to your piece? You find this out, not by looking at one issue, but by skimming several issues scattered over several years. Look over the list you have put together and find out which journals have the largest readership, are the most prestigious, have the quickest turn around time—whatever criteria are important to you. After you have decided in which journal you would most like your piece to appear, find out the style and format your manuscript needs to follow. Should notes appear at the end, separated or combined with references? What type of cites should you use in the text? Do you need an abstract? How many copies should you send? Are fees required. If so how much? This type of information can usually be obtained by perusing the most recent issue of the journal. If you still have questions, it is worth a phone call to the journal's editorial office.

Shifting to the role of the editor, he or she is in the position to perform crucial gatekeeping roles, especially if she is the editor of an official journal for a discipline, e.g., *Criminology, American Political Science Review, American Sociological Review.* She has the authority to launch a new author or a new work into the field or to hold back the person or the work. Publication, especially in a major journal, can play a crucial role in a young academic's career. It can mean the difference between gaining tenure or losing one's position. Even for older scholars, publication in a major journal can be the key to a promotion, a better job offer, or winning an award.

But the discipline places constraints on the editor's freedom and authority. For official journals, those constraints can be formidable. There is the strong expectation, for example, that every submitted manuscript will be sent out for review; in practice, about 95 percent of the manuscripts are sent out to two readers. Perhaps a third of those manuscripts, including the ones that are clearly unworthy or inappropriate, could be rejected by the editor and staff. But "form" requires outside reviews for all.

Other restraints include strong expectations that the journal will not publish manuscripts that receive negative reviews. This is the case even though in the editor's judgment the manuscript would make a contribution and is publishable.

What kinds of manuscripts are likely to receive favorable reviews from an editor and negative reviews from readers? Some, perhaps the largest group, are probably technically flawed, not up to snuff by the most recent methodological or theoretical standards. But the category may also contain some of the more imaginative, more pathbreaking pieces. A "gifted maverick" is more likely to fall by the wayside in the process. His or her imagination, innovation, or iconoclasm may not receive positive appraisal from the competent yeomen who are good at catching errors and omissions but might miss a "gem"; or at least the unusual, provocative, or outside the mainstream, submission. My advice to editors is to take more chances. Livelier, brasher issues would be the result. And, yes, there would be more debate, more argument, and not so much on technical issues, as on what contribution the article makes, how it fits into the current state of the discipline, whether it is on the cutting edge, and whether it refutes current schools of thought.

One innovation that could be introduced in the name of editorial discretion is to have a portion of the journal set aside for editors' selections, articles about which the editor openly declares: these are my choices; they did not meet peer review or they were not sent out for review. They have been published because they are iconoclastic, irreverent, provocative, and maybe pathbreaking, useful, or important. It is not likely that the editor would take advantage of the pages set aside for him or her in every issue, but they would be there when and if needed, perhaps even accompanied by the readers' critical comments and the author's rejoinder.

I also think some changes should be made on the matter of multiple submissions of the same piece to different journals. I think both authors and editors should have the option of multiple submissions. An

author should inform each editor that he or she is submitting the manuscript to more than one journal. The author should also inform each
editor as soon as the manuscript has been accepted and she or he has
agreed to publish it in the first journal that is willing to do so. An editor, on the other hand, has the right to refuse to consider a manuscript that is under review elsewhere. The editor needs to say so up front
and right away.

But, I would urge that the editor not take that tack; he or she could
miss out on some good pieces. Why not use the multiple submission ploy
as a way of getting faster turn around time from readers? A little competition in the system might make everyone happier. The author would
hear results faster; the editor who is on top of things comes off with the
best manuscripts and the process would take half the time. It seems to
work in book publishing and for some journals, as well—for example,
in law reviews.

The editor's role in nonofficial scholarly journals is somewhat different, and the biggest difference is in the greater autonomy and freedom he or she is likely to have. First of all, the editor should, and can,
play a more provocative role. Such editors should feel comfortable
about soliciting manuscripts rather than waiting for pieces to come in
over-the-transom. They should solicit for special issues that they plan
to run or just because they have heard of, or read, the work of scholars
of whom they think well. Special issues that are organized around substantive themes or methodological or theoretical orientations can be very
exciting. The opportunity to discuss and debate within the pages of
these smaller journals should be taken advantage of by using different
formats: symposia, dialogues among authors of major pieces, followed
by comments. The editor might purposely solicit pieces that represent
opposing viewpoints, arrive at different conclusions, recommend different research or social action strategies, and then after they have
appeared in print, give the readers, in the form of letters to the editor,
a chance to be heard.

The editor might be more visible in the pages of such a journal by
calling for a new way of looking at some aspect of the discipline; or by
calling attention to the need for research on a social problem; or by offering a critical assessment of a major theoretical or ideological orientation
currently applied in the discipline; or by asking rhetorical questions
about "where" the discipline is headed, "why" it has lost its voice, and
"how" it has become so circumscribed. In other words, the irony here
is that the editors of smaller, less prestigious journals, may in fact have
greater influence, and make more of an impact on the discipline and the
world of ideas than editors of the larger official journals, because their
roles have become so limited. Should the editors of smaller journals
choose to take advantage of their greater autonomy, they can function
both as gatekeepers and initiators of knowledge and ideas. After they

have completed their tour of duty they are more likely to leave their imprint than are editors of the official journals. They will have something that they can point to and say, "I was responsible for that. I made the difference here." The readers are also more likely to remember the journal as being under the editorship of a particular individual during various periods of its history. Editors of official journals are more likely to fade into the woodwork.

So, future editors, if you want to mold, create, and leave your mark, it is the unofficial journals that you should seek to edit. If on the other hand, you crave the gratification and experience of being in the center, at the pulse of a discipline, look toward "official" major journals. The opportunities they provide for learning about the ferment that is going on, the type of work that is being done, and how such work is evaluated are much greater. These editors play more passive roles, but they may be actively learning a lot more about where the field is and where it is likely to be going.

The decision about which type of editorship one seeks out might in part be a function of age, especially professional age. The editorship of an official journal may suit older scholars, those who see themselves as having done their major, most creative work; not unlike the decision of some professors to become deans. Taking on the editorship of a smaller and nonofficial journal is more likely to allow the editor to continue to exercise creativity and imagination. The editor has more control and autonomy, and there is greater opportunity to leave a mark. His or her ideas, views of the discipline, notions of the direction in which the field should go permeate the pages of the journal.

It would be unusual to go through 40 years of a career and not run into some trouble. Briefly I'll review one of three cases that I reflect on with gratification.

In 1990 I was asked to help conduct a fact finding study of political and criminal prisoners in Israel. There would be three people in the delegation: a representative of the human rights organization, who spoke Arabic; my daughter, an attorney who has served as a guard in a men's prison in the United States, and is fluent in Hebrew; and myself. I had some experience studying prison conditions in the United States, Western Europe, India, and China. At the time of our visit, Israel was the only country in the Middle East that had granted the human rights organization permission to visit and speak directly with inmates in its police and military run prisons. The three of us visited four prisons, two police lock-ups, and five military camps.

Unfortunately, the delegation differed in the interpretation of what they saw, and in their evaluation of Israel's treatment of criminal and political prisoners. As a result, two different reports were eventually written and published.[13] Prior to the publication of the two separate reports the human rights organization stated that they would not publish a report based on the 1990 investigation. Instead they said they would wait a year or so, and then go back in the hope that it would then be possible to gain access to prisons in other countries in the Middle East. I protested that decision and I told a representative of the human rights organization that Judith and I would release the report we had prepared on our own, and not in any way make them a party to our conclusions. The person I spoke with had no problems with that decision so we went ahead and released our report to the media. That is when all hell broke loose. The Director of the organization wrote a letter to the then Provost and Acting President of the University that stated:

> A number of journalists to whom my colleagues and I have spoken have told us that the University press office has been publicizing an attack on a division of Human Rights Watch by Professor Rita Simon. I write to let you know of this and to ask you to look into the matter and let me know why the University should lend its imprimatur to Ms. Simon's efforts. If you are not already aware of the problem, I think you will soon discover that it can only do harm to your university.
>
> It is difficult for me to understand what advantage your university could derive from publicizing an effort by one of its faculty that warrants descriptions as being work of such dismal quality and where that faculty member is also susceptible to a charge of unethical conduct.
>
> After you have had a chance to look into this matter, please let me hear from you. Your comments will help to determine whether I undertake an effort to make the University community generally aware of this matter.

Excerpts from the Provost's response appear below:

> I have your letter of April 19 and its attachments. I am puzzled by your letter inasmuch as you must be aware that the publicizing of a faculty member's work—especially of so distinguished a scholar as Rita Simon—does not constitute an "imprimatur" as you suggest. Our voluminous faculty publications and other achievements draw both praise and protest, which I perceive to be normal for a university in a free society. I am not sure what it is you want me to "look into."

To my knowledge, nothing more was heard from the human rights organization.

In the sixth decade of my life I ventured into a new arena that I describe briefly in this last section.

I had studied a good deal of the research literature on women's roles and status in American society, and I pulled together data on women in the labor force, the relative educational attainments of men and women, and the wage differentials between men and women over some five decades. I continued to read in the popular media about how the radical feminists portrayed women as victims and men as their enemies. I thought something should be done to set the record straight and to make a better match between rhetoric and data. With the collaboration of Cathy Young, who emigrated to the United States from the Soviet Union in the early 1980s and currently earns her living as a journalist, I founded the Women's Freedom Network (WFN) in the fall of 1993.

Essentially the Women's Freedom Network views women as competent, responsible individuals who do not need special protections and dispensations from the state; nor do they need to have standards lowered for them to be able to compete effectively for jobs or acceptances to institutions of higher education. The Women's Freedom Network believes that there are no "male" and "female" standards of excellence, morality, or justice. The rhetoric of victimization trivializes real abuse, demeans women, and promotes antagonism instead of partnership between the sexes. The WFN believes in empowering individual women rather than the state and its bureaucracies, and therefore advocates a full and open discussion of the role of government and the private sector in creating equal opportunity.

We currently have about 1,200 supporters who receive our bimonthly newsletter. In my role as President, I have served as the major fundraiser, have organized national conferences, and joined with board members to give talks at regional meetings, receptions, and other conferences. None of the officers receive a salary or stipend from WFN.

Women's Freedom Network is my first venture in founding a social movement. I believe the decision to do so was a direct outgrowth of my work in the academy, on women's movements, on women immigrants, and the various studies I have done about crime and the criminal justice system. Thus, in bringing this professorial memoir to an end, I return to an old and familiar theme: data matter and it is incumbent upon us to check and to carefully distinguish between bogus and real data. That is what I see as an important role that the Women's Freedom Network performs. Thus, I do not find any inconsistency in serving as President of the Women's Freedom Network and in carrying on my usual teaching and research activities.

One final comment: as I reread this essay and think back over the almost half century that has gone by since I started graduate school and continued on as a faculty member, I feel extraordinarily lucky and grateful. Over all these years I have been rewarded monetarily and by professional recognition for doing work that I have found enjoyable, and meaningful. In thinking back, there are a few things I might have done differently but, on the whole, I have had the wonderful opportunity to choose and work on problems that I believe are important and the outcome of which might make a difference. I am very grateful.

## Endnotes

1   *The Jury and the Defense of Insanity*, Little Brown, Boston, 1967. Reissued, Transaction Books, 1999.

2   "Of Nepotism, Marriage, and the Pursuit of an Academic Career," (with Shirley Merritt Clark and Larry L. Tifft), *Sociology of Education*, Vol. 39, No. 4, Fall 1966.

3   "The Woman Ph.D.: A Recent Profile," (with Shirley Merritt Clark and Kathleen Galway), *Social Problems*, Fall 1967.

4   *Transracial Adoption* (with Howard Altstein), Wiley-Interscience, 1977.

   *Adoption, Race and Identity* (with Howard Altstein), Praeger, 1992.

5   *Women and Crime*, NIMH Monograph, Center for Crime and Delinquency, 1975. Also Lexington Books, 1975.

6   *The Criminology of Deviant Women* (with Freda Adler), Houghton Mifflin, 1979.

7   *The Crimes Women Commit, The Punishments They Receive* (with Jean Landis), Lexington, 1991.

8   "Women and Crime the World Over," (with Nina Chernoff), *Gender Issues*, Vol. 18, No. 3, Summer 2000.

9   *Women's Movements in America: Their Achievements, Disappointments, and Aspirations* (with Gloria Danzinger), Praeger, 1991.

10   *Rabbis, Lawyers, Immigrants, Thieves: Women's Roles in America*, Praeger, 1993.

11   "Black-White Friendships," (with Daniel H. Simon), *Champaign Life*, June 1983.

12   *Editors as Gatekeepers* (with James Fyfe), University Press of America, 1994.

13   "Prison Conditions in Israel," (with Judith D. Simon), *Moment*, Vol. 16, No. 3, June 1991.

# 12

# Unwinding: Reflections on a Career

James F. Short, Jr.

## Introduction

For most of my life I seem to have been in a hurry—to get some-where, to do something or to do it better; all-too-often, alas, to "catch up." As a result, I have found it difficult to slow down and to unwind—to "really retire." My wife attributes this, in some measure, to "ego," by which she means that staying professionally active is ego-satisfying, per-haps implying that I am too much invested in the work that has been a preoccupation for so many years.

She is probably correct. My slight feelings of guilt over this con-fession are assuaged, however, by the sheer enjoyment I experience in being a sociologist, a criminologist, an observer of the human condition, and participant in the academic life, all of which I have found to be tremendously satisfying. Ego investment in what is most meaningful in one's life is, after all, generic to the human species. I still enjoy the rhythms of the academic week and year, and the opportunities that liv-ing in a university community affords; not the least of which is the asso-ciation with colleagues and ideas. In this day and age, the latter can, of course, be achieved via email and the Internet, telephone and travel; but there is satisfaction in local availability.

This universal condition of human existence was brought home to me with special poignancy nearly half a century ago when I paid a brief visit to William F. Ogburn, my mentor at the University of Chicago. Ogburn had retired at the close of the summer session in 1951, just as I had completed my Ph.D. program. He continued to have an office at the university, however, and that is where we met.[1]

I greatly admired Ogburn. He was "hard-nosed" about sociology but intrigued by new methods and the insights that they might provide. We had become friends toward the end of my graduate student tenure and he had sent a warm congratulatory note to me when *Suicide and Homicide* (1964)—a joint project based on Andy Henry's and my dissertations—was published. Always restrained, as befitting a southern-born gentleman, he greeted me with a smile. When I inquired as to his well-being, he replied, "You know, I don't see or hear as well as I used to. Sex isn't as important to me as it used to be, and my tennis game has suffered; but there is one thing that never changes: the old ego" (pointing to his head)![2]

A hard lesson, indeed, and I can attest to both the veracity and the insights in the old man's remarks! (At the time, Ogburn was younger than I am at this writing.) Although I choose to believe that ego is not the only reason for staying professionally active, there can be no doubt that I and many others continue to work in semi-retirement in part because our work boosts our egos. One tries to keep such concerns under control, however, and an experience early in my career reminded me of the value of humility. Dorothy Swaine Thomas wrote a review of *Suicide and Homicide* for *Science* magazine. The review was not complimentary, and I was devastated, especially because Thomas was a pioneer in studying social aspects of the business cycle. I also thought the review was unfair in its criticism. I quickly prepared a point-by-point refutation, and sent it to Andy Henry, urging that if he agreed, we should send it to *Science*. Andy's reply was cryptic. Although he agreed with my critique, he did not think we should seek its publication. Instead, he said, "Next time, let's write a better book."

Andy's advice was a lesson in humility. I knew there were weaknesses in the book—more than Thomas had identified. Fortunately, more favorable reviews soon appeared in sociological journals. There was another lesson, as well: controversy is, after all, the essence of science. Criticism should be taken in good grace. We should learn from it; and do better next time.

## Biographical Background

My background was small town and strongly Protestant—"about as WASPish as one can get" (see Short, 1969).[3] That 1969 essay also addressed many of the influences that have informed the topics to be addressed in this one. Chief among them, to summarize, were the very early installation of personal responsibility for one's conduct, a strong work ethic, and belief in the redeeming power of education—faith that the "truth shall make you free" in the terminology of my Baptist upbringing (Northern—now American Baptist—emphatically not Southern). I continue to hold to that faith despite the important insight that much that passes as truth is socially constructed.

My father was Principal of the high school in the rural community in which I spent all twelve years of common school. His position was an honored one, and one that suffered less than most throughout the great depression. His salary one year, as I recall, was $1500, and he sold—or attempted to sell—encyclopedias (Britannica, as I recall) during at least one summer. We had a large vegetable garden and occasionally raised potatoes on farm land that my grandfather had given to my mother. Being Baptists was politically advantageous because the local power structure, such as it was, tended to be dominated by Irish Catholics and German Lutherans. In matters of religion, Baptists were a minority and, in this sense, politically nonthreatening.

Growing up in that small town, and having nearby uncles and aunts who were farmers provided many work opportunities very early on: water boy and gate opener, later driving horse-drawn grain and "bundle" wagons for the threshing run, beginning at age 6. These were great learning experiences, and I quickly discovered a lot of jobs that I did not care to make my life's work![4] Summers were not all work, however. Dad's stable job and a small income derived from the farm permitted occasional travel opportunities, including one long cross-country trip to California when I was ten,[5] and two summers during which my parents ran a summer camp in the Black Hills for the South Dakota Baptist Convention. The first of these, when I was still a pre-teen, provided my first experience with a minority population, when Indians from the Pine Ridge reservation came for a week's camping experience.[6] For the second, when I turned 17, my "middle brother" and I did the "scut" work for the camp, and checked out all the teen-age girls.

With this modest "real world" experience, following graduation from high school I enrolled at Shurtleff College, a small Baptist institution located in Alton, Illinois. Shurtleff was where Mom and Dad had met, and where it was supposed that I, too, might find a "life helpmate" (such was the language commonly employed in such matters). I did not find a wife, but much to the consternation of some of my relatives (not my parents) I did fall heavily for a lovely Japanese-American girl from Hawaii. This was in the fall of 1942, when the United States was at war with Japan. In retrospect, I am surprised that it never occurred to me that dating an obviously Japanese young woman might be viewed askance by the local populace or by my fellow students. Neither occurred, at least to our knowledge; and we enjoyed what was then, I suppose, a typical freshman romance.[7] I felt frankly liberated to be away from the strong ties of parents and other relatives, loving though they were. I had gone to Shurtleff on scholarships, and enjoyed musical and athletic activities.[8]

I also enlisted in the U.S. Marine Corps Reserve during that first year in college, and on July 1, 1943, was sent to a newly formed "V-12" program at Denison University, located in Granville, Ohio ("Mary Worth's" community). Granville, a small community once described as "more New England than New England," was "back east" from my Illinois roots, and my liberation from those roots continued. Established to train future Navy and Marine Corps officers, the V-12 program required that we be in uniform, attend regular drills, live in dormitory barracks, and follow a prescribed curriculum. A few elective options were permitted, however, and it was at Denison that I took my first sociology and criminology courses. I also found time to date a lovely girl from nearby Newark, Ohio, and sing for a "gospel team" comprised chiefly of former Wheaton College students—a clear reminder of the continued influence of my early religious upbringing.

Denison was a wonderful experience. We were, of course, always conscious of the war and our potential role in it; but it was still college. The war's urgency became more personally intense when our unit was sent to Parris Island for boot camp in late Fall, 1943. That was another liberating experience, despite the shaved heads and rigid restrictions, and the obvious reservations—bordering on contempt—that our noncommissioned officers felt for all of us budding "shave-tails."[9] We were confined to barracks, as Christmas and New Years came and went. Parris Island was followed by a brief stint at Camp Lejeune, in North Carolina, while we awaited assignment to Officers Candidate School in Quantico, Virginia. Events occurring while I was in training at Quantico radically changed the course of history. President Franklin Roosevelt died and victory was achieved by the Allies in Europe. I was commissioned a Second Lieutenant in the USMCR in June of 1945 and, after a brief leave, was sent to Camp Pendleton. While awaiting assignment there, further events transpired to radically alter not only history, but my personal fate. Nuclear bombs were detonated over Hiroshima and Nagasaki, and the war in the Pacific theater ended. Immediately thereafter I joined a small contingent of officers which, after a brief stop in Guam, became part of the occupation forces in Japan.

In September, 1945, I was assigned to "Baker" (B) Company, 8th Marine Battalion, 2nd Marine Division. I "grew up" a lot during my service in Japan, and it was there that my sociological and criminological curiosity was informed and piqued in many ways (see Short, 1988). Following discharge from the Marine Corps I returned to Denison where, on my first night back on campus, I met the beautiful young woman to whom I have now been married for more than 52 years. Graduate school at the University of Chicago followed, and it was there that I took the first steps toward becoming a "real sociologist" (see Short, 1969).

I offer this perhaps overly long "introduction" to my personal odyssey because these learning experiences tell a great deal about the choices I have made, and such advice as I feel comfortable in dispensing for would-be criminologists.

## Working Habits

My background helps to explain why I have nearly always enjoyed a relatively high level of activity—working and playing. Early in my teaching career I asked for 8 o'clock classes, so as to get on with it, and to free time for research. Although I have had to slow down, and now find it easier to do so, I prefer to walk fast, and I "work out" regularly. Now that gardening has become my primary hobby I even enjoy pulling weeds. Indeed, I recommend such mindless activity as a welcome relief from the concentration required for research and writing. I enjoy chopping wood and all the many tasks that having a cabin on Priest Lake, Idaho, entails (especially with son Michael)—as well as the "fun things," of course (especially when I can do them with daughter Susan and/or her children).

A 12-hour teaching load at Washington State University (then the State College of Washington) and my passion for research led me, after my first year of full-time teaching, to apply to the Social Science Research Council for a Faculty Research Fellowship. For three years the SSRC fellowship funded half of my academic year salary, plus a summer stipend, to facilitate my research on self-reported delinquency, a topic to which Clifford Shaw had first directed me (see Short, 1982; Meier, 1988). It was in the course of this work that I learned to appreciate the difficulties, and the rewards, of field work and collecting my own data—lessons that, alas, many budding social scientists never experience in this age of easily accessible large scale data sets. Despite the great advantages of such data sets, I strongly recommend that all graduate students be required to grapple with the problems of collecting data on their own, preferably in a field work setting.

Electronic computing was in its infancy when I returned to the University of Chicago to direct the Youth Studies Program (YSP), in June, 1959.[10] The lone computer on the University of Chicago campus at the time was a UNIVAC I, housed in the basement of the Administration Building. It was slow, difficult to program, and cantankerous. Electronic data management was not well developed at the time, even for easily quantifiable data. This proved to be the undoing of several proposed reanalyses of data from the YSP (for which I have received several requests over the years), a situation that I deeply regret, and one that truly does inspire guilt feelings. Fortunately, support from the National Consortium on Violence Research (NCOVR) has recently made possible the digitalization of a large volume of field observations of gangs, and a fine WSU graduate student (Lorine Hughes) is analyzing the data for her dissertation research. The YSP thus has been given new life that, we hope, will permit still other investigators to use the data. When compared with data from ongoing research, such as Mercer Sullivan's and Jeffery Fagan's studies in New York, and Elijah Anderson's in Philadelphia, it is my hope that these data will help to advance the group process perspective that was the YSP's major product.

Becoming comfortable with writing on the computer was a struggle for me. Fortunately, I had learned to "touch type" while I was in high school, but for many years I wrote every article and chapter in long hand, and I revised almost continuously—as I still do. I shudder to think of the hours of retyping that this writing strategy inflicted on numerous secretaries.

Computers have also facilitated—exacerbated might be a better word—my penchant for working on more than one project, paper, or chapter at a time. I strongly recommend switching among tasks as a means of avoiding burn out. I often do so when I reach a point of diminishing returns for the investment of time and energy required of any one task—call it writer's block, occasional boredom, or simply growing weary of concentration on one task.

## What I Think I Have Learned

Despite my appreciation of the social constructionist position, I am strongly oriented toward data, and to the comfort zone it provides—assuming, of course, the data meet reasonable standards of reliability and validity. I worry a great deal about these standards and recommend strongly that anyone starting out in the field do likewise. It was that concern that guided my first efforts to measure delinquent behavior by means of self-reports, and to compare such data with official records of offending. To this day, whenever possible, I "triangulate" self reports, other types of survey data, and ethnographic and other types of observational data.

Direct observational studies are, I believe, of critical importance for improving the rigor of both empirical analyses and theoretical development. An incident that occurred early in the YSP is illustrative (see my "Foreword" to Jacobs, 1999). A graduate student observer's report of an evening spent with one of the gangs we were studying alerted us to the importance of intimate, detailed knowledge of places and activities. The observation took place in a pool hall where young and old from the community met and socialized. Outsiders, unless they were legitimized by regulars, were unwelcome. At one point in the evening the detached worker assigned to the gang asked our observer if he was aware of drug traffic taking place in the pool hall. He was not, although it was happening literally in front of his eyes. He had noted that an attractive girl occasionally took the pool cue from one of the gang members, but the young man's behavior appeared little different from those of others in the group. In fact they were quite different, for he alone among the gang members was selling heroin (he was also the only "hard drug" user in the gang, several of whom smoked marijuana). The girl, a prostitute who sold drugs, left the more dangerous aspects of the task (carrying and delivering heroin) to the gang member, who in fact did not know the identity of her customers. She made the contacts with customers and collected the money, whereupon she relieved her confederate (our gang member) of his pool cue. The boy who was carrying the drug then placed the purchase in the pocket of a coat that was hung casually on the wall, from which the customer could complete his or her purchase.

The point is not that our graduate student's observations would have been inaccurate; rather, they would have been incomplete without the detached worker's more sophisticated knowledge. And so it is with many "variables," "factors," and "risks." The lesson: be alert to problems of validity as well as reliability. Do everything you can to ensure that your data reflect the reality of phenomena you wish to measure.[11]

Similar interests in the extent to which observations can be generalized, their validity, and how we interpret them, propelled my focus on risk analysis. "Material culture," especially in the form of technology, was the driving force of Ogburn's theory of social change (Ogburn, 1924). Because change has become so much a part of virtually all sub-fields of the social and behavioral sciences, with notable exceptions it has waned as a special topic in its own right. My re-entry into the field was indirect, stimulated by an excellent graduate student, Donna Randall, who chose as her dissertation topic, "women in a toxic work environment" (see Randall & Short, 1983). This, in turn, directed my attention to risk analysis, a field of great importance to the "hard sciences," engineering, medicine, and among economists and a few psychologists, but until that time largely neglected by sociologists and other social scientists (but see Perrow, 1984, Douglas & Wildavsky, 1982). With the encouragement of WSU colleagues, Bill Freudenburg and Gene Rosa, I chose as the topic of my American Sociological Association presidential address, "The social fabric at risk: Toward the social transformation of risk analysis" (Short, 1984).[12]

Risk analysis forced me to become better acquainted with organizational theory and research, and it brought me into closer contact with other sociological colleagues from other places, most notably Lee Clarke, with whom I enjoyed a productive collaboration (Short & Clarke, 1992; Clarke & Short, 1993); as well as colleagues from other disciplines, such as economics, law, and political science. It certainly helped me to become a better generalist and a better scientist.[13]

It also provided a unique opportunity. In the spring of 1991 I was approached about becoming involved in efforts of officials in Clark County (Las Vegas), Nevada, to study the effects of a proposed high-level nuclear waste facility to be located (literally) *in* Yucca Mountain. With pass-through funding from the U.S. Department of Energy, Clark County and other "affected areas of local government" (counties, municipalities, and tribes) were provided with funds to assess and prepare for possible impacts of such a facility on local populations, their property, etc. With the aid of consultants, Clark County chose to appoint a Peer Review Committee (PRC) to monitor and advise the County's Nuclear Waste Division's (NWD) efforts in this context.[14] I was honored to be asked to chair the Committee which, like the State's Technical Review Committee (TRC) and its research team, was comprised of distinguished social scientists and experts in fields such as transportation and emergency management.

The PRC lasted for four years. The Committee reviewed evolving plans for the transport of HLNW through and around Las Vegas, technical aspects of HLNW disposal (including visits to the Yucca Mountain site and to the Waste Isolation Pilot Project for transuranic wastes, located near Carlsbad, New Mexico), as well as emergency management plans in the event of an accidental release of radiation in the course of HLNW transport or a repository malfunction, and studies of possible economic and social impacts of the construction and operation of the repository.

Participation in the PRC was exhilarating, and an unparalleled opportunity to work with a fine group of colleagues, including many who were "wrestling with the beast" of this seemingly intransigent problem. Although it was clear from the beginning that Clark County officials were less interested in "social effects" than was the State, attention to such effects was a condition of my acceptance of the PRC chairmanship, and a bona fide effort was promised. The State's TRC had made great strides in this area, but their focus was largely on individual perceptions and behaviors. PRC members hoped to broaden this focus to include institutions and organizations in the larger community. Halting efforts were made over a period of nearly four years, but in the end, diminished funding and the realities of local and national politics prevented their realization. Despite persistent prodding by the PRC, studies of the social impacts of the proposed repository continued to be resisted by the NWD (and, I suspect, by other county officials and community influentials). The effort was hampered by increasingly hostile relationships between the NWD and the research contractor—a situation that I failed to spot and deal with effectively. Difficulties experienced by the contractor in carrying out initial research designs also occurred, contributing materially to the deterioration of the research effort. Beyond such problems, however, it was not clear that the Committee's efforts were appreciated; indeed they were viewed with suspicion. NWD staff turnover was a continuous problem, and NWD priorities often seemed directed more toward maintaining staff (whose record of achievement left much to be desired) than toward the goals we felt had been mutually agreed upon. The lesson: be aware of the difficulties of conducting research in social policy settings. Realpolitik is a tough arena in which to conduct research, especially when the setting is emotionally and politically charged.

It was time to pull back, in any case, and I resigned in the spring of 1995, and the PRC was, in effect, dissolved. Although the DOE continued (and continues) to study the technical feasibility of the Yucca Mountain site and to seek the advice of third parties, including the National Academy of Sciences, funding of research concerning social effects of HLNW disposal was severely restricted, especially at the State level.[15] The results of the State's funding of social effects research resulted in landmark contributions in the form of "well over 300 reports, presentations, articles, books, and chapters in books" (Flynn et al., 1995:xi).

Study of risk analysis and the Nevada experience further convinced me that even the most technical problems have important, often critical, social components; and that solutions to technical problems often require recognition of social dimensions of those problems. Early in my graduate studies I learned from Clifford Shaw that professional and technical training often leads to the neglect of the people who are most affected by decisions made on the basis of professional and technical criteria. Shaw pointed to the overlapping distributions of crime and settlement houses, social work professionals, and social agencies. Instead of drawing the "obvious" conclusion that the overlap was due to the *need for professional services* in the same areas in which crime was concentrated, he asked why crime continued to flourish in these areas despite the presence and the best of intentions of such agencies. While some may argue that Shaw's suggested solution to problems of crime and juvenile delinquency—to involve local people, and indigenous leaders, in the planning and carrying out programs aimed at crime prevention and rehabilitation of offenders—has also failed to prevent crime, the *principle* of involving stakeholders in solutions to their own problems is now far more acceptable among human services professionals. Indeed, it has become doctrinal among many professionals, which might not entirely please Shaw!

Risk analysis typically is concerned with highly technical problems: how to ensure the safety of industrial designs or of the location and construction of toxic waste disposal sites, for example. The contribution that social science makes to this conundrum lies in promoting the realization that technical solutions, by themselves, are insufficient to truly solve many of these problems—that the problems are often as much political and social as technical. Many in the risk analysis community, with strong support from the National Research Council (National Academy of Sciences; see Stern & Fineberg, 1996), know this. As a result, those who are most affected by technical problems (or those who are about to be so affected by proposed solutions)—that is, stakeholders—increasingly are involved in the search for acceptable and successful solutions to problems that heretofore have been viewed solely in technical terms. Resistance continues, however, particularly among those with traditionally narrow views of the nature of technical problems. The parallel with criminology regarding "solutions" that would exclude attention to "root causes" of crime is compelling.

## Risk, Theory, and Social Policy

The vocabulary of risk is now widely embraced in many areas of social concern; so much so that identification of risk factors has, for some, become a substitute for theory. This is lamentable and potentially tragic for the social and behavioral sciences. I am reminded of the hoary debate in graduate school concerning "multiple factor theories," which are not theories at all. Theories explain, or attempt to do so. Facts, factors, and indicators of risk do not explain; they must *be explained*. That, together with its primary role in stimulating empirical research, is the province of theory.

Reliance on "facts," *per se and without theory*, is especially egregious in the context of policy advocacy. Facts are, of course, critical to theory testing, and invaluable to social policy. But all data suffer from problems of reliability and validity, and data in the social and behavioral sciences typically are bound by limitations of time, place, and other types of contexts.

Preoccupation with policy advocacy often leads us to be over-confident in the reliability and validity of our research—our measures, analyses, and theories. In my view, our stance with regard to social policy should follow an "enlightenment" model, rather than an "engineering" model (Janowitz, 1972; Short, 1968; 1975). That is, our primary efforts should be directed toward obtaining knowledge of fundamental personal, interpersonal, group, and organizational structures, cultures, and processes. The principle applies to every type of human behavior and social problem. We should be prepared to advise practitioners, politicians, and publics concerning what we learn; and we should be willing to discuss possible implications of what we have learned for social policy. But we must be honest and straightforward regarding the limitations of our data, our findings, and our theories; and we should not become embroiled in policy advocacy. We should not have to be reminded that, as has been written of policy scientists, "self restraint . . . should be their hallmark in the face of uncertainty or ignorance . . ." (Eulau & McCluggage, 1985:71).

This position is sometimes difficult to maintain, particularly when one feels strongly about issues. I hold strong personal and political views concerning many issues, including those to which I have devoted much of my professional life. I often feel strongly about policies and programs that ostensibly are designed to address these issues; and I feel free to advocate, or to oppose, such policies *as a responsible individual citizen, but not in my capacity as a sociologist/criminologist.* To do otherwise would, in my view, undercut the credibility of the social and behavioral sciences, and my credibility as a scientist.

I hold to this position regarding professional organizations, as well. I do not believe it is appropriate—indeed, that it is quite inappropriate—for professional associations to engage in policy advocacy. I believe it is incumbent upon such organizations to defend scientific principles of inquiry and analysis, but that those principles should not be compromised by engaging in advocacy for policies that, inevitably, involve political decisions, as well as uncertainties related to relevant knowledge bases and conditions of policy implementation (see Short et al., 2000). I hasten to add that occasional disagreements with colleagues in this respect has done little to diminish the pleasure I have experienced while participating in the governance and other activities of professional associations

Action-research *collaboration*, as opposed to a narrow focus on whether social policies and action programs "work," can, in my experience, be mutually rewarding. When I was asked by the University of Chicago and the YMCA of Metropolitan Chicago to study the latter's "detached worker program" I argued, successfully, that the research should be directed toward data gathering in the interest of theory testing and building, rather than evaluation of whether the program reduced delinquent behavior. My rationale then, as now, was that this strategy would be more productive in terms both of advancing knowledge about youth gangs and of service to the YMCA program. I met frequently with the detached workers and their supervisors, told them about our research and what we were finding, and tried to answer their questions as best I could. As a result, neither the workers nor YMCA officials felt threatened by our research and a productive relationship was maintained.[16]

Having thus delivered myself of these strong views, over the course of a long career, I have participated in a number of policy-oriented efforts in addition to the PRC and TRC programs in Nevada, including the President's Commission on Law Enforcement and Administration of Justice (President Johnson's "Crime Commission"); the National Commission on the Causes and Prevention of Violence; the Committee on Law and Justice of the National Research Council, and that committee's Panel on the Understanding and Control of Violent Behavior; the National Consortium on Violence Research (NCOVR); and, most recently, the Academic Advisory Committee for the National Campaign Against Youth Violence.

Each of these efforts has been personally and professionally rewarding, and in each I have held steadfastly to the enlightenment model. There is a "flip side" to both the enlightenment and engineering models of participation in the policy process. The charge is made that participation in such efforts subjects one to the risk of cooptation and of shoring up corrupt regimes. Although such concerns must be taken seriously, and guarded against, both as citizens and scholars I believe we have a responsibility to participate in efforts to address problems for which our training and experience are relevant. Moreover, as scholars who enjoy the support of the larger society, our work is critical to the proper functioning of democratically representative government.

Support of the enlightenment model sometimes places me at odds with colleagues who prefer a more activist role of policy advocacy. Disagreement often centers as much on the quality of scholarly work and the manner in which it should be presented, as it does on the question of advocacy, per se. In my experience, however, the shrillness of policy advocacy often is based more on ideology than on science. Ideology and personal bias play important roles in everyone's thinking and actions, of course, but ideologically-driven inquiry and argument are the bane of scientific thinking. I try to act according to ideological principles embodied in many of the world's great religions, including the Judeo-Christian traditions in which I was reared; and I believe strongly in the traditions of democratic, representative government. These beliefs motivate much of my research and the social and political causes with which I am associated. They also guide my relationships with others. My advice in all these matters: we must strive to be decent human beings and to be objective in research endeavors and in interpreting and responding to the research and scholarly efforts of others. Although complete objectivity is an unattainable ideal, we must strive for it nonetheless.

## Conclusion

Ambition is both necessary and to be feared. Until a few years ago I had, in fact, never thought of myself as particularly ambitious. I was mildly shocked when a friend, the then Executive Vice President of Washington State University, remarked that he had not been aware of my *ambition* to become President of the American Sociological Association (having once been defeated for the post, I had recently agreed to be nominated by petition).[17] My surprise was genuine. I thought then and continue to believe that service in professional associations is a professional obligation—albeit an honor, and an enjoyable obligation for the most part, as well as a lot of hard work—rather than a proper goal of personal ambition. I recognize how richly I have been rewarded by my participation in such activities—especially how much I have learned and profited from the personal contacts and relationships that they have facilitated.

My advice, then: be ambitious, work hard, and enjoy the ride! I am rarely bored with life, and see no reason why—given good health and an active mind—one should ever be. I believe that one should embrace life with all its challenges and opportunities. For me, this has meant avoiding too narrow concentration on any single specialization. Working in risk analysis forced me to become better acquainted with literatures that I had neglected—research and theory in organizations, for example. It facilitated my return to earlier interests in technology and social change, and helped me to become a better and more general sociologist. I highly recommend that a second "specialization" be a part of career planning.

As for the future, I will never read all the books that I want to read, listen to all the music that I know I would enjoy, cultivate the perfect garden, witness all the events and entertainments that living in a university community affords and modern travel and communications systems make possible—or be as good a sociologist/criminologist as I would like to be. I am told that many scholars "quit trying" toward the end of their careers. I cannot imagine why, except for lack of physical or mental capacity. That will happen to me, I am certain—and I hope I will know when it does. In the meantime, I plan to keep trying, because I am having too much fun to quit.

## Acknowledgments

I owe much to the University of Chicago, past and present, personally and professionally: in addition to Ogburn, Clifford Shaw, and through him Henry McKay, Solomon Kobrin, Joe Puntil, and others associated with the Illinois Institute for Juvenile Research and the Chicago Area Project; Ernest W. Burgess, Everett and Helen Hughes, Ethel Shanus, Sam Kincheloe, Phil Hauser, and Albert J. Reiss, Jr., each of whom in his/her own way did a great deal to socialize me during my graduate student years and after; as did fellow graduate students, especially Andy Henry and Harold Finestone. Chicago was a much more exciting place when I returned to conduct the gang research, in 1959. Peter Rossi, Jim Davis, Morris Janowitz, Jim Coleman, Dudley Duncan, Don Bogue, Elihu Katz, Peter Blau, Mayer Zald, Harrison White, and, of course, Fred Strodtbeck, had joined the faculty, bringing new perspectives and energy; Desmond Cartwright and Ken Howard, from the Department of Psychology brought their skills and insights to the YSP research team.

For one who has maintained affiliation with a single institution over the course of half a century, my life has been enriched by a number of special opportunities and career moves. The SSRC Fellowship brought me into contact with Albert Cohen, from whom I learned a great deal and whose collaboration and friendship I will always cherish. Returning to Chicago for the gang research proved to be fateful for my career, as did service as Co-Director of Research (with Marvin Wolfgang) for the National Commission on the Causes and Prevention of Violence. The latter followed upon my four-year tenure as Dean of the Graduate School at Washington State University, in the course of which I had the pleasure of working with two fine WSU Presidents, Clement French and Glenn Terrell. A fellowship at the Center for Advanced Study in the Social and Behavioral Sciences (1969-70) and a visiting professorship in law and sociology at Stanford University, (1975), visiting fellow appointments at the Institute of Criminology and Kings College, University of Cambridge (1976) and the Centre for Socio-Legal Studies and Wolfson College, University of Oxford (1986) were especially enjoyable and stimulating.

Washington State University colleagues, especially in the Department of Sociology and the Social and Economic Sciences Research Center, have been remarkably tolerant of my frequent absences, and supportive of my far-flung activities. Over the course of a long career I have benefited in untold ways from friendships, collaborations, and relationships with too many such to acknowledge individually. I cannot let this opportunity pass, however, without acknowledging the special relationship that I have enjoyed with Jack P. Gibbs and Charles Tittle. Jack, whom I have known since he was a graduate student at the University of Oregon, has done me the honor of "introducing" me as president of each of three professional associations (Pacific Sociological Association, American Sociological Association, and American Society of Criminology; see Gibbs, 1998)—and in the process managed to inject humor to a usually humorless and often dreary proceeding! I admire his values, his guts, and his bull headedness in sticking to his guns regarding sociology/criminology (even when I disagree with him). Like Jack, Charles is a brilliant scholar; he is perhaps the hardest worker I have ever known and, without question, the best mentor of graduate students in my experience. Except for his urging I would not have agreed to stand for election as President of the American Society of Criminology; and without the assistance of Charles and his wife, Debra Curran, who served as Program Chair, I could not have performed the duties required of the office. The three of us, along with Bob Bursik and Colin Loftin, formed a "shadow cabinet" that kept me on an even keel and made it all a lot of fun. Charles—his friendship and all around colleagueship—has been a critical influence, personally and professionally, for more than a decade. Finally, because they continue to seek my advice and ask that I serve on dissertation committees, many of the graduate students Charles helped to recruit and train are a source of gratification, and at times inspiration.

# A Few of My Favorite Readings

Anderson, E. (1999). *Code of the Street: Decency, Violence, and the Moral Life of the Inner City*. New York, NY: W.W. Norton. This book, together with Anderson's other books and articles, ranks with the very best among urban ethnographic work.

Coleman, J.S. (1988). "Social Capital in the Creation of Human Capital," *American Journal of Sociology,* 94 Supplement:S95-120.

Sampson, R.F., J.D. Morenoff & F. Earls (1999). "Beyond Social Capital: Spatial Dynamics of Collective Efficacy for Children," *American Sociological Review*, 64:633-60. Sampson and his colleagues have mounted the most sophisticated research ever undertaken—theoretically as well as empirically—in the rich tradition of the Chicago School.

Schwartz, G. (1987). *Beyond Conformity or Rebellion: Youth and Authority in America*. Chicago: University of Chicago Press. A rich, comparative study of youth and adult relationships in Illinois communities; a most relevant, but under-appreciated book.

Shaw, C.R. & H.D. McKay (rev. edition, 1969) *Juvenile Delinquency and Urban Areas*. Chicago: University of Chicago Press. I recommend the revised edition because it includes McKay's analysis of more recent data and some intriguing findings. My "Introduction" is also of interest.

Stern, P.C. & H.V. Fineberg (eds.) (1996). *Understanding Risk: Informing Decisions in a Democratic Society*. Washington, DC: National Academy Press. This book is a thoughtful assessment of problems in both risk assessment and management. Advocacy of involvement of stakeholders in the entire process is based on sound sociological research and theory.

Sullivan, M.L. (1989). *"Getting Paid": Youth Crime and Work in the Inner City*. Ithica, NY: Cornell University Press; perhaps the finest example of the use of multiple methodologies, including intensive field observation, for studying inner-city youth groups.

Thrasher, F.M. (1927; abridged ed., 1963). *The Gang: A Study of 1,212 Gangs in Chicago*. Chicago: University of Chicago Press. The classic work on gangs. The abridgement deletes much that had little to do with gangs, *per se*, my Introduction updates the Chicago gang picture at a time when our research was ongoing.

Toby, J. (1957). "Social Disorganization and a Stake in Conformity," *Journal of Criminal Law, Criminology, and Police Science*, 48 (May-June):12-17. The first statement of an important principle of great significance to crime and delinquency.

Wilson, W.J. (1987). *The Truly Disadvantaged: The Inner City, the Underclass, and Public Policy*. Chicago: University of Chicago Press. Perhaps the most influential of Wilson's works, this book documents the emergence of a permanent underclass in some U.S. cities, and its consequences.

## My Most Important Work

Short, J.F., Jr. (1999). "Characterizing and Managing Environmental and Technological Risks: Some Requirements for a New Paradigm." In W.R. Freudenburg and Ted I.K. Youn, eds., *Research in Social Problems and Public Policy*, 7:325-355; the most recent of my publications in risk and, as such, representative of my thinking about the area.

Short, J.F., Jr. (1998). "The Level of Explanation Problem Revisited," *Criminology*, 36:3-36; because, in the interest of more general theory, it is both a methodological and a theoretical critique of explanatory models. The article was my ASC presidential address.

Short, J.F., Jr. (1997). *Poverty, Ethnicity, and Violent Crime* (Boulder, CO); because it brings together my work and the work of others concerning these elusive phenomena.

Short, J.F., Jr. (1990). "Gangs, Neighborhoods, and Youth Crime," *Criminal Justice Research Bulletin*, 5, No. 4:1-11. This paper may have been the first application of "social capital" to criminology.

Short, J.F., Jr. (1990). *Delinquency and Society*. Englewood Cliffs, NJ: Prentice-Hall. This volume, in the Foundations of Modern Sociology Series, is the most comprehensive assessment of my own work as it relates to the field of juvenile delinquency. Regrettably, it is out of print.

Short, J.F., Jr. (1984). "The Social Fabric at Risk: Toward a Social Transformation of Risk Analysis," *American Sociological Review*, 49:711-725. My ASA presidential address, this paper called for sociological attention to an area of importance to understanding social change—a challenge that has since been taken up by an increasing number of sociologists and other social scientists.

Short, J.F., Jr. (1965). *Group Process and Gang Delinquency* (with Fred L. Strodtbeck; Chicago, IL: University of Chicago Press). Including several chapters written with other colleagues, this book brought together our first attempts to test theoretical insights concerning street gangs, and to develop a group process perspective that has yet to be fully appreciated, despite important contributions by Mercer Sullivan, Elijah Anderson, Malcolm Klein, John Hagedorn, and others.

Short, J.F., Jr. (1954). *Suicide and Homicide: Some Economic, Sociological, and Psychological Aspects of Aggression* (with Andrew F. Henry; Free Press); an early attempt to treat empirically the theoretical idea that suicide and homicide represent alternative extreme expressions of aggression. The theory continues to generate research and theory (see Unnithan, et al., 1994).

## References

Clarke, L. & J.F. Short, Jr. (1993). "Organizations and Risk." *Annual Review of Sociology*, 19:375-399. Palo Alto, CA: Annual Reviews.

Coleman, J.S. (1988). "Social Capital in the Creation of Human Capital." *American Journal of Sociology*, 94 Supplement:S95-120.

Douglas, M. & A. Wildavsky (1982). *Risk and Culture*. Berkeley, CA: University of California Press.

Duncan, O.D. (ed.) (1964). *William F. Ogburn on Culture and Social Change*. Chicago, IL: University of Chicago Press.

Eulau, H. & V. McCluggage (1985). "Proliferation and the Institutional Structure of the Congressional Committee System." In G. Suttles & M. Zald (eds.) *The Challenge of Social Control: Citizenship and Institution Building in Modern Society: Essays in Honor of Morris Janowitz*. Norwood, NJ: Ablex.

Gibbs, J.P. (1998). "Introduction of James F. Short, Jr.: November 21, 1997." *Criminology*, 36:1-2.

Heimer, C.A. (1987). "Social Structure, Psychology, and the Estimation of Risk." *Annual Review of Sociology*, 14:491-519. Palo Alto, CA: Annual Reviews.

Henry, A.F. & J.F. Short, Jr. (1954). *Suicide and Homicide: Some Economic, Sociological, and Psychological Aspects of Aggression*. Glencoe, IL: Free Press.

Janowitz, M. (1972). "The Professionalization of Sociology." *American Journal of Sociology*, 78:105-135.

Meier, R.F. (1988). "Discovering Delinquency: A Biographical Sketch of James F. Short, Jr." *Sociological Inquiry*, 58 (Summer):231-239.

Nye, F.I. & J.F. Short, Jr. (1957). "Scaling Delinquent Behavior." *American Sociological Review*, 22:326-331.

Ogburn, W.F. (1938, 1950). *Social Change*. New York, NY: Viking Press.

Perrow, C. (1984). *Normal Accidents: Living with High-Risk Technologies*. New York, NY: Basic Books.

Randall, D.M. & J.F. Short, Jr.(1983). 'Women in Toxic Work Environments: A Case Study of Social Problem Development." *Social Problems*, 30:4:410-424.

Sampson, R.J. & S.W. Raudenbush (1999). "Systematic Social Observation of Public Spaces: A New Look at Disorder in Urban Neighborhoods." *American Journal of Sociology*, 105:603-651.

Short, J.F., Jr. (2000). "Technology, Risk Analysis, and the Challenge of Social Control." In H.N. Pontell & D. Shichor (eds.) *Contemporary Issues in Crime and Criminal Justice: Essays in Honor of Gilbert Geis*. Englewood Cliffs, NJ: Prentice Hall.

Short, J.F., Jr. (1999). "Characterizing and Managing Environmental and Technological Risks: Some Requirements for a New Paradigm." In W.R. Freudenburg & T.I.K. Youn (eds.) *Research in Social Problems and Public Policy*, 7:325-355.

Short, J.F., Jr. (1998). "The Level of Explanation Problem Revisited: Presidential Address, American Society of Criminology." *Criminology*, 36:3-36.

Short, J.F., Jr. (1997). *Poverty, Ethnicity, and Violent Crime*. Boulder, CO: Westview.

Short, J.F., Jr. (1994). "Trace Substances, Science and Law: Perspectives from the Social Sciences." *Risk: Health, Sasfety & Environment*, 5:319-335.

Short, J.F., Jr. (1988). "Aleatory Elements in a Criminologist's Career." *The Criminologist*, 13, no. 3 (May-June):1, 3, 6-7.

Short, J.F., Jr. (1984). "The Social Fabric at Risk: Toward a Social Transformation of Risk Analysis." *American Sociological Review*, 49:711-725.

Short, J.F., Jr. (1982). "Life History, Autobiography, and the Life Cycle." In J. Snodgrass (ed.) *The Jack-Roller at Seventy: A Fifty-Year Follow-Up*. Lexington, MA: Lexington Books.

Short, J.F., Jr. (1980). "Evaluation as Knowledge Building: And Vice Versa." In M.W. Klein & K.S. Teilman (eds.) *Handbook of Criminal Justice Evaluation*. Beverly Hills, CA: Sage.

Short, J.F., Jr. (1969). "A Natural History of One Sociological Career." In I.L. Horowitz (ed.) *Sociological Self-Images: A Collective Portrait*. Beverly Hills, CA: Sage.

Short, J.F., Jr. (1967). "Action-Research Collaboration and Sociological Evaluation." *Pacific Sociological Review*, 10:47-53.

Short, J.F., Jr. (1957). "Differential Association and Delinquency." *Social Problems*, IV:233-239.

Short, J.F., Jr. & L. Clarke (eds.) (1992). *Organizations, Uncertainties, and Risk*. Boulder, CO: Westview.

Short, J.F., Jr., R.A. Tennyson & K.I. Howard (1963). "Behavior Dimensions of Gang Delinquency." *American Sociological Review*, 68:571-579.

Short, J.F., Jr., M.A. Zahn & D.P. Farrington (2000). "Experimental Research in Criminal Justice Settings: Is There a Role for Scholarly Societies?" *Crime & Delinquency*, 46, 3 (July):295-298.

Stern, P.C. & H.V. Fineberg (eds.) (1996). *Understanding Risk: Informing Decisions in a Democratic Society*. Washington, DC: National Academy Press.

Sullivan, M.L. (1989). *"Getting Paid": Youth Crime and Work in the Inner City*. Ithica, NY: Cornell University Press.

Unnithan, N.P., L. Huff-Corzine, J. Corzine & H.P. Whitt (1994). *The Currents of Lethal Violence: An Integrated Model of Suicide and Homicide*. Albany, NY: State University of New York Press.

# Endnotes

[1]    I am uncertain as to precisely when this visit occurred. I traveled often to Chicago and, with the support of a Faculty Research Fellowship from the Social Science Research Council, I spent part of one summer there in the mid-1950s studying self-reported delinquent behavior among inner-city boys, focussing especially on members of gangs (see Cohen and Short, 1958). It was during this summer, probably in 1955, that my visit with Ogburn took place.

[2]    Ogburn was not possessed of false modesty; he was very much aware of his place in the history of social science (see Duncan, 1964).

[3]    It is noteworthy that, upon reading this characterization, my parents did not know the meaning of the acronym.

[4]    Part-time work during this period also included working with a local electrician and a variety of tasks in a small, local coal mine. Later, between high school graduation and college enrollment, I worked in a steel mill in Alton, Illinois, and for a time sold shoes at a local store and waited tables in the college dining room. I continued the latter job in the fraternity house in which I lived after returning from military service.

5   My first experience with "real crime" occurred during this trip. We were camping near Boise, Idaho, when the cover to the two-wheeled trailer that held the family tent and other camping provisions was stolen.

6   In "A Natural History" I also discuss the belief, and in many cases the boast, that a black person had never spent the night in our town; not, that is, until a quartet of singers from Piney Wood College (a small Negro college from the south) came to perform at the Baptist church. The quartet was travelling in a small trailer that was parked on the church lawn. My father joined other men in the congregation to watch over the trailer for the night, following their performance.

7   The only family resistance to my relationship with my Japanese-American girlfriend came from a Bible quoting, farmer-preacher uncle who wrote me of the evils of racial mixing!

8   One of my scholarships was for basketball. I had never played football (it was not a varsity sport in our high school) but, because my father's brother had been a star football player at Shurtleff, the coach suggested that I turn out. I did so and made the travelling squad, but served mainly as practice fodder for the real football players.

9   While I was at Denison I discovered that I was near-sighted. I was fitted with prescription lenses, a further mark of indistinction among NCOs. Rifle range instructors were clearly surprised when I made "expert rifleman." Men who wore glasses were not expected to know how to shoot straight! What they didn't know was that I had been the proud possessor of guns, from BB-guns, to "22s" and a 12-gauge shotgun from an early age.

10  Mary Henry and Kelma Short (Andy's wife and my wife, respectively) performed the hundreds of statistical analyses of suicide, homicide (and other crime), and business cycle relationships on hand-operated electric calculators that were located in the Business School at the University of Chicago.

11  I recognize the value of such methods as videotaping in efforts to document indicators of "disorder in neighborhood public spaces" (see Sampson & Raudenbush, 1999).

12  1984 proved to be something of a turning point for sociological interest in risk analysis (see Clarke & Short, 1993). The first treatment of the topic published in the *Annual Review of Sociology* was Carol Heimer's (1987) "Social Structure, Psychology, and the Estimation of Risk."

13  Randall Collins (1986) argues that in order to become a well-informed specialist one must be reasonably expert in more than one special field; an argument that I endorse heartily.

14  The State of Nevada had, several years earlier, mounted a similar effort, also largely funded by DOE, including a Technical Review Committee (TRC) for monitoring and oversight. The TRC was chaired by distinguished geographer Gilbert White. Kai Erikson was a member of the TRC, and later its Chairman. Bill Freudenburg, my former colleague at Washington State University, was a consultant to the TRC, and more than a dozen other social scientists, including psychologists, economists, geographers, anthropologists, and political scientists conducted research under its auspices.

15  Following my resignation as PRC chair, I was appointed to the TRC. Although the State continued to support social affects research until federal funding virtually ceased, research funding for affected units of local government was continued at

substantial levels. Ironically, at this writing (more than five years after the PRC's dissolution), research on possible economic and other social affects of the proposed repository has surfaced again within the NWD and, in part, in collaboration with the State Agency for Nuclear Projects. Perhaps we did some good, after all.

[16]    Long after this relationship had been affirmed, I learned that a YMCA lay committee had determined that the "experiment" of hosting the research enterprise was to be watched closely and closed down in the event the research proved to be cumbersome, embarrassing, or hostile!

[17]    The Vice President was Wallis Beasley, formerly the department chair who had hired me fresh out of graduate school.

# 13

# Doing Well in the Slow Lane

Don C. Gibbons

I have more than once offered comments on my life as a criminologist and have borrowed a line from a skit on the television program, "Saturday Night Live," in which comedian Garrett Morris portrayed a Latino major league baseball player whose frequent response to queries from sports writers was: "Beezball has been berry berry good to me." In like fashion, I have reported that "criminology has been very very good to me." Of course, by itself, that observation is of little significance to anyone other than myself. However, I have some more general comments to offer about criminology, drawn from nearly a half-century of involvement in this field.

I began undergraduate criminology in the late 1940s, received a doctorate in 1956, and taught full-time from 1956 to 1992. Over this period, I was an observer as criminology grew from a small sub-area of sociology, involving a relative handful of scholars, to a large, multidisciplinary, and relatively free-standing field of study, carried on by a very large number of persons, most of whom identify themselves as criminologists or as criminal justice specialists.

More to the point, I have been more than simply a passive observer of the growth of criminology. For one thing, I have made some modest contributions to the research in the field, including a study of differences between male and female juvenile offenders, an investigation of rural crime, and a series of surveys of public attitudes and perceptions regarding deviance, crime, and the criminal justice system. Still, most of my activity has been as a reporter of, and critic of, the growing knowledge base in criminology. More specifically, I have written several basic textbooks, two books dealing with criminological theorizing, and three other works. As a criminologist, I have spent much of my time mulling over questions of the sort, "What does it all mean?"

Also worth noting is that I was Editor of *Crime & Delinquency* from 1985 to 2000. During my stewardship, the journal was operated as a "cottage industry," in that I read, reviewed, and copy-edited all of the 2,000 or more manuscripts that were submitted to it. Also, as Editor, I received and read a large number of review copies of books in criminology. As a result, I have a good bit to say about the literary quality of the scholarly products of contemporary criminologists.

Moving to a different matter, the concept of "career," defined by *Webster's New World Dictionary* as "one's progress through life," is a familiar and often-used one in reference to such occupations and professions as medicine or law, which frequently involve an orderly series of steps or stages through which persons proceed: from undergraduate student to medical school to an internship to advanced training in a medical specialty, etc. The career notion has also been employed in criminology, both with regard to the patterning of criminal conduct over time and to the unfolding of academic careers.

One thing that we have learned from research is that "careers" in crime often involve various twists and turns, "false starts," and considerable blundering about on the part of offenders. Much the same is true of criminologists in that the progress through life of many of them is often affected by mundane, chance occurrences of one kind or another. The pages to follow include a number of comments about criminological careers, drawn both from my own experiences and from those of fellow criminologists.

Finally, an account of my criminological career, and particularly of doing well in the slow lane, may be instructive to persons who are about to enter the field. I speak of "the slow lane" in order to highlight the fact that I spent virtually all of my academic life, first at San Francisco State College (now, University), and later at Portland State University. These institutions emphasized undergraduate teaching and were characterized by heavy teaching loads, both in terms of classes taught and students enrolled in them. Also, both were lacking in the secretarial assistance and other resources which support the work of scholars in research-oriented universities. Although I was involved, between 1976 and 1991, in a doctoral program in Urban Studies at Portland State which included a criminal justice "track," this was a modest venture involving only a small number of students.

What is most noteworthy about all of this is that a large share of the jobs that appear in the "Position Announcement" section of *The Criminologist*, the official newsletter of the American Society of Criminology, are in second-tier colleges and universities, rather than in major research-oriented institutions or, in other words, they are in the slow lane. And, my case indicates that it is possible to sustain a scholarly career in the slow lane. As I have already noted, I managed to author or co-author eight books and about 75 published articles during my years of teaching. Additionally, I was President of the Pacific Sociological Association in 1984 and have also twice been nominated as President of the American Society of Criminology (although I lost both times). I am listed in *Who's Who in America*. Finally, I am one of the 101 persons who have been elected as Fellows of the American Society of Criminology (as of November 1999), since the beginning of that organization. In short, I have done fairly well at the business of criminology.

## Becoming a Criminologist

I grew up in a small lumbering and oyster-processing town in Washington state. I was an indifferent student in high school during World War II, mainly because, like my fellow male schoolmates, I was unable to see much of a future beyond impending military service.

My entry into the Navy on my eighteenth birthday in June 1944 was a life-changing event, for it was there that I first began to entertain the possibility of going to college. After being discharged from the Navy, I spent the summer of 1946 working in a lumber mill and then, GI Bill in hand, headed off to the University of Washington in the fall, probably more to escape from the mill "green chain," "choker-setting" in the woods, or a life of harvesting oysters, than to pursue knowledge. I had tried my hand at all three of these lines of hard physical work while in high school and those brief tastes were enough to push me toward "the life of the mind."

Once enrolled, I quickly realized that my initial plan to become an artist was unrealistic. I then explored some other possibilities, including public school teaching. Still later, I enrolled in sociology, which I found to be more to my liking. I eventually came into contact with Clarence Schrag, one of two criminologists on the Washington faculty and a person possessed of a powerful intellect and great personal charisma. I was one of a number of persons upon whom he had a significant impact.

I received a BA in 1950 and then proceeded on to graduate school, initially intending to earn a master's degree and become a correctional worker. I obtained an MA in 1953 and then got a summer job with the Seattle City Planning Commission. At the end of the summer, I was offered a well-paying, full-time job, but my wife urged me to continue on toward a Ph.D. and I managed to wangle a teaching fellowship at the last moment.

Another fortuitous event occurred in my last year of graduate work, when Schrag and Norman Hayner, the other full-time criminologist, both were appointed to administrative positions in the state correctional system. Instead of looking outside for persons to replace them, the sociology department turned to Donald Garrity, another graduate student, and to me to teach the upper-division criminology courses. As we struggled mightily to organize our thoughts and to keep one jump ahead of our students, we stumbled on to the fairly inchoate view that criminals come in a variety of forms and began to organize our lectures around that germ of an idea, filched mainly from Schrag's claims about "types" of prison inmates.

Garrity got a job at San Francisco State in 1956 and I went off to an uncertain future at the University of British Columbia. After a year there, I moved to San Francisco State, where I spent the next 12 years. Garrity and I continued to work on what eventually become known as the "typological approach," and published several papers on that theme, in which we tried to identify the major variables around which offenders might be sorted into relatively distinct types.

I expanded upon this typological perspective in *Changing the Lawbreaker* (1965). That book identified a number of alleged "types" of juvenile and adult offenders and also put forth a "different strokes for different folks" argument about correctional treatment, in which offender types were matched to specific treatment strategems. As an aside, I eventually began to distance myself from typological notions because the research literature that accumulated in the 1960s and 1970s indicated that, among other things, offense specialization was actually fairly rare among offenders (Gibbons, 1985).

Although a good many criminologists find writing to be an onerous task, I am not one of those persons. Accordingly, I turned fairly quickly to a larger project, namely, *Society, Crime, and Criminal Behavior*, which appeared in 1968. Next came *Delinquent Behavior*, first published in 1970, and *Becoming Delinquent*, co-authored with Peter Garabedian in 1970. I continued to write while at Portland State University and coauthored *Becoming Delinquent* with Joseph F. Jones in 1975 and *Criminal Justice Planning* with Joseph L. Thimm, Florence Yospe, and Gerald F. Blake, Jr. in 1977. My last two books, *The Criminological Enterprise* (1977) and *Talking About Crime and Criminals* (1994) center on the development of modern criminology and critiques of major lines of theorizing.

## Criminology as Work

The late Donald R. Cressey, a major figure in twentieth century criminology, had a standard response to his former students who had entered academia and who complained of being under-appreciated and overworked, to wit: "Work harder!" In somewhat the same way, I have sometimes tweaked complaining colleagues, suggesting to them that "criminology beats working," that it is a "license to steal," and that it is not "real work." These seemingly cynical comments were intended to draw attention to the fact that those who are engaged in the academic life enjoy a great many pleasures and privileges that are not experienced by those who work in lumber mills, the woods, or upon oyster beds!

Happily, complaining abut one's lot in life is apparently not all that common among criminologists. I know a goodly number of them who view criminology as a calling rather than simply a job, or in other words, who take the pursuit of criminological knowledge very seriously.

While criminology certainly should be taken very seriously, and while individual criminologists ought to work diligently at the criminological enterprise, they probably should not take themselves too seriously. Fame is often fleeting in this field and few monumental "breakthroughs" in knowledge have been made by theorists or researchers to date. Indeed, contrary to Andy Warhol's forecast, a goodly number of criminologists are likely *not* to be famous in the future, even for 15 minutes! Accordingly, those criminologists who allude to "the corpus of my work" and the like probably ought to stop doing so and to speak, as I do, simply about "my stuff."

What should a trained criminologist know? Ideally, he or she should know about the history of the field; all of the perspectives, past and present, that have informed it; every theory that has been produced; all of the research and every publication; and all of the books and monographs that have ever been written, in short, everything.

However, it was clearly an impossible task for anyone to read and keep up with the entire literature, even in the 1950s, before that literature had grown exponentially. Nonetheless, over the years, I made a serious stab at mastering a sizable chunk of the knowledge-in-print. And, I recall a number of occasions in the 1960s when my friend and former colleague, Peter Garabedian, asserted to other persons that: "Gibbons really knows the literature."

One of my habits, both at San Francisco State and at Portland State, was to tend a sort of "trap line" in the university libraries, going every week or so from floor to floor, paging through the current issues of a large number of journals, both in the social sciences *and* in other fields as well. Criminologists ought to cast their nets widely when searching through periodicals for grist for their criminological mills. I often found valuable material, not only in such journals as *The American Journal of Orthopsychiatry* or *The Social Service Review*, but also in such places as *Harvard Business Review*. For example, it was there that I came upon Argyris's (1954) report on human relations in a bank, which suggested the hypothesis that some of the problems that have propelled some persons into embezzlement have more to do with social relations in the workplace than with idiosyncratic personality problems.

There is also material of criminological significance to be found in publications such as *Atlantic Monthly*, *Harper's*, or *Vanity Fair*. For example, ex-offender Everett DeBaun's (1950) account in *Harper's* had much to say about the nature of professional armed robbery and, similarly, various essays in *Vanity Fair* have thrown light upon rapacious conduct, drug use, and other behavioral excesses of executives and movie stars who travel in the fast lane in Hollywood.

Early on, I developed some techniques of "speed reading" so that I became adept at skimming many of the articles that came to my attention, as well as the books that I examined in the "new books" section of the libraries. I also carried a batch of note cards on which I jotted down bibliographical information on many journal articles, along with brief summaries of their contents. However, while it is sometimes possible to skim materials, much of the time there is no substitute for a full and careful reading of articles and books. For example, an informed judgment about such books as Jack Katz's (1988) *Seductions of Crime* or Michael Gottfredson and Travis Hirschi's (1990) *A General Theory of Crime* can only be had from very careful study of them.

This brief account of the tactics that I employed to get a handle on and to maintain a hold on the criminological literature emphasizes a single point, namely that while it is not possible to know everything, with some effort, one can come to grips with a significant chunk of contemporary criminological knowledge. However, I would *not* suggest that criminology should be a single-minded, monkish pursuit. In my case, among other things, I have put together a successful 50-year marriage, run 13 marathons (including Boston), developed some skill at watercolor painting, and become a tolerably decent downhill skier, as well as doing criminology in the slow lane.

## Some Thoughts on Criminology in the Twenty-First Century

As I have already noted, criminology was for the most part a small sub-area of sociology at the time that I became involved in it in the late 1940s. Further, some persons who were engaged in criminology often identified themselves as "penologists" who focused upon crime control and correctional programs, while others spoke of themselves as criminologists and centered their attention mainly on causal processes in criminality and delinquency. The textbooks of the time sometimes bore titles such as *Criminology and Penology*, reflecting this division of labor. It is fair to say that a spirit of optimistic liberalism characterized many of the penologists, that is, most of them assumed that, with a bit of effort, the police could be professionalized, prisons could be made more humane, and criminologists could construct effective intervention and rehabilitation programs which would lead to significant reductions in lawbreaking.

In the intervening years, "penology" virtually disappeared from the criminological lexicon, but the corrections-causation bifurcation has continued. The companion field of criminal justice which arose in the late 1960s involves a considerable number of persons whose major interests are focused on the police, courts, and corrections. Then, too, some self-identified "criminologists" continue to zero in mainly on the criminal justice system while others continue to focus principally on the causation side of the equation.

I do not have space here to say much more about penology and criminal justice. However, I would indicate that we know considerably more about the workings of police agencies, correctional institutions, and other components of the criminal justice system than we did in the 1950s. And, as a result, we have tempered our earlier, overly optimistic assumption that criminologists would soon become highly influential advisers to those in power by providing them with scientifically based recommendations regarding criminal justice policy. The fact is that we are of more than one mind with regard to what ought to be done about "the crime problem." The policy recommendations of contemporary criminologists are often more accurately described as informed but conflicting opinions than as scientific pronouncements (for evidence on this point, see Rubin, 1999; Gibbons, 1999).

I also do not have space for even a fairly cursory examination of all of the varied lines of theorizing and research on causal questions that have developed in the past 40 years but would direct the reader to two of my books (Gibbons, 1979, 1994) for discussions of these matters. What I propose to do here is to provide a brief summary of the current state of criminological theorizing and to offer some conjectures about where the field is headed.

In the 1940s and 1950s, when I made my initial moves toward a career in criminology, the relatively small band of theorists and researchers of that time took it as self-evident that crime and delinquency existed, that they could be subjected to investigation, and that factual conclusions could be reached as to their causes, and accordingly, they simply got to work at doing criminology.

Also, in the 1940s and 1950s, the major research accomplishments of criminology were relatively few in number, consisting principally of Sheldon and Eleanor Glueck's studies of careers of juvenile and adult offenders, the gang investigations by Clifford Shaw and Henry D. McKay, and a few other reports. As for theory, Edwin H. Sutherland's paired arguments about culture conflict and differential association were about the only game in town.

The situation at the start of the twenty-first century is very different, for contemporary criminology involves a much-expanded body of empirical evidence about the social forces and social processes involved in lawbreaking. Additionally, the criminological enterprise has become markedly ecumenical, with contributions coming not only from sociology but from various other directions as well: sociobiology, psychology and psychiatry, economics, political science, and geography, to name a few.

What about contemporary criminological theory? To begin with, most of us employ a catholic definition of theory which includes virtually every written or verbalized explanatory statement, from very narrow to very broad ones, and from rigorously stated to markedly fuzzy ones.

Fuzzy theories are considerably more common in criminology than are rigorous ones. The former are stated in the conventions of everyday language, often in a rambling fashion, and with implicit or unclear assumptions, vague concepts, ambiguous propositions, and the like. As a result, criminology often resembles a debating society engaged in interminable arguments about what a particular theorist has said or about the extent to which the evidence does or does not support his or her theory.

As criminology has grown in recent decades, the list of what passes for theory has expanded dramatically. Also, some of these arguments reflect very different assumptions about the nature of knowledge than those which guided criminologists in the past. A partial enumeration of current theories is sufficient to support this claim: various sociobiological theories; a host of arguments which stress individual differences and/or psychopathology; differential association and social learning arguments; routine activities theory; evolutionary ecological theory; a number of rad-ical-Marxist perspectives; a collection of control theories, including low self-control arguments; rational choice views; feminist viewpoints; left realism claims; critical and constitutive criminology; peacemaking criminology; various strain theories, and many others.

Perhaps we should view this situation positively and, as the bumper sticker advises, we should "celebrate diversity." However, there are some criminologists, myself included, who are uneasy about contemporary criminology. For one thing, some persons are of the view that it is time for sociological criminologists to "bring sociobiological arguments in," that is, to begin the difficult job of probing the forms in which, and the extent to which, sociobiological factors are bound up with social and psychological influences in lawbreaking.

Some criminologists are also troubled by what they see as the proliferation of perspectives without many net gains in the way of more precise and more powerful theories. There has been considerable talk in recent years about theoretical integration, that is, about achieving a "bigger bang for the buck," by taking ingredients from a number of separate arguments and combining them into a single formulation which will "explain more of the variance" in lawbreaking. However, it seems to me that we first need to sharpen our existing formulations before we embark upon theoretical integration. There is little to be gained from efforts to join two or more imprecise theories into a larger, but still imprecise argument.

Having said this, I should add that I do *not* expect that we will move in these directions any time soon. My guess is that there will be more rather than less building of fuzzy theories in the future, if for no other reason than that the creation of plausible but imprecise theories is considerably easier than is formal theory construction. Absent significant pressure from outside of the field, such as growing disenchantment on the part of politicians and the general public with the products of criminology, criminologists are not likely to change their ways. In short, I see little reason to raise an alarm about a crisis in criminological theory or to proclaim that the field is fractured and that the center will not hold. As far as I can tell, few persons, inside or outside of criminology, are concerned about the problem of theoretical disarray, thus it is not a real problem. But, in my opinion, there is another, little-acknowledged flaw in contemporary criminology which is a serious threat to the viability of the enterprise and it is to it that I now want to turn.

## Criminologists and the Write Stuff

### Is There a Problem Here?

Drawing mainly upon our experiences with the production of *Crime & Delinquency*, former Assistant Editor Kathryn Ann Farr and I have written several editorial opinion pieces that drew attention to a serious problem in criminology, namely, flawed writing which is endemic in the field, or in other words, we argued that: "There is a lot of bad writing out there" (Farr & Gibbons, 1989; Gibbons, 1995; Gibbons & Farr, 1998). Also, we included considerable "chapter and verse" in the way of examples of flawed writing in those essays.

However, my impression is that our remarks were often ignored by many criminologists. For one thing, some of them do not read *Crime & Delinquency*, while others who subscribe to it do not read all of the articles. Then, of those who have read one or another of our essays, many probably have concluded, sometimes mistakenly, that "they aren't talking about me, I write well." Others, while conceding that Farr and I have a point, may have thought: "OK, but what's the big deal?"

The "big deal" is this: the criminological enterprise centers almost entirely on "talking about crime and criminals," either in lectures to students or in books, journal articles, and other written products. Thus if we cannot deliver a reasonably lucid lecture in a fairly articulate fashion, we are in trouble. And even more important, if we cannot master the standard rules of composition and the essentials of clear writing, we are in even more trouble. Why should we expect noncriminologists to pay much attention to us if we write in obscure and/or ponderous ways and if we fracture the English language? Learning to write reasonably well should be a central feature of taking criminology seriously.

## Some Disclaimers

Although the remarks to follow are critical of much of the writing of contemporary criminologists, I would not try to pass myself off as an expert in the rules of English composition. I have long forgotten most of what I may have learned in high school about such matters as split infinitives and the proper uses of "me" and "I." Still, I can recognize subject-verb inconsistencies, misspelled words, egregiously screwed up syntax, and kindred problems that are common in criminological writing.

I also make no claim to being a peerless wordsmith who can knock out dazzling prose at one sitting before a word processor. Quite the contrary, virtually everything that I have written for publication has gone through multiple revisions and much honing and polishing, and even then, I have been less than entirely satisfied with the end result.

One other disclaimer is that I have no interest in "outing" individual criminologists who, in my opinion, are poor writers. My concern is with bad writing, rather than with singling out a few inept writers from a much larger group of equally inept authors. At the same time, I am obliged to invoke some evidence to support my comments and cannot simply mimic humorist Dave Barry and assert in parentheses that: ("I am not making this up!") Accordingly, I shall offer a number of examples of flawed writing, culled from the papers and books I have read in recent years, but without explicitly identifying the persons who penned these materials, Still, I realize that it would not be all that difficult to identify the authors, were one interested in doing so.

## Exhibit A

In our discussions of the writing problem in criminology, Farr and I emphasized three points, one of which is that *bad writing takes a variety of forms*. One can identify a number of instances of criminological works, particularly books, which are essentially unreadable. Badly written papers are also very common but less visible in that many of them are rejected by editors at an early stage and thus they never see the light of day in print. More commonly encountered are books and journal articles which are inelegantly written and shot through with flawed syntax and the like, but which, with some effort, can be read and understood. Second, *flawed writing exists at all levels within the academic hierarchy*, so that it is not solely graduate students and recently minted Ph.D.

persons who write badly. Finally, flawed writing is an *institutional problem as well as an individual one*. At least for most of us, the ability to write is an acquired skill, but graduate programs have generally been derelict in their responsiblity to make sure that students learn to write reasonably well.

Now, consider some evidence. On the readability dimension, the most striking case of unreadability I have encountered in recent years is a 1999 book on globalization and crime. Globalization is a fact of modern life and it probably is also true that crime is affected by it, so that a book on crime and globalization should be inherently interesting. Moreover, it ought to be possible to write about these matters in straightforward prose. However, the book in question is likely to kill any interest that most people have in this topic because page after page of it consists of familiar words that have been strung together in sentences which are syntactically correct but which are so clouded that even after several readings, most of us would probably still not know whether any of it makes sense.

Some criminologists have complained in recent years about the unreadable character of other books, and in particular, about a number of works by persons who identify themselves as critical criminologists or postmodernists. However, while some of these books do contain a fairly heavy measure of odd terminology and expressions, with a bit of effort, most of them can be read and understood.

Among flawed books, the most frequently encountered ones are those that are easy to read but which contain various "warts" and "blemishes" that detract from them: misused words, misspelled authors' names, shifting tenses, and fractured syntax. I have encountered a large number of books that are marred in these ways.

As an aside, my impression is that flawed books are becoming more common, probably in considerable part because of major changes in the publishing industry. One of the consequences of mergers such as that of Prentice Hall with Simon and Schuster, which in turn, was taken over by Viacom, is that publishing companies no longer spend much money on copy editors, who in the past often cleaned up the defective manuscripts.

Turning to journal submissions, the surfeit of these that I have examined over a 15-year period often contained the same flaws I have noted above: misspelled words, incorrect citations, subject-verb problems, shifting tenses, and flawed syntax. In addition, many of them included excess verbiage, as for example, when writers asserted that they carried out a study "in the context of Seattle," when in actuality, they simply did a study in Seattle. Even more troubling were numerous instances of sentences which were technically correct in terms of syntax, but in which the authors asserted things quite different from what they intended. One of the most hilarious of these involved two scholars who wrote of Einstein and asserted that "the practical utility of certain of his ideas was not recognized until after his death from adventures in space!" In another case, an author claimed that "we need more interview data from rapists like Diane Scully and Joseph Marolla," who, in fact, were persons who interviewed rapists! Still another criminologist asserted that Travis Hirschi, who wrote about social bond theory, was a cause of delinquency! In yet another paper, dealing with workplace crime, the author asserted that: "One of the more effective tools in preventing dishonesty in the workplace is to treat employee theft as a serious matter and make it part of the formal policy of the organization!" Finally, in another submission, the authors wrote that "A subsequent warrantless search of —'s home by the probation officer accompanied by the investigator uncovered cocaine, which was used at a subsequent criminal proceeding!" If so, this gives a new meaning to "the high court!"

As an aside, I don't want to be a modern-day Ned Ludd, but I do want to voice a concern or two about computers and writing. My impression from a number of papers that I have perused in recent years is that their authors knocked them out in a single sitting before a computer, without any effort to hone and polish them. While computers are indeed remarkable and highly useful tools in writing, those authors often placed too much confidence in them. There is no computer that is capable of preventing writers from penning such sentences as those in the paragraph above. Similarly, while a spell check can prevent the misspelling of "affect" and "effect" or other similar sounding words, it cannot tell us when these words are misused. Even more to the point, computers cannot automatically rid a manuscript of excess or overly flowery verbiage, nor can they determine the adequacy of the overall structure of an essay. These tasks can only be performed by the author or authors.

## *Accounting for Flawed Writing*

What are the immediate factors that are involved in the flawed writing exhibited by graduate students, recent recipients of doctorates, and established scholars in criminology? Farr and I have identified these as *ineptitude*, *sloth*, and *hubris*. Many persons in criminology are bad writers, largely because they failed to learn much about English composition and "the tricks of the trade" of good writing anywhere in their educational experiences.

By sloth, I mean that I have also encountered a number of authors who have the ability to turn out satisfactory work but who are simply not concerned about doing so. A considerable share of the papers that were published in *Crime & Delinquency* during my editorship had initially been returned to the authors as in need of considerable further work. After I held their feet to the fire, the authors cleaned up their work and made it publishable. Finally, hubris refers to an extreme form of indifference exhibited by self-important senior persons in the field, for whom proofreading and the like are matters to be left to so-called "lesser folk" such as editors.

## Dealing With Flawed Writing

So, what is to be done about flawed writing? At the individual level, the obvious answer is that inept writers must be encouraged to undertake serious efforts to increase their writing skills. On this point, Farr and I (1998) have drawn attention to a number of resources that can be employed for this purpose and we have also offered advice and guidance to persons who want to sharpen their writing.

However, as I have already noted, the flawed writing problem calls out for an institutional response as well as for individual efforts to do better. The plain fact is that relatively few graduate programs in criminology provide any sort of systematic training in professional writing. On this point, in my work for *Crime & Delinquency*, I routinely sent authors a thoroughly marked-up copy of their paper and a single-spaced letter usually running to three or more pages, identifying and commenting upon the "warts" and "blemishes" in the paper. On a number of occasions, I later received responses from newly hired Assistant Professors who asserted that they had learned more about writing from this single encounter than from their entire graduate experience! Such reports do not speak well for graduate training.

What about mentoring as a solution to the writing problem? The notion of mentoring has received a fair amount of attention in criminology and criminal justice in recent years, including the creation of an American Society of Criminology award for superior mentoring. At first glance, the proposal for mentoring seems obvious and unexceptionable, particularly in that *Webster's New World Dictionary* defines a mentor as a "wise, loyal advisor," while "professor" is described as a college teacher of the highest rank. It could be argued that these are virtually synonymous terms, save for the qualifier that one can engage in mentoring without being a professor. And, if mentoring is central to "the professing trade," it follows that all of those who are employed as professors should be engaged in acts of mentoring on a daily basis.

Still, I am uncomfortable with some aspects of mentoring proposals. For one thing, the idea of mentors and their pupils is misleading insofar as it implies that education is a one-way process in which professors teach and students learn. The fact is that the former are often as much indebted to some of their students for insights and intellectual stimulation they have received from them as the other way around.

An even more important point is that, as far as attacking the flawed writing problem is concerned, it is not enough to simply urge professors to do a better job of guiding their students, because many would-be mentors are themselves in need of a crash course on how to write!

If the situation is as I have described it, it seems palpable that *graduate departments need to take seriously the responsibility for training students in the craft of writing*. What should departments do in the way of concrete efforts to face up to this responsibility? First and foremost, training in writing must be given the same degree of emphasis as is now placed upon other curricular responsibilities, such as training in theory, methodological competency, and other tasks that are now fairly standard in criminology programs. The details as to what sorts of training in writing should be offered and by whom are best left to departmental faculty, but I suggest that these might include the identification of skilled writers in the department, creation of courses on professional writing led by these persons, and efforts to get less-skilled faculty members into programs through which they might improve their writing. Finally, departments may need to employ the resources of Departments of English and to take other steps to draw upon outside persons.

## Conclusion

My contribution to this book about the lessons of criminology has focused upon the criminological enterprise, or in other words, on the professional activities of criminologists. Most of my observations had to do with scholarly "careers" in criminology, of which there are a number of variants. On the one extreme are the large number of individuals who earn the Ph.D., obtain a job in some college or university, and then as far as scholarly accomplishments are concerned, are never heard from again. On the other extreme are those relatively rare persons such as Edwin H. Sutherland, who has often been acknowledged as the most notable American criminologist of all time. Indeed, even though he died in 1950, Sutherland's influence upon the field continues to be very strong (Gibbons, 1994:19-23). A host of different career patterns can be identified between these end points, including those of persons such as Maurice F. Parmelee, the author of the first full-blown American criminology textbook and of a number of other books in the 1920s, but who subsequently became almost completely forgotten (Gibbons, 1974). Still other criminologists, including Donald R. Cressey, Edwin M. Lemert, and others, attained considerable fame during their lifetimes and continue to be recognized in the annals of the field.

My account of my life in criminology indicates that, with a good deal of hard work, it is possible to do reasonably well in the slow lane. Also, I have argued that in order to do well, either in the fast or the slow lane, criminologists must be able to write about the accomplishments of the field and about their own efforts in a clear and effective manner. We have few if any products to give or sell to others, beyond written accounts of our research findings and our theorizing.

# References

Argyris, C. (1954). "Human Relations in a Bank." *Harvard Business Review*, 32(September-October):63-72.

DeBaun, E. (1950). "The Heist: The Theory and Practice of Armed Robbery." *Harper's*, 200(February):69-77.

Farr, K.A. & D.C. Gibbons (1989). Why Can't John and Jane Write? More Observations from the Editor's Desks," *Crime & Delinquency* 35(April):309-315.

Garabedian, P.G. & D.C. Gibbons (eds.) (1970). *Becoming Delinquent*. Chicago, IL: Aldine.

Gibbons, D.C. (1999). "Review Essay: Crime, Criminologists, and Public Policy." *Crime & Delinquency*, 45(July):400-413.

Gibbons, D.C. (1995). "Unfit for Human Consumption: The Problem of Flawed Writing in Criminology and Criminal Justice and What to Do About It." *Crime & Delinquency*, 41(April):246-266.

Gibbons, D.C. (1994). *Talking About Crime and Criminals*. Englewood Cliffs, NJ: Prentice Hall.

Gibbons, D.C. (1985). "The Assumption of the Efficacy of Middle-Range Explanations: Typologies." In R.F. Meier (ed.) *Theoretical Methods in Criminology*, pp.151-175. Beverly Hills, CA: Sage.

Gibbons, D.C. (1977). *The Criminological Enterprise*. Englewood Cliffs, NJ: Prentice Hall.

Gibbons, D.C. (1974). "Say, Whatever Became of Maurice Parmelee, Anyway?" *Sociological Quarterly*, 15(Summer):405-416.

Gibbons, D.C. (1970). *Delinquent Behavior*. Englewood Cliffs, NJ: Prentice Hall.

Gibbons, D.C. (1968). *Society, Crime, and Criminal Careers*. Englewood Cliffs, NJ: Prentice Hall.

Gibbons, D.C. (1965). *Changing the Lawbreaker*. Englewood Cliffs, NJ: Prentice Hall.

Gibbons, D.C. & K.A. Farr (1998). "The Good, the Bad, and the Ugly: Dealing With Flawed Writing in Criminal Justice." *Crime & Delinquency*, 44(July):464-474.

Gibbons, D.C. & J.F. Jones (1975). *The Study of Deviance*. Englewood Cliffs, NJ: Prentice hall.

Gibbons, D.C., J.L. Thimm, F. Yospe & G.F. Blake, Jr. (1977). *Criminal Justice Planning*. Englewood Cliffs, NJ: Prentice Hall.

Gottfredson, M.R. & T. Hirschi (1990). *A General Theory of Crime*. Stanford, CA: Stanford University Press.

Katz, J. (1988). *Seductions of Crime*. New York, NY: Basic Books.

Rubin, E.L. (1999). *Minimizing Harm*. Boulder, CO: Westview.

# Epilogue

Mary Dodge

For me, the "lessons" in this volume encourage a unique type of introspection for criminologists that involves evaluating what we have done and planning for where we personally are going. As someone in her fourth year of teaching and writing, my comments on the foregoing chapters are from the perspective of a relative newcomer to criminology and criminal justice, a person further down on the academic totem pole. I want to reemphasize some things in the chapters that struck a responsive chord in my mind or related importantly to my postdoctorate experience of one year at California State University, Los Angeles, and, as of now, three subsequent years on the faculty of the graduate school of public affairs, University of Colorado at Denver. I also want to share some of the things that I have learned during my brief time on the job so that the perspective of a newcomer can supplement somewhat the views of veterans.

I found a virtual (and reassuring) consensus among the writers that becoming a successful criminologist is an evolving process, with the likelihood of a number of bumps and detours along the route. Dedication, perseverance, wise choices, and some luck all apparently contribute to upward movement in the discipline's pecking order. Satisfaction largely will be personal. There may be tangible rewards, but academic work has a better than average quota of sharks out there, looking for blood, and it often appears that everybody is so busy doing his or her own work that they have precious little time to attend to what others are accomplishing unless it bears directly on their own immediate research concerns.

For me, the "lessons" set forth in the foregoing chapters were much more than recitations on how to get along and get ahead in criminology and criminal justice. There was not only information about the high points and the downsides of the writers' careers, but more importantly there came through for me a sense of commitment to a life tied to the discipline and a considerable satisfaction with the rewards, personal and professional, that such a life has to offer. To be sure, Gary Marx notes that there are other things in this world besides work, and these pleasures need to be cultivated. Several of the writers though, most notably Jim Short, point out, a bit shyly, that they tend to be almost irremediably task-oriented and somewhat driven in regard to research and writing.

For myself and my co-editor, one of the things that we learned from our work on this book was the reliability of those who had agreed to prepare chapters. In most such enterprises, with a more eclectic roster of contributors, inevitably some drop out along the way and others submit their manuscripts far after the deadline. Shrewd editors, I'm told, set an artificially early submission date, but nonetheless still are often held up from meeting the actual deadline by putative contributors who somehow have not quite gotten with the task. But every one of our writers met the deadline, and a good number had the material to us much earlier than the date that we set. I suspect that such diligence and dependability is one of the hallmarks of a successful career.

The book offers insights and wisdom that represent an accumulation of more than 500 years of experience. Many of the writers were trained in fields other than criminology and criminal justice and, as Malcolm Klein observes, "criminology is a tenuous molding of disparate fields." This can be a considerable asset because it allows a multifaceted phenomenon such as criminal behavior to be looked at from different perspectives and results in a more full-bodied scrutiny of the behavior. Scholars are able to unite under an expansive umbrella to provide fully fleshed-out portraits rather than what results from traditionally limited disciplinary inquiries.

I am an accidental criminologist, like so many of the contributors to this volume. I first became involved in the study of deviance while I was working for a master's degree in clinical psychology. I knew a lot about Freud, Jung, and Skinner, but had never heard of Sutherland, Merton, or Hirschi. I found exposure to a theories of crime class akin to landing unexpectedly on an alien planet. A panicked trip to the library changed the course of my career. That day, I discovered the seductions of criminology (a phrase, though altered, borrowed from Jack Katz) not in integrated theoretical models, but in books such as Clifford Shaw's *The Jack Roller*, Howard Becker's *Outsiders*, and *Tally's Corner* by Elliot Liebow. Inspiration, as noted by several contributors, is handed down by those who have become "virtual gods in the field" for good reason.

For many of us who manage to jump over graduate school hurdles, the most severe challenge is to find lifestyle equilibrium in an academic position. Teaching, doing research, writing, and serving the university and the community are demanding and time-consuming tasks. Even the most intensive efforts at satisfactory time-management can be subverted by students, deans, and department chairs—not to mention family and friends. It took me some time to appreciate that involvement in non-writing chores often was a subconscious tactic to avoid writing even though I know, and many of the writers of this book emphasize, that scholarly production is the sine qua non of success in the realm of higher education. A successful career apparently means having to accept that your classes could be better prepared and that some departmental memoranda will merely be skimmed, not absorbed.

Indeed, writing itself has built-in dilemmas. I once heard a senior scholar tell a group that she adhered to what she called "the 82 percent practice of writing." She would send off an article that she knew could be improved by 18 percent with a good deal more effort. She presumed, usually accurately, that it would be published as it then stood. Her explanation was personal: there came a time, usually at the 82 percent level, when she became a bit bored with the work and wanted to move on to something new and more appealing.

Academic life for me has posed stark contrasts in terms of interactions. Teaching and committee work call for social skills and, at times, political savvy. In comparison, writing often seems best accomplished in isolation at odd times of the day and night. Mostly, I miss the opportunity that I had as a graduate student to work continuously on a subject. Inevitable interruptions typically involve a considerable waste of time trying to recapture the tone and reabsorb the earlier segments of the writing. If I could work on something each day I could move forward routinely without having to go back after a time lapse.

In this regard, I always remember graduate school advice that had first been set out by novelist Ernest Hemingway: Always quit writing when you are ahead. You should stop not when you are stymied but when you know exactly where you are heading. In that way, it will be easier to jump start the next installment.

I have found that teaching is the easier part of the job, though course preparations and new material require a substantial time investment. My reliance on varying approaches has helped to make even a particularly heavy teaching load manageable. Films, guest speakers, small group exercises, and an emphasis on classroom discussions are helpful. "Smart classrooms" with modern equipment help us to become directors, producers, and actors vying for the attention of our students. Mastering technologies such as PowerPoint, Blackboard, and the Electronic Hallway, as well as developing Web sites, offers a new set of challenges and advantages.

I've also learned that taking 10 or so minutes before class to sit quietly in your office and think about the forthcoming session is priceless for reducing any anxiety engendered by teaching. And I've found out the hard way to have a back-up plan in the event of no-shows or equipment failures.

Initially, I had been convinced that I was prepared if I remained one step ahead of my students. There is too much agony involved in not really knowing as much as you can absorb about the full range of what you are teaching. I also quickly learned that by far the best teaching technique is to admit ignorance when you are unable to answer a decent question satisfactorily. It often seems a good idea to ask the there-always-is-at-least-one eager student to try to locate the answer in the library or on the Internet.

In the end, though, these chapters tell me that the emphasis is on publishing. In the first article in the book, Frank Cullen sets the theme "Publish, publish, publish," he writes, an admonition likely to send chills down the spine of an untenured, expendable assistant professor. I read Cullen's words soon after I had a spate of rejections on articles that I was convinced were quite good. Feeling rather sorry for myself (I rank high on the self-pity scale) and beginning to have doubts about my abilities, I took his advice to heart: "Get over it, improve the manuscript, and resubmit it to other journals." I got over the knee-jerk reaction that the reviews were based on myopic visions and hidden agendas and sat down and rewrote the pieces. In some instances, I had forgotten to heed the advice I give to students: "Always consult those gurus of grammar, Strunk and White (William Strunk, Jr. and E.B. White, *The Elements of Style*). Indeed, Don Gibbons's comments in this book on writing produced a slight twinge of contrition about my own writing "warts" and "blemishes." I found a perverse satisfaction in the fact that many of the present luminaries in the field also had faced and surmounted the same blows to the ego.

When asked about my specialty, I am likely to reply that I am an opportunist. I understand that there are clear advantages to becoming an expert in a particular area. But I find the need to collaborate is crucial to my career and may take me in unexpected directions. Research, writing, submitting grant applications, consulting, and having a voice in public policy seldom are accomplished alone. I have also learned that, for me, diversity in research helps maintain a sense of excitement.

The essays also convinced me that retirement in criminology is something of a fiction. A number of contributors to this book have embraced retirement as allowing them more time to write. Despite a late start in my own career, I am still an academic spring chicken. I find it difficult to imagine retiring. I liked the observation by Frank Cullen that academia is a wonderful life—"the kind of life people retire to."

For me, it became essential to find a leisure activity that removed me from the world of criminology and criminal justice. Endeavors such as gardening, biking, or, in my case, rock-climbing, are imperative for balancing our personal and professional lives. On a recent scary climb of a 140-foot spire called Montezuma's Tower, a fellow climber asked what I was thinking as I hovered far above the ground. "It's great," I said. "I haven't once thought about work." I know that there always will be unread books, papers to grade, and research work to be done. A scholarly career can be all-consuming. A temporary refuge, far removed from that scene, may be the key to keeping sane and productive.

# About the Authors

**Gilbert Geis** is a Professor Emeritus in the Department of Criminology, Law, and Society at the University of California, Irvine. He is a former president of the American Society of Criminology and recipient of its Edwin H. Sutherland Award for outstanding research. He has also been given research awards by the Association of Certified Fraud Examiners, the Western Society of Criminology, the American Justice Institute, and the National Organization for Victim Assistance.

Geis received his undergraduate degree from Colgate University and his Ph.D. from the University of Wisconsin. He taught at the University of Oklahoma (1952-1957) and California State University, Los Angeles (1957-1972) before joining the Irvine faculty. He has held visiting appointments in the School of Criminal Justice, State University of New York, Albany; the Institute of Criminology, Cambridge University, the Faculty of Law, University of Sydney; and the College of Human Development, Pennsylvania State University. During the fall semester 1996, he was a Distinguished Visiting Professor at John Jay College in New York City.

Geis has published more than 350 articles on various aspects of crime and criminal justice. His most recent books are *A Trial of Witches* (with Ivan Bunn); and *Crimes of the Century: From Leopold and Loeb to O.J. Simpson* (with Leigh Bienen).

**Francis T. Cullen** is Distinguished Research Professor in the Department of Criminal Justice at the University of Cincinnati. He received a Ph.D. (1979) in sociology and education from Columbia University. Professor Cullen has published more than 150 works in the areas of crime and deviance theory, corrections, and white-collar crime. He is author of *Rethinking Crime and Deviance Theory: The Emergence of a Structuring Tradition* (1984) and is co-author of *Reaffirming Rehabilitation* (1982), *Corporate Crime Under Attack: The Ford Pinto Case and Beyond* (1987), *Criminological Theory: Context and Consequences* (1989 and 1995), *Criminology* (1992), *and Combating Corporate Crime: Local Prosecutors at Work* (1998). He also has co-edited *Con-*

*temporary Criminological Theory* (1994), *Offender Rehabilitation: Effective Correctional Intervention* (1997), *and Criminological Theory: Past to Present—Essential Readings* (1999). Professor Cullen is a Fellow of the Academy of Criminal Justice Sciences and of the American Society of Criminology. He has served as President of ACJS and as editor of *Justice Quarterly*.

**Charles R. Tittle** is Professor of Sociology and the Goodnight/Glaxo-Wellcome Endowed Chair of Social Science in the Department of Sociology and Anthropology at North Carolina State University, Raleigh, North Carolina. He holds a B.A. (1961) from Ouachita Baptist University, and an M.A. (1963) and Ph.D. (1965) from the University of Texas in Austin. He has served on faculties at Indiana University, Bloomington; Florida Atlantic University; and Washington State University; and he edited *Criminology* 1992-1997. Having authored four books and numerous journal articles and anthology chapters, he is best known for work on deterrence, social status and crime, and control balance theory.

**Malcolm W. Klein** is Emeritus Professor of Sociology at the University of Southern California. He is a Sutherland Award winner of the American Society of Criminology, and author or editor of 14 books on delinquency measurement, treatment of juvenile offenders, juvenile justice systems, criminological evaluation, cross-national research, and street gangs. He has served on various state and federal advisory committees and lectured at several dozen universities in the United States and Europe. He is currently working on two new gang books, is heavily engaged in a cross-national gang research program, and serves as consultant and expert witness in numerous gang-related court trials.

**Frank R. Scarpitti** is the Edward and Elizabeth Rosenberg Professor of Sociology at the University of Delaware, where he has been a faculty member since 1967. He earned his B.A. degree at Cleveland State University and his Ph.D. at Ohio State University in 1962. He received the American Psychiatric Association's Hofheimer Prize for Research (1967), and served as President of the American Society of Criminology (1981), and as Chair of the Crime, Law and Deviance Section of the American Sociological Association (1997). His books and articles have addressed issues related to mental illness, juvenile delinquency, female crime, group therapy, organized crime, and substance abuse treatment programs. He is married to the former Ellen Canfield and is the father of a daughter, Susan, and a son, Jeffrey.

**Joan McCord**, Professor of Criminal Justice at Temple University, earned her Ph.D. in Sociology from Stanford. Currently Co-Chair of the National Academy of Sciences Panel on Juvenile Crime and Vice President of the International Society of Criminology, she is a past-President of the American Society of Criminology. Her empirical research ranges from studies of the etiology of crime to patterns of crime and the effectiveness of intervention programs. She received both the Prix Emile Durkheim from the International Society of Criminology and the Edwin H. Sutherland Award from the American Society of Criminology for her contributions to research.

**Gary T. Marx** is a retiring but not shy Professor Emeritus from M.I.T. He received his Ph.D. from the University of California at Berkeley. He is the author of *Protest and Prejudice, Undercover: Police Surveillance in America*, and co-editor of *Undercover: Police Surveillance in Comparative Perspective,* among other works.

**Jackson Toby** studied with Professors Talcott Parsons and Samuel A. Stouffer at Harvard and learned from them the importance of both theory and research, working in tandem, to advance scientific understanding. The title of Stouffer's book of his collected articles, *Social Research to Test Ideas*, expresses Professor Toby's conception of sociological research. My Ph.D. dissertation, "Educational Maladjustment As a Predisposing Factor in Criminal Careers: A Comparative Study of Ethnic Groups," (Harvard, 1950) investigated why second-generation Italian-American boys had higher delinquency rates than second-generation Jewish-American boys and called attention to the different cultural resources for legitimate social mobility in the traditions from which these youngsters came. Professor Toby has been listed in *Who's Who in America* for more than 30 years.

**John Irwin**. After a normal early childhood and diverse and wild teenage years that included burglary, robbery, and drug use, I was sent to prison where I served five years. There I began preparing myself for a different life, one that would include higher education. I began taking college courses in prison, continued my education upon release and eventually received a Ph.D. in sociology. Because of my earlier involvements in crime and imprisonment, my academic concentration was in criminology with a particular focus on the prison. I was professor of sociology at San Francisco State University for 27 years during which time I continued to study imprisonment. In all of these studies, which resulted in five books, I employed "participant observer" methods and attempted to reveal the experiences of the research subjects-the prisoners-and to present their humanness.

**Richard Quinney's** works in criminology are contained in several books, including *The Social Reality of Crime, Critique of Legal Order, Criminology, Criminal Behavior Systems, Class, State, and Crime, and*

*Criminology as Peacemaking*. His autobiographical writings are contained in *Journey to a Far Place, For the Time Being*, and *Borderland*. The development of his work in criminology—as reflected in his writing—is presented in his recently published book *Bearing Witness to Crime and Social Justice*. Richard Quinney is professor emeritus of sociology at Northern Illinois University.

**Julius Debro**. The opportunity to convey to the reader insights into a personal view of the field of Criminology and Criminal Justice is a privilege that comes only once in a lifetime. I am indeed grateful that I was given the opportunity to contribute to the writing of such a book. As one grows older, one reflects upon those people who have made a difference in one's life. Most people help because of a sense of dedication but my mentors helped because they wanted to make a change and bring young African-Americans into the academy. Julian Roebuck kept me in school at the Master's level at San Jose. Robert Carter gave me my first opportunity in research and introduced me to the graduate school at Berkeley. Gordon Misner, Jerome Skolnick, Shelly Messinger, Herman Schwendinger, Paul Takagi, Tony Platt, and David Matza guided my studies and Howie Becker allowed me to interview him for my first article and he has remained a true mentor over the years. Bart Ingraham, helped me through a very difficult dissertation and without Bart, I would not have completed the degree. Peter Lejins helped me in getting over my hostility toward whites and also assisted in my education in International Criminology. Dr. Lejins was a true Icon at the University of Maryland. Without Dr. Lejins, there would not have been a Ph.D. program in Criminology/Criminal Justice. His influence on my life is very difficult to measure. He retired in 1979 because he had reached the mandatory retirement age of 70. Today, we no longer have age discrimination. Someday, we may no longer have racial, ethnic, and gender discrimination.

As one reads the names of my mentors, one may be struck by race, ethnicity, and gender. All are white males with one exception. In 1968 when I entered Graduate School, there were no black Professors on regular faculty and only one white women and she never received tenure. We have come a long way, baby!

**Rita J. Simon** is a sociologist who earned her bachelor's degree at the University of Wisconsin and her doctorate at the University of Chicago in 1957. Before coming to American University in 1983 to serve as Dean of the School of Justice, she was a member of the faculty at the University of Illinois, at the Hebrew University in Jerusalem, and the University of Chicago. She is currently a University Professor in the School of Public Affairs and the Washington College of Law at American University. In 1966 she received a Guggenheim Fellowship. From 1978 to 1981 she served as editor of *The American Sociological Review*, and from 1983 to 1986 as editor of *Justice Quarterly*. She is currently editor of *Gender Issues*.

**James F. Short, Jr.** is Professor Emeritus, Washington State University. He was Director of Research (with Marvin Wolfgang) of the National Commission on the Causes and Prevention of Violence (1968-69), a member of the National Academy of Science, National Research Council Committee on Law and Justice, and that committee's Panel on the Understanding and Control of Violent Behavior. He served as Editor of the *American Sociological Review* and as President of the American Sociological Association, the Pacific Sociological Society, and the American Society of Criminology. His most recent book is *Poverty, Ethnicity, and Violent Crime*. He is a member of the Academic Advisory Council of the National Campaign Against Youth Violence, and advisory committees for the National Consortium on Violence Research and the National Youth Gang Center. He has received many honors, including the Edwin H. Sutherland Award (ASC), the Bruce Smith Award (Academy of Criminal Justice Sciences), the Paul W. Tappan Award (Western Society of Criminology), and the Guardsmark Wolfgang Award for Distinguished Achievement in Criminology. He is the namesake for the James F. Short, Jr. Best Article Award, created by the ASA Section on Crime, Law, and Deviance.

**Don C. Gibbons** is Emeritus Professor of Urban Studies at Portland State University. He received his B.A., M.A., and Ph.D. all from the University of Washington. Prior to going to Portland State, he taught for 12 years at San Francisco State College. His criminological work has centered on the development of offender typologies and surveys of citizen' attitudes about crime and criminal justice. He is also the author of a number of textbooks and other works in criminology. While "doing criminology," he also found time to run 13 marathons and learn downhill skiing. Also, he remains a rabid fan of University of Washington football!

**Mary Dodge** has her M.A. in clinical psychology from the University of Colorado at Colorado Springs and her Ph.D. in criminology, law and society from the School of Social Ecology at the University of California, Irvine. Currently, she is an assistant professor at the University of Colorado at Denver, Graduate School of Public Affairs. Prior to coming to CU, Denver she taught at California State University, Los Angeles. She teaches a variety of courses for the Master of Criminal Justice program, including Juvenile Justice Administration, Nature and Causes of Crime, Judicial Administration, White-Collar Crime, Social Deviance, Women and Crime, and Domestic Violence in the Criminal Justice System. Her recent research has appeared in *Courts and Justice, Con-*

*temporary Issues in Criminology, International Journal of the Sociology of Law, The Prison Journal, Police Quarterly,* and *Journal of Contemporary Criminal Justice.* Her research interests include white-collar crime, fraud in assisted reproductive technology, juvenile informants, women in the criminal justice system, and policing.